THE READING OF BOOKS

THE READING
OF BOOKS

HOLBROOK JACKSON

UNIVERSITY OF ILLINOIS PRESS
Urbana and Chicago

First Illinois paperback, 2001
Manufactured in the United States of America
P 5 4 3 2 1

♾ This book is printed on acid-free paper.

Library of Congress Cataloging-in-Publication Data
Jackson, Holbrook, 1874-1948.
The reading of books / Holbrook Jackson. — 1st Illinois pbk.
p.   cm.
Originally published: New York : Scribner's, 1947.
Includes bibliographical references and index.
ISBN 0-252-07041-0 (acid-free paper)
1. Reading. I. Title.
PN83.J3   2001
418'.4—dc21   2001027821

To

GLADYS BURLTON

In memory of all books which lay
Their sure foundations in the heart of Man;
Whether by native prose or numerous verse,
That in the name of all inspiréd Souls,
From Homer, the Great Thunderer; from the Voice
Which roars along the bed of Jewish Song;
And that, more varied and elaborate,
Those trumpet-tones of harmony that shake
Our shores in England; from those loftiest notes
Down to the low and wren-like warblings, made
For Cottagers and Spinners at the wheel,
And weary Travellers when they rest themselves
By the highways and hedges; ballad tunes,
Food for the hungry ears of little Ones,
And of old Men who have surviv'd their joy . . .

WILLIAM WORDSWORTH, *The Prelude* (1805), v, 193–208

CONTENTS

PREFACE

The central idea of the theme discussed in this book—that reading can be an art and the reader an artist—is implicit in all my work since and including *The Anatomy of Bibliomania*. It was referred to briefly but with more precision in the Preface to *Maxims of Books and Reading* (1930), and, as that volume was issued by the First Edition Club for members only, I have welded most of it (not more than a thousand words) into the Introduction which follows and the chapter entitled the 'Reader as Artist'. The rest of the volume is new. The title of that chapter was to have been the title of the book but as it was thought to be ambiguous it was abandoned for the present but more general title, suggested by my daughter, Gwendolen, as a companion to an earlier work, *The Printing of Books*. I have pleasure in thanking my friends Gladys Burlton and Duncan Williams for reading the proofs and making several valuable suggestions, but I exonerate them from any complicity in the opinions expressed or responsibility for any errors that may have escaped detection.

HOLBROOK JACKSON

INTRODUCTION

There have been many essays on the art of reading, but so far as I am aware, no writer, even when accepting reading as an art, has treated the reader as an artist. There are books on the art of reading but they deal with everything but reading as an art. They always deal with the craft or technique of reading and generally with the craft or technique of reading books which the writer of the dissertation happens to like, or, even, to have written. Such books are little more than special pleadings for personal preferences. They are acts of persuasion rather than attempts at elucidation. Their object is invariably to subject the reader to the will of the writer, rather than to help him to realise himself through his reading. In the following pages I treat books as the media of an art and the reader as an artist. I show that the reading of books involves in some measure, often considerable, experiences similar to those generally associated with the writing of books. I make no claim to finality for my conclusions, and would ask the reader to look upon this work as an experimental study of literary experiences. I shall be content if I have succeeded in doing no more than blaze the beginning of an interesting and possibly useful trail.

It is risky at any time to attempt an unbiased opinion, and especially at a time when literary method is changing through the penetration of new ideas: our own period for example. Modern thought and imagination have been deflected from tradition and convention by theories like the 'survival of the fittest', 'materialistic interpretation of history', the 'will to power', the 'Marxian dialectic', and more recently the development of psycho-analysis and the exploration of 'the unconscious'. These influences can be traced throughout the arts, but, as might be expected, they are particularly obvious in literature both communicative and expressive. Criticism has had to be adjusted to meet new conditions and during the process of adjustment the backchat of the leaders of literary opinion has exhibited many of the characteristics of propaganda in wartime.

Indulgence in the *tu quoque* turns discussion into dispute and destroys or limits opportunities for that literary guidance for which there is a steady demand.

This book is not about purposeful reading, nor about reading to gratify authors or critics or teachers. There is no advocacy of 'great books', 'classics' or other literary 'high-lights'; I believe that nothing is more likely to destroy an authentic gift for reading than undue insistence upon established masterpieces, or the favouring of a list of some enthusiast's 'Hundred Best Books'. The only hundred best books is the hundred that is best for you. Nor should a potential graduate in bookmanship read what he ought to read. But although he may free himself from external interferences, or open attempts at the subjugation of any natural taste he may have, reading is not free of its own conditions. No art is free. Whether it is painting or poetry, building or governing, living or reading, art is hedged about by conditions imposed by technique, form, materials, circumstances and traditions, each of which can be and often is dictatorial and even tyrannical. The so-called freedoms of art are probably attempts on the part of the artist to hide his bondage. A free verse is as illusory as a free state. If verse were free it would not be verse just as a consistently free state would soon be a state of chaos.

In the following pages I show how this kind of dilemma may be circumvented, the method advised being 'mind your own business', which in this context is reading, not writing. I put the case for the reader, but without claiming to exhaust so large a theme. The problems of reading, not those of writing or appraising, are emphasised, but the reading I have tried to expound does not rule out the pleasure or the necessity of textual and technical appraisement. The points of view of the connoisseur and the bellettrist are not despised, but they are beyond the scope of this volume, and since the majority of writers upon the art of reading deal with that aspect of the subject, there is no reason to re-travel a well-worn path, not, however, because it lacks interest or legitimacy, but because it is accepted and familiar. My concern is less with method than with effect. A synthesis is more than implied and its end is a person rather than a book. It is not necessary or desirable to go beyond the personal, for a person adequately developed compasses the world in the cosmogony of himself. For that reason the object of this treatise is not books solely as works of art but books as one of the means of the art of living; and the artistry upheld is not appraised as a thing in itself, but as a method of implementing a fuller life.

If reading is to be an art, it follows that the reader must have special qualifications. Much will depend upon the quality of his mind and the quality and extent of his reading. But the qualifications required do not end there, the technique indicated demands alertness of the senses, the mind, and the imagination. The reader must exercise these three faculties in a controlled appreciation of a book if he is to share the writer's aesthetic experience without being prevented from distilling it into an aesthetic experience of his own.

Bookmanship is the art of adjusting literature to life. It is concerned with the functional character of books in so far as they serve life rather than a particular livelihood. Life in this connection is to be understood as personal living, not so much as how other people live as how you live or wish to live. Bookmanship thus becomes the faculty of uniting a book with the life of a reader. It means also that a reader must read for himself, and, first and last, to please himself. No other reason is given and no compulsion or persuasion is implied or suggested.

I am not, however, trying to create a new type of reader, still less to add to the existing list of ideal readers, but to define a class. Within the class there is room for many variations. Only the imitative reader who habitually follows a fashion, or the reader who reads what he ought to read, is black-balled. The reader of my imagining is a blend of the 'gentle reader' of tradition and the more contemporaneous 'fit reader'. In his make-up there would be room for Stendhal's 'passionate few', Meredith's 'acute but honourable minority', and Walter Pater's 'grave' or 'susceptible' reader, as well as for the 'fit reader' who 'reads to discover how life seems to another, partly to try how his attitudes will suit us, engaged as we also are in the same enterprise'.[1] I think it is obvious that if the reader is to achieve artistry he must be prepared to devote an athletic attention to what is worth reading, as well as to be capable of avoiding or throwing out what is of less repute. 'Every book', according to a dictum of Henry Fielding's, 'ought to be read with the same spirit as it is writ,'[2] but if this is too great a demand and beyond the capacity of reasonable fitness, the reader worthy of the name should, in Pater's words, be capable of a 'minute consideration' for writing which 'in every minutest detail . . . is a pledge that it is worth the reader's while to be attentive'.[3] So keeping this concept of fitness

[1] I. A. Richards, *Science and Poetry* (1926), 46. [2] *Tom Jones* (1749). Intro. Bk. iv. [3] *Appreciations* (1889), 10.

well in mind we may now proceed more or less comfortably upon our adventure with reasonable hope of reaching, if not agreement, at least intelligent disagreement, on the involved and contentious problem of the art of reading.

CHAPTER I

THE READER AS ARTIST

'A sufficient reader shall often discover in other men's compositions, perfections farre-differing from the Author's meaning, and such as haply he never dreamed of, and illustrateth them with richer senses.' MONTAIGNE, *Essays*, (Dent i, 128).

'Good reading is an art.' R. W. EMERSON, *Journals* (1914) v, 24.

'The meaning of any beautiful created thing is at least as much in the soul of him who looks at it, as it was in his soul who wrought it. Nay, it is rather the beholder who lends to the beautiful thing its myriad meanings and makes it marvellous for us, and sets it in some new relation to the age, so that it becomes a vital portion of our lives, and a symbol of what we pray for, or perhaps, of what, having prayed for, we fear that we may receive.'—OSCAR WILDE, *Intentions* (1891).

---

i

The art of reading is not a virtue or a duty, but a faculty which at no time has won the allegiance of more than a small if satisfied following; but it has the virtue of being one of the few entirely disinterested occupations. When we read solely to please, or in other words to express ourselves we rob no one, hurt no one, annoy no one, compete with no one, and expect nothing in return but the pleasure of the experience. We may desire at times to share some of these experiences, but first and last we read to ourselves and for ourselves whatever reasons we may give, and, in an increasingly regimented world this faculty is a precious possession and should be jealously protected as it may well be the last resort of individual expression.

I refer to that kind of reading which has no practical or useful purpose, ignoring for my immediate argument, but not despising, books devised for education or instruction, although even technical books may produce effects other than those immediately intended. Reading, with or without an ulterior object forces us, inevitably, to readjust our minds and our emotions to the conditions brought about by the simple contact of reader and writer. Approval is not always necessary. Clash of interests, differences of opinion, and even lack of understanding may startle dormant consciousness into activity, when an immediate and harmonious adjustment may lull rather than awaken the mind.

The books I have in mind comprise what Thomas de Quincey called the 'literature of power' as distinct from its antithesis the 'literature of knowledge',[1] they are those books which express rather than inform: books from which the reader may learn nothing but by which he may become something. The range is wide for it includes poetry, fiction, essays, travel, biography, autobiography and history as well as philosophy and even, to some extent, science; with excursions (which De Quincey might not have permitted) into the expository realms of theology, politics and law. But it requires no undue stretching of the idea to include in my category of books that are books for this purpose, say, the sermons of a Donne or a Jeremy Taylor, the orations of a Demosthenes or a Churchill, or the dissertations of a Blackstone or a Maine, for in works of that kind the special pleadings are as personal in origin and character as they are in the more subjective of histories, such as those of Gibbon or Macaulay.

So when I use the word 'literature' I refer to all that kind of writing which has for its object expression, interpretation, or description, rather than that which is concerned primarily with facts or information. There is, however, no fixed frontier between the two classes because it is not possible to eliminate the writer from even the most objective writings, and it is not easy to sweat literature

---

[1] This classification was first used by De Quincey in his 'Letters to a Young Man Whose Education has been Neglected', published in the *London Magazine*, 1823: 'I . . . use the antithesis power and knowledge as the most philosophical expression for literature (that is *Literae Humaniores*) and anti-literature (that is *Literae didacticae*—παιδεία!)'. The idea was amplified in his essay on 'Alexander Pope' (1848), *Works*, ix.

of purpose without falling into the booby-trap of art for art's sake. The end of reading is living, not reading—even the best books.

ii

It is not my intention to applaud or expound books as instruments of culture, their use to that end being well established, but rather to present a case for their less appreciated use as a means of self-expression. In doing so it will be necessary to distinguish between knowing and experiencing as you would distinguish between learning and living, and to remember always that reading is not merely a pastime, nor a method of indulging a taste for fine writing, any more than it is solely a means of absorbing information. Books are as varied and as extensive as life, and reading, like living, is largely composed of repetitive operations, but seldom in the same circumstances or under identical conditions, and sometimes illuminated by unique and memorable events and experiences.

With reading, as with living, we regret opportunities lost more than opportunities taken, even when the supervening experiences have been disappointing or unfortunate. Yet the reader has every chance of good fortune for books are ubiquitous, inexhaustible, and of infinite variety. He might at first be dismayed by such accessible opulence. But even in the Reading Room of the British Museum besieged by the invitations of four million volumes he need not be downhearted, for no reader, however learned, has read everything or could read everything. Nor has any reader read everything that is readable, or that he ought to read, or that is wise, good, or otherwise excellent according to this or that point of view. But it is a curious fact that the best readers continue to be disturbed by the gaps in their bookish experiences, when they ought to know that the better the reader, the more obvious the gaps will be. Good reading has depth rather than breadth and the quintessence of bookmanship is selection. The writer as writer roves the world of life and letters and selects what is peculiar to himself and his needs. The reader as reader does the same with literature. Reading, like living, should be qualitative not quantitative if it is to give that kind of pleasure which by deepening and refining the sensibilities extends the boundaries and augments the quality of our lives.

To regret that one has not enough time to read all books, or even all the best books, is useless, like regretting that one cannot visit all the desirable places of the world, or experience every exquisite sensation. Reading, like painting or sculpture, reveals its artistry at every stage. It begins but it need not end. It just stops or goes on and should suffice at every pause. All the stars and all the heavens in a page—or a sentence. Reading should be three parts gloating, dreaming, pondering upon the thing read. We all have our moments of gluttony when we can't get enough and tend to bite off more than we can chew: but to chew is best. Many books are not essential. If a book is any good you find something worth pondering on every time you open it no matter how many times you have read it. Nietzsche wanted cow-like readers: those who chew the cud. He was not disinterested but he was right. Good readers ruminate. To scamper through a book is like bolting your food: you miss the flavour and risk dyspepsia. There are, however, degrees of slowness. You must taste in order to assimilate. Taste is perception, assimilation understanding.[1]

iii

In addition to their use as instruments of knowledge and culture books have a wider if less definite use in the service of a universal desire for rest, escape and recreation. But as this function does not include all the services rendered by books, it must not be supposed to classify the aims of readers irrevocably, for objectives overlap and readers are often found enjoying several of the advantages offered by books simultaneously. Rest, escape and recreation are generalisations within the experiences of most readers, and lend themselves to examination without undue emphasis upon idiosyncrasy.

iv

Reading for rest, or passive reading, needs no explanation. It is the familiar, and within bounds, harmless habit of reading without thinking, when, for one reason or another, feeling is barren and thought a burden. It is the nihilism of thought, a form of anaesthesia, for where no mental effort is made no impression is left upon the mind and consequently no result is registered, or the mind and the imagination are walled-in with trite concepts and stale abstractions. Direct memory plays but a small part in such reading. Books thus approached may be totally forgotten, or remembered only on re-reading. But if they serve no mental purpose some of the impressions may strike deeper than others and lie fallow pending the awakening touch of a future experience. Yet the results of the idlest reading are

[1] See Notes.

not always so slight; casual impressions of both life and letters often strike deep when we are scarcely aware of their penetrations, and, though forgotten at the time, they reveal themselves later as permanent inmates of our consciousness.

V

Reading to escape is the use of books as 'loopholes of retreat' from life, the world, circumstances, which, in the end, whatever you call it, is yourself. Reader and writer meet here on common ground:

> *Then as th'earth's inward narrow crooked lanes*
> *Do purge sea water's fretfull salt away,*
> *I thought, if I could draw my paines,*
> *Through Rhyme's vexation, I should them allay.*
> *Grief brought to numbers cannot be so fierce,*
> *For, he tames it, that fetters it in verse.*[1]

The aim is not an escape from life but the substitution of one kind of life or one kind of consciousness for another, in the hope, not always consciously formulated, that it will afford relief from boredom, anxiety, sorrow, or whatever condition of living may have become tedious, painful, or intolerable.

At all times books have been used to relieve temporary annoyances, minor (and sometimes major) anxieties, or boredom, yet it is often argued that to use them in this way is like resorting to drugs or drink for relief which should be sought in action. But whether you 'glut your sorrow on a morning rose', or:

> *. . . take a large hoe and a shovel also*
> *And dig till you gently perspire*

the remedy must be judged by results. Books are known to be efficacious, and not always the best books, 'the compilers of salacious memoirs and of contemporary reminiscences, the writer even of commercial fiction and of negligible drama, have a right to exist which they share with the licensed victualler. They supply drams to the brains of men too weary to think and too much caught up in the machine to feel.'[2]

But the desire to escape is not always morbid nor due to misfortune.[3] Everyone has experienced the convenience of books as aids to escape

[1] John Donne, *The Triple Foole.* [2] Ford Madox Hueffer, *The Critical Attitude* (1911), 65. [3] See Notes.

from the tedium of a railway journey or a sea voyage. Macaulay, who may often have been wrong-headed but was nearly always healthy-minded, and being neither recluse nor misanthrope, did not hesitate to use books to escape from the tedium of travel and the stress of affairs, as well as from his fellow men. When stationed in India, he reflected that the 'best rule in all parts of the world, as in London itself', was 'to be independent of other men's minds,' and his method of releasing his own mind from obtrusive companionship on the long voyage to the East in 1834, was reading. He read 'insatiably', and even he was proud of the extent and variety of his achievement. The list of books read on the voyage includes: The *Iliad* and *Odyssey*, *Virgil*, *Horace*, Caesar's *Commentaries*, *Bacon*, *De Augmentis*, *Dante*, *Petrarch*, *Ariosto*, *Tasso*, *Don Quixote*, Gibbon's *Rome*, Mill's *India*, all the seventy volumes of *Voltaire*, Gismondi's *France*, and the seven thick folios of the *Biographia Britannica*. Macaulay not only read on one voyage what might well have served a cultured reader for a lifetime, but he remembered and compared and criticised and made notes and wrote to friends about what he was reading, showing that he could escape at will from the world of men into a very complete world of his own fashioning.

The modern objection to what is now generally known as 'escapist literature' is paradoxical, most of the objectors being revolutionaries who would willingly shatter this world to bits and remould it nearer to their own desires—or to those of the latest ideologist. They ignore the possible inference that as escapist literature has always existed it must satisfy some need, and further that since the demand for it is considerable at the present time, the need must be greater.

All literature is impelled by desire for escape or self-realisation: escape from personality or realisation of personality. Avoidance or acceptance of personality and its attendant emotions, are, in fact, equally escapist, and the two desires are closely related, each of them, whether it is born of deep resolve or shallow irritation, indicating an impulsion towards change of condition.[1] Desire to escape is not necessarily degenerate, still less a sign of defeat. It may be a desire for liberation. There is a vast difference between, say, the *Imitation of Christ* and *Mein Kampf*. Each promises a method of escape, one from the material world, the other from political conditions.

---

[1] 'Retrospective regionalism was a retreat from contemporary confusion; as a movement [in U.S.A.] it ended in mere quaintness.' Granville Hicks, *Proletarian Literature* [n.d.], 355.

18

The *Psalms of David* and *Pilgrim's Progress, News from Nowhere,* the *Rubáiyát of Omar Khayyám* and *Thus Spake Zarathustra,* are as escapist as the 'Ode to a Nightingale', the 'Scholar Gipsy', or the 'Blessed Damozel'. The desire to escape is not peculiar to mankind, it is common to all forms of life. Every living thing is running away from something or developing defences which make running away unnecessary. The desire to escape from the annoyances and perils of civilisation is instinctive and salutary:

> *He who fights and runs away*
> *Lives to fight another day*

is a popular adage, and timidity has possibly played as great a part as bravery in the development of the species. It is sometimes difficult to distinguish one from the other.

It would be no exaggeration to say that the desire to escape from the 'fever and fret' of life has been the greatest of all literary stimuli from Homer to Shaw, Proust and Rilke.[1] The difference between ancient and modern escapists is that the moderns are inquisitive about the life from which they would escape. They have, like Kipling's soldier, a nostalgia for the world they condemn—

> *. . . it never done no good to me*
> *But I can't drop it, if I tried.*

vi

Reading for recreation (which is the main theme of this book) may include reading for rest and escape, but it is consciously creative, recharging the spirit with vitality, acting positively as a stimulant to invigorate and encourage. By this method you may rest and be refreshed, or escape from yourself to meet yourself on better terms. It is a change that recuperates, a mode of life rather than a substitute for life. It is an instinctive pursuit of designs for living and at its best a contribution to the art of living.

vii

But when each of the above generalisations has been considered it will be found that much that is of value in books is not to be caught

[1] 'I do not read poetry as a critic; I read it as a human being in need of solace, refreshment and peace.' W. Somerset Maugham, *Books and You,* 21.

in their nets. There is, for instance, an indefinable quality with an equally indefinable technique which is common to all fit readers and to all readers capable of ultimate fitness. It is innate and instinctive, and although it can be developed by its owner, it cannot be acquired, and deliberate attempts to guide it are apt to mislead. To impose rules or opinions on such a delicately balanced mechanism is to disturb the balance and weaken the sense of perception or direction in thought and feeling. Fit readers find their own way from start to finish and they rarely take the wrong turning. They know by instinct what is eligible for the canon of good literature. The first line, almost the first word, of a poem tells them whether the rest is poetry or not. They can tell *biblia* from *a-biblia* almost by touch! Nor is approval of an author essential to enjoyment. If you have this instinct for books, you may be charmed and disenchanted simultaneously. An irritant may provoke pleasure as well as evoke consciousness of hitherto unapprehended characteristics and qualities.

Books resemble people or the characters in a novel. 'There are', says George Saintsbury, 'characters in fiction that one adores, or at least loves, and others (it is an equal compliment to their authors) that one hates. There are yet others that one admires, laughs at, would like to quarrel with, and in a dozen other ways recognises as rightly created under the conditions of novel creation.'[1] In *Hortus Inclusus* Ruskin refers to a book 'of a character at once prosaic, graceful and simple, which will disenchant and refresh you at once'. Prosaic, graceful, simple, disenchanting and refreshing! These qualities are all ambiguous and matters of opinion; except, perhaps, 'simple'—but no, not even that, for what is my simplicity may be your complexity. Some readers may be merely disenchanted by a book, others refreshed by it as well. Books which do no more than disenchant may be second-rate, but first-rate disenchanters invigorate and enlighten. Bernard Shaw, for example, disenchants and refreshes. So do Schopenhauer, and Montaigne, and Nietzsche, and Turgenev, and Anatole France, and Voltaire, and Samuel Butler . . . realists, pessimists, ironists . . . their wine is never sugary and it rarely goes to the liver, though some of the vintages go to the head.

viii

Even books which are technically bad may give pleasure, and they have other uses as well.[2] An ingenious anthologist once supported

---

[1] 'Trollope Revisited,' *Collected Essays* (1923), 340.   [2] See Notes.

this idea with a compilation called *Half Hours with the Worst Authors*. Samuel Butler took a peculiar delight in books which aroused his puckish contempt. He was 'immediately fascinated' with A. C. Benson's *Life of Archbishop Benson* much as he had been with Hallam, Lord Tennyson's *Life of Alfred Tennyson*—'only more so—for bad as the *Life of Tennyson* was, the *Life of Archbishop Benson* is worse.' In much the same mood Joseph Conrad 'enjoyed' *The Gadfly* by E. Voynich. 'It is perfectly delightful,' he told Edward Garnett, 'I don't remember ever reading a book I disliked so much.'[1] Unreadable books are known to have value for the student and the historian, but they cannot be recreative as well unless we remember that the term is relative. Bancroft, author of the *History of Central America*, for instance, is now, according to Aldous Huxley, 'almost unreadable; but for the sake of what he may be made to mean by future alchemists of the mind, he deserves all respect.'[2] Van Wyck Brooks pays a similar left-handed compliment to Mark Twain's novel, *The Gilded Age*. 'It is not a good novel; it is, artistically, almost an unqualified failure. And yet, as inferior works often do, it contains the very spirit of its time; it tells, that is to say, a story which, in default of any other and better, might well be called the Odyssey of Modern America.'[3] It all depends upon the immediate object of your reading. Alchemists of the mind may revel in an outmoded *History of Central America* and be bored by *Beyond the Mexique Bay*. The observer of literature would want to know why: he is not necessarily convinced when he learns that so high an authority as Sainte-Beuve has called *Salammbô* unreadable.[4] It is the history of these expressions which counts, not the expressions themselves.

ix

If books were solely purveyors of knowledge they could not serve such a variety of purposes. We need not take anything from them, but they can help us to recover from ourselves, from our inner lives, qualities, treasure, which might otherwise go unheeded. Everyone contains within himself dormant characteristics which can be awakened by the touch of art, and more conveniently and more permanently by those arts which are enshrined in books. Literature

[1] *Letters from Conrad: 1895–1924.* Ed. Garnett (1928), 101. [2] *Beyond the Mexique Bay* (1936), Albatross Ed., 130. [3] *The Ordeal of Mark Twain* (1922), 55–6. [4] *Journals of the Goncourts.* Trans. Galantière (1937), 135.

contains seeds which can develop only in the mind of the reader. The fertilisation of those seeds depends upon the nature of the ground, and their growth is affected by the presence or absence of intelligence, imagination, culture and experience of life. It is the presence or absence of the first three which differentiates. Experience is qualified by intelligence and imagination and culture because the approach to life is much the same as the approach to letters. What we find in a book is life transmuted into words, and life, as we know, can be more ambiguous than letters. Life and letters, indeed, are fundamentally identical, and appreciation as well as impression depend upon sensitiveness qualified by experiences, both vital and imaginative.

x

To obtain these results the method of reading should be concentrated rather than extensive. To read well it is not necessary to be 'well read'. On the contrary, the well-read man is often one who has accumulated knowledge at the expense of imagination. He is a scholar not an artist, educated rather than experienced. Yet although experience of reading is deepened when accompanied by mental and imaginative alertness, the mere memory of half-forgotten bookish experiences which were not even enjoyable at their inception may have a similar effect. Most general reading is little more than skimming; much is forgotten as the eye glances over the page, noting phrases, ideas, incidents, when they stick out, with no intention of remembering them. But these casual impressions are recorded and often recalled under the impression that they are original. Ideas are propagated more by this sort of unconscious plagiarism than by propaganda or education. Perhaps subconscious pilfering is the basis of intelligence, for the mimetic faculty is one of the impelling forces of life.

Many readers can recall instances of such automatic reactions, and some have been recorded. One of the best and most familiar is in the *Grammar of Assent* where Newman considers 'how differently young and old are affected by the words of some classical author, such as Homer and Horace'. To the boy those passages 'are but rhetorical commonplaces, neither better nor worse than a hundred others which any clever writer might supply, which he gets by heart and thinks very fine, and imitates, as he thinks, successfully, in his own flowing versification.' But they 'come home to him when long years have passed, and he has had experience of life, and pierce him, as if he had never before known them, with their sad earnestness and vivid exactness. Then he comes to understand how it is that lines, the birth of some chance morning or evening at an Ionian festival, or among the Sabine hills, have lasted generation after generation, for thousands of years, with a power over the mind, and a charm, which the current literature of his own day, with all its glorious advantages, is utterly unable to rival.'

The peculiarity and probably the charm of such experiences, however, is that we do not understand them. We have never learned why lines born of some chance morning or evening at an Ionian festival, or among the Sabine hills, have become so precious to us. All we know is that they are precious, and just as the current literature of our own day, with all its advantages, has been utterly unable to rival them, so the current science of our own days, with all its knowledge, has failed utterly to explain the miracle.

xi

Such reading with its final test of individual sensibility adopts a similar attitude to that of the artist towards phenomena. But just as it is impossible to turn an ordinary man into an artist by educational methods, so it is impossible to make a reader by rule or precept. Readers are born not made, and what is not there cannot be developed. Thousands of children are taught to draw or paint, millions are taught to write and read, but few become painters or poets—or readers. The reason is obvious. If the germ or gift is there all is well. Reading may become an art if the reader is equipped with a sensitive independence of choice and a desire to apply it with that passionate rigour which is a condition imposed by all artistry.

A book may thus be one of the media of an art as well as a work of art.[1] It is a device by means of which a reader may apprehend himself more vividly and more satisfactorily than he could if left to his own resources in a world of confused sensations and experiences. Books properly understood and used should co-ordinate the experiences of reader and writer, producing a harmony out of two assertive

---

[1] Two modern poets have recognised this idea in their analysis of the technique and effect of *Sunset*, a poem by E. E. Cummings, which presents 'a complicated recipe for a sunset experience', and if used 'turns the reader into a poet'. Laura Riding and Robert Graves, *A Survey of Modernist Poetry* (1927), 41.

forces, that of an author who says in effect, 'I am,' and of a reader who says, less consciously but not less effectively, 'I become'. But the reader does not become the author, he becomes himself. Goethe had this idea of the dæmonic power of books when he told Eckermann that we 'learn nothing' by reading Winckelmann but 'we become something'.[1]

xii

I am aware that such an attitude towards books may seem anomalous to some readers, but the anomaly is only apparent, based as it is upon the popular conception of a writer as invariably the creator of objective works, when the reverse is more often true. But in respect of this inevitable display of exhibitionism, writer and reader have much in common. They are both performers and each plays a part to himself, and often for himself, whether before an audience or not. If, as Somerset Maugham holds, the writer is 'the Comedian who never loses himself in the part, for he is at the same time spectator and actor',[2] the same may be claimed for the reader who must involuntarily place himself in the attitude of the writer without losing his own identity, for he is at the same time reader, or spectator, and (by proxy) writer, or actor, as well. When he seeks to unveil the writer he unveils himself and the subsequent revelation is also a creation.

But that after all is only one phase of art. There is artistry in perception, in point of view, and in attitude. To be an artist you must first possess a sensibility which will give distinction and significance to what you perceive, and with that gift and the power to use the results of imagination you remain an artist whether you have a public or not, or whether you make something tangible or not; for just as a violinist may perform for himself alone and be an artist, so may a reader become an artist by using books to express himself to himself. When you enjoy, that is absorb, a poetical or prose work, you re-create it for yourself in your own mind. It becomes your own.

If writing, therefore, is existence to the writer (that is to say, the point at which expression and consciousness merge), if the writer writes to become himself or to discover himself, for becoming and discovering are allied, so also is reading to the reader. The reader reads to express, to discover, to become, but books not pens and paper are the media of his art. The reader has many other points of

---

[1] *Conversations* (Everyman Ed.), 173.   [2] *The Summing-Up* (1938), 99.

resemblance to the writer; one of the most important is that both are subject to the same general conditions of life. Their responses to these conditions are different not in kind but in depth and quality of expression; the same degree of response existing between reader and reader, as, indeed, between artist and artist. There are no means of measuring degrees of aesthetic experience, but we all know that they exist. Everyone to a greater or lesser degree is conditioned intellectually and emotionally by his environment and the differences between creation and absorption are technical. Reading as well as writing is a part of the technique of the art of literature. One may write books, another read them, and some do both; but the unresolved intentions and the immeasurable qualities of the processes are identical.[1]

Reading, then, is the art of extracting essences from books for our own, not the author's benefit, but it happens that the best of those essences are extracted when we read in a spirit of give and take. Without capacity for occasional self-abandonment a reader is not fully equipped for his job. Virginia Woolf, who was distinguished both as reader and writer, put the case for this form of creative collaboration when she said, 'Do not dictate to your author; try to become him. Be his fellow-worker and accomplice. If you hang back, and reserve and criticise at first, you are preventing yourself from getting the fullest possible value from what you read. But if you open your mind as widely as possible, then signs and hints of almost imperceptible fineness, from the twist and turn of the first sentences, will bring you into the presence of a human being unlike any other.'[2]

Youth is the period for such abandonments for then there is pleasure and advantage in submitting to the dominance of a book. We enjoy the feeling of being overwhelmed, and the opportunity of temporarily losing identity in the mind of another is an experience which sometimes takes the place of a passionate friendship. J. H. Shorthouse, author of *John Inglesant*, felt the strange power which

[1] 'A poet may be able to appreciate the merit of each particular Part of his own poem as well, or (if he have a well-disciplined mind) better than any other can do; but the *effect* of the whole as a whole, he cannot from the very nature of things (from the fore-knowledge of each following part, from the parts having been written at different times, from the blending of the pleasures and disgusts of composing with the composition itself, etc.) have the same sensation as the Reader or auditor to whom the whole is new and simultaneous.' S. T. Coleridge, 1811, *Unpublished Letters*. Ed. E. R. Griggs (1932), ii, 64. [2] 'How One should Read a Book.' *The Common Reader*, second series (1932), 259.

could subsist between reader and writer at such times. He refers to
the 'affection . . . that springs up between the author and those of
his readers who appreciate him, or sometimes, failing that, the
friendship which seems to exist . . . between myself and the book
itself; it seems to me that a favourite book knew me'.[1] The idea is
supported by a contemporary writer, L. A. G. Strong, who says that
'The discovery of a poem which really means something to you,
which becomes a part of your private world, is like the discovery
of a friend: and, like a friend, it gives you more at every meeting.'[2]

The fit reader whilst preserving his willingness to share an
experience, is active rather than passive. If there is a correct
attitude it is that of Edward Dowden. In the early days of his
professorship in Ireland he writes, 'I have always felt dominated by
Goethe when I approached and stayed long with him', but, he
added, 'I always at the same time felt something protesting against
the influence.'[3] He felt that there was something weak about
unconditional surrender, and he feared the influence of Goethe.
With Wordsworth it was different: 'What is peculiar to Wordsworth
rather than what he possesses in common with other poets, and his
earlier writings rather than his later, drew me into one long trance
of communion with him, which for a while—for some years—
excluded every other influence of a profound kind, and was to my
life what the sunrise seen by the wanderer from a "bold headland"
was to the day which followed it.'[4] This influence was one of
'absolute harmony—almost identity'. Yet Dowden never quite lost
his identity when reading the poems even of Wordsworth—'it
seems to have been appropriating without surrendering itself really
for a moment;'[5] and again he says 'I read Wordsworth a great deal,
and find my own in his pages',[6] and in the end, after having been
'enveloped' by Wordsworth, he can 'go in and come out at will',
revering and loving him, but retaining his independence.[7]

xiii

Reading is an adventure with some of the characteristics of the
chase. Yet when we adventure among masterpieces with the object,
say, of tracking down Pater's 'last lurking delicacies of colour and
form', not finally for the sake of their colour and form but for what

[1] *Life* (1905), 41. [2] *Common Sense About Poetry* (1932), 162. [3] *Fragments from Old Letters* (1914), 48. [4] *Ib.*, 79. [5] *Ib.*, 12. [6] *Ib.*, 59,
[7] *Ib.*, 64.

impelled those qualities, we are explorers rather than hunters, observers rather than devotees. We confer, exchange, and compare ourselves with them. We win most not by absorbing them wholly, nor yet by following them implicitly, but by holding our own and remaining ourselves. Paul Valéry had this sense of exploration centred in self. When he was studying Leonardo da Vinci, he wandered so far into his subject that he did not know how to return but consoled himself with the thought that 'every road leads back to oneself'.[1]

It is only by temporarily losing ourselves that we may hear those inward intimations which are often awakened by a book and are its best reward. For an author can give us little compared with what we may take from him. The best he can do is to make us aware of inward riches which we already possess. 'What the writer does', says Katharine Mansfield, 'is not so much to *solve* the question but to *put* the question.'[2] The skilled reader, in Montaigne's phrase, 'puts his ear close to himself, and holds his breath and listens.'

⟩ When Schopenhauer said that reading was merely thinking with other people's brains, he was right. Reading is even further in that direction. It is becoming someone else for the time being and running the risk of remaining so. When we read we do not so much enter into the souls of others; we let them enter into us. We become Shakespeare or his characters—Hamlet, Falstaff, Antony, Touchstone. When we read Schopenhauer we become Schopenhauer, which was probably what Schopenhauer intended. When we read Whitman we may become Whitman, which was what Whitman intended although he seemed to deny it when he said that his best disciple was the one who learnt how to destroy the master. And that also is what all fit readers intend. They do not read in order to become someone else. They read in order to become more fully and more distinctly themselves. They go forth from themselves and after a while they return home having gained something and lost something. Thus reading becomes an experience, and although it may begin by prolongation through the imagination of the author's experience, it ends by becoming a part of the reader's consciousness, by a process of absorption, in itself an experience which can in certain circumstances be as impressive as that which originally inspired the author. Far from being a question of subjection no great book can be adequately appreciated unless it is read with something

[1] *Introduction to the Method of Leonardo da Vinci.* Trans. McGreevy (1920), 14. [2] *Letters* (Albatross Ed.), 163.

of the quality that went to its making. We can't all hope to be geniuses, nor is that necessary or desirable, any more than it is necessary or desirable that all readers should become writers: the end of reading is living, not reading or writing. Reading should tune our sensibilities to such a pitch that we are able to respond to the poet in the book and the poet in ourselves: a book is not read until the reader becomes its equal.

The test of such an experience is a desire to prolong it. Every sensitive reading of the kind should be followed by a feeling of satisfaction and reluctance to take up another book. We are content to brood on our new experience and to resent, for the time being, interference with what seems to be an established state of mind. A writer must, therefore, persuade or fight us before we accept him. Cunninghame Graham is convinced that the writer and the reader are sworn foes: 'The writer labouring for bread, for hopes of fame, from idleness, from too much energy or from that uncontrollable dance of St. Vitus in the muscles of the wrist which prompts so many men to write (the Lord knows why), works, blots, corrects, rewrites, revises, and improves; then publishes, and for the most part is incontinently damned. Then comes the reader cavalierly . . . and gingerly examining the book says it is rubbish, and that he wonders how people who should have something else to do, find time to spend their lives in writing trash.'[1] A writer must batter down the barricades of our prejudices, our criticisms, our resentments, and our complacencies, which are attempts to maintain our mental and spiritual possessions, and to conserve what we are. Great books are great victories rewarding instead of despoiling the vanquished. We benefit by surrender if we retain our integrity.

xiv

Literature in itself, however, is not an infallible passport at the frontiers of a reader's mind. The validity of a book is not always or instantly apparent even to the experienced observer. Confidence between author and reader is essential to acceptance, and many authors take pains to establish it. But confidence is neither simple nor easy to achieve. Writers who openly condescend to their readers by excessive brightness or ill-judged persuasiveness generally defeat their aim. The fit reader suspects salesmanship whether in the blurb or in the text, and even legitimate attempts to establish confidence

[1] R. B. Cunninghame Graham, *Thirteen Stories* (1900), Pref. ix.

are liable to be mistaken for the confidence trick. On the other hand, neglect to establish confidence may mean loss of readers. The chief obstacle is the natural and ineradicable interest of a writer in his own work and his belief that what he has to say will be comprehended automatically by the reader. This does not often occur, and in the last resort confidence in a book must depend upon the reader. There are doubtless many varieties of confidence, and two of the most useful have been segregated by Anthony Trollope, 'which two kinds the reader who wishes to use his reading well should carefully discriminate'. They are confidence in facts and confidence in vision. 'The one man tells you accurately what has been. The former requires simple faith. The latter calls upon you to judge for yourself, and form your own conclusions. The former does not intend to be prescient, nor the latter accurate. Research is the weapon used by the former; observation by the latter. Either may be false—wilfully false; as also may either be steadfastly true. As to that, the reader must judge for himself.'[1]

XV

The battle of the book should be a courtship ending in collaboration. An author should win our allegiance by opening windows and doors to the spirit, drawing blinds from imagination and perception, and thus helping us to perceive and savour more of life than would otherwise have been possible. At the same time a book is no more than an introduction, or, better, a passport: an introduction to oneself *apropos* of an author—a passport to our own territories. But we must explore the promised land independently, further aid is unnecessary, for we are enriched by the process of inspecting other minds even though we get no further or more distinct help from them. The danger is that the book which inspires should become a substitute for life rather than an extension or enrichment of life. The risk of such a sequel has stricken even writers of genius with bibliophobia. They have seen their own books become caves in which readers hide, instead of frontiers to new worlds into which they hoped their readers would penetrate. These magnanimous anxieties must not be confused with that more prevalent bibliophobia born of resentment against the legitimate changes which books bring about. Timid bibliophobes are jealous of these quiet,

[1] *Autobiography* (1883). Ed. Michael Sadleir (1923).

irresistible influences, not knowing when they may disturb pet ideas or dispel vested illusions. For a book is not the end of a voyage but the beginning.

xvi

Literature, whether imaginative or perceptive, has the power to stir our emotions as well as our imaginations. That is what De Quincey meant when he said that 'literature seeks to communicate power'. Power as he understood it was being 'made to feel vividly, and with a vital consciousness, emotions which ordinary life rarely or never supplies occasions for exciting, and which had previously lain unwakened, and hardly within the dawn of consciousness—as myriads of modes of feeling are at this moment in every human mind for want of a poet to organise them' when, he asks, 'these inert and sleeping forms *are* organised, when these possibilities *are* actualised, is this conscious and living possession . . . power, or what is it?'[1]

A book may also become a power by creating a revolution in the spirit by adding something to perception not hitherto possessed, just as it may rectify the emotions by inducing the 'vital consciousness' defined by De Quincey, or what Wordsworth called a 'new composition of feeling'.[2] But that is not all. The sharpening of the perceptions, the rectification of the emotions, needs no defence. A book which achieves so much justifies itself. Mere novelty of perception or of thought or feeling has no intrinsic value, except in special circumstances. If literature did no more it would be of less value than it is. But it can do more. It can re-awaken imagination and stimulate perception[3] so that the reader may not only add new wealth to his inner resources, but regain that which he has lost by indifference or by the inevitable erosion of the years.

A great book never loses this power to revive, restore, or stimulate consciousness. Its resources are inexhaustible. For that reason, doubtless, the competent reader is not always running after new books. The contrary is often, and probably always, more evident. Competent readers do not necessarily object to new methods or new ideas: they invariably return to old and familiar books because these alone create an illusion of permanence by stimulating recognition

[1] *Op. Cit., ante,* 14. [2] Letter to Prof. John Wilson ('Christopher North') *Memoirs,* i, 196. [3] 'If I have any relish for the beauties of nature, I may say with truth, that it was from *Virgil* and from *Thomson* that I caught it.' James Beattie, 22, vii, 1778. *Letters and Writings* (1824), ii, 3.

of things already known. The method varies but the result is the same. By recalling us to what we already possess books recover sensations and experiences from the limbo of unconsciousness. It is doubtful if they do anything better worth doing.

Writers have always aimed in some measure at some such recovery of the past, but not until recent years have the resources of memory been so intensively explored. Contemporary emphasis of this tendency, augmented by psycho-analysis and the development of the psychological novel with their insistence upon the past, is probably a symptom of our shaken and, perhaps, disintegrating civilisation. As security decreases and the pace of living increases we seek alternatives, and turn willingly from the shifting sands of the present to the ghostly security of the past, for although opinion of what has been may change, we feel that the past is secure. That feeling in itself is a consolation to a generation which is painfully aware of its shattered ideals and possessions; and for the same reasons we are increasingly suspicious of the future. But the past has not always been in favour or the future in disrepute. At the beginning of the century there were attempts to challenge the present with a philosophy of the future. H. G. Wells devoted several novels and essays to anticipations of the shape of things to come, and he addressed the Royal Society on *The Discovery of the Future*. Later, an Italian journalist, Marinetti, inaugurated a Futurist Movement with a manifesto which he and his followers scattered over Venice from the tower of the Campanile, exhorting the Venetians to destroy their festering antiquities and replace them with structures of concrete and steel.[1] Neither advocate got very far. On the contrary, Wells did no more than extend the present, and Marinetti became bogged in a decomposing civilisation under the illusion that he was bounding forward. His noisy philosophy with its war whoops and slogans, its praise of speed and machines, was a reversion to barbarism, aided and abetted by science. These results were to be expected, for the future is an illusion and the present too near at any time to be clearly understood; only the past is real and its reality increases as we and the world grow older.

xvii

Among the novelists who have deliberately and successfully exploited the subliminal past are Henry James and Marcel Proust.

[1] See Notes.

31

Their object was the same but where James desired to show in a variety of stories and novels the reactions of numerous individuals under the influence of what he called the 'sense of the past', Proust sought in one long novel to recover his own past, or an imaginative conception of it, in order to extend consciousness and prolong personal sensation. He realised that in the processes of time an impression apparently insignificant at its inception becomes a 'precious image', a symbol enshrining sensations more important and possessing a more immediate reality than more recent experiences. The reason is that past impressions determine future behaviour, and thus what he calls 'resurrections of memory' become an important phase of his technique of living. The method is something more than remembering; it is creative memory based upon research, and whilst it remains an art it keeps close to the technique of science. Proust's researches into the remote fortresses of the memory have for their object not the recovery of forgotten or half-forgotten experiences, but the recovery of time and the arrest of those erosions which gradually waste the territories of the mind. He believes in our inseparableness from the past and seeks to bring the 'embodiment of Time' into strong relief in his work.[1] It is necessary to point this out because the aim although clearly indicated in his title, *A la Recherche du Temps Perdu*, is often overlooked by English readers, because the title given to the translation, *Remembrance of Things Past*, is obviously based upon a too literal interpretation of the epigraph from Shakespeare's *Sonnets*:

> *When to the sessions of sweet silent thought*
> *I summon up remembrance of things past . . .*

His intention is not remembrance but recovery, or even discovery. Of this there is evidence throughout the novel, and especially in the last volume which has the significant title, *Le Temps Retrouvé*, which indicates an exploratory aim, as undoubtedly its achievement is recovery. In this epic of remembrance Marcel Proust has recovered his past life by re-living it imaginatively.

He goes further than most writers towards recognising the resemblance between reading and writing, and he is a convinced advocate of the rights of the reader. This is hinted at several times in his last volume and, if there were any doubt, revealed clearly in this passage: 'In reality, every reader, as he reads, is the reader ᴏ.

[1] *Time Regained* (*Le Temps Retrouvé*, 1927). Trans. Stephen Hudson (1941), 432.

himself. The work of the writer is only a sort of optic instrument which he offers to the reader so that he may discern in the book what he would probably not have seen in himself. The recognition of himself in the book by the reader is the proof of its truth and *vice versa*, at least in a certain measure, the difference between the two texts being often less attributable to the author than to the reader.'[1] Further on in the same book he reasserts this idea pointing out that it would not be correct to say that whilst writing his novel he was thinking of 'those who would read it as my readers, but the readers of themselves, my book being only a sort of magnifying glass. . . .'[2] In short, Proust looks upon the processes of reading as variations of the processes of writing, the difference being operational rather than functional.

The processes of reading, however, are still obscure, although there is a growing body of evidence and opinion which should help towards a reasonable explanation. This is especially true of more recent references to reading. In the past books were accepted in the main for their functional value as impartial contributions to knowledge or recreation. They were informative, consolatory, hortatory, amusing, and, as such, taken at their face-value. The chain of enthusiastic dissertations in praise of books from Richard de Bury to Frederic Harrison now seems to be composed of rather smug simplifications. There is little attempt to go below the surface or to analyse the effect of reading on individual temperaments, the assumption being that books are good for you whoever you are or whatever your status, social or temperamental, and that all readers live on the same plane of intelligence and are expected to have identical responses and reactions to the printed word. In our own time the approach to reading is often broader and deeper. We no longer skim over the surface of books, we dive into them. And, although Proust goes to the opposite extreme, it is undoubtedly true that when we dive we bring up not the author alone, but ourselves and the author, and sometimes ourselves alone.

The process has again been expounded by Proust in a description of the working of his own creative memory, and that something similar happens to the reader is supported by Virginia Woolf in some illuminating comments on the process of reading which follow closely her not entirely disinterested advocacy of abandonment to the author—for it must be remembered that Virginia Woolf was a

---

[1] *Ib.*, 265–6. [2] *Ib.*, 415.

writer first although one of the most profound and subtle readers of her time. In this passage she makes it quite clear that reading does not depend upon first impressions even if these have been received with the utmost understanding. Such impressions are inevitable and important but they are no more than half the process. If we are to get complete pleasure from a book the initial process must be followed by another. It might be called a period of fermentation similar to that which takes place in the mind of a writer before his impressions or experiences crystallise into a work of art. Virginia Woolf does not go quite so far. She says: 'We must pass judgment on these multitudinous impressions; we must make of these fleeting shapes one that is hard and lasting. But not directly. Wait for the dust of reading to settle; for the conflict and the questioning to die down; walk, talk, pull the dead petals from a rose, or fall asleep. Then suddenly without any willing of it, for it is thus that Nature undertakes these transmissions, the book will return, but differently. It will float to the top of the mind as a whole. And the book as a whole is different from the book received currently in separate phrases. Details now fit themselves into their places. We see the shape from start to finish; it is a barn, a pig-sty, or a cathedral. Now then we can compare book with book as we compare building with building.'[1]

xviii

There is little difference between this theory of reading and Wordsworth's theory of poetry.[2] It is the process with which we are familiar as 'emotion remembered in tranquillity', or as I should prefer it, experience remembered, or, better, distilled in tranquillity. This process is probably at work in the creation of all poetry as well as in all creative reading. Wordsworth, however, is not the best illustration of the idea when applied to reading; for that we must turn to his friend and inspirer, Coleridge, who gave to metaphysics what was meant for poetry, and whose poetic experiences were largely distillations of what he had read. He drugged himself with literature as well as with laudanum, and even the most fantastic images and incidents in his greatest poems are not creations in the popular sense but transmutations of bookish memories. Through the researches of John Livingstone Lowes we are able to trace the growth of *The Ancient Mariner* and *Kubla Khan* from memories of

[1] 'How Should One read a Book,' *The Common Reader*, Second Series (1932), 266–7. [2] See *post*, pp. 91–4.

what the poet has read, and to understand how imaginative genius has transmuted matter-of-fact into fantasy.

This investigation of the mechanism of one of the most subtle and imaginative of English poets would have been impossible if Coleridge had not possessed a lifelong habit of filling notebooks with memoranda of his reading. *The Road to Xanadu* is an examination of these memoranda apropos of two poems which have hitherto seemed devoid of material or earthly associations. *The Ancient Mariner* and *Kubla Khan* take you into the realm of dreams and seem to be made of ethereal stuff which is tarnished and coarsened even by contact with words. The *Note Books* are studied for the purpose of discovering what Coleridge read and what was the method of his reading: 'Few more significant questions can be asked about any man, and about Coleridge probably none.' What he read 'stuck like limpets in his memory' because he read 'with a falcon's eye for details in which lurked the spark of poetry'. It is not forgotten that Coleridge was a genius, 'But after making all allowance for those elements which are unique in Coleridge, as the incommunicable essence of every genius is unique, there remains a precious residuum which is peculiar to no individual, but which inheres in the nature of the imaginative faculty itself.' If 'to track a poet like Coleridge through his reading is to lay bare . . . what touched the springs of his imagination',[1] further examination of the working of such a 'precious residuum' which, in varying degrees is a common possession, will help us to realise how the unconscious storage of bookish memories may affect less gifted readers.

Lowes compares subconsciousness to a deep well into which impressions and memories are dropped to mature or to be forgotten according to the creative power of the individual. Coleridge is perpetually adding to and taking from this haunt of hidden treasure. 'One after another vivid bits from what he read dropped into the deep well. And there, below the level of conscious mental processes, they set up their obscure and powerful reaction. Up above, on the stream of consciousness (which is all that we commonly take into account) they had floated separate and remote; here in the well they lived a strangely intimate and simultaneous life. . . . Facts which sank at intervals out of conscious recollection drew together beneath the surface through almost chemical affinities of common elements. . . . And there is Coleridge's unconscious mind, while his

[1] John Livingstone Lowes, *The Road to Xanadu* (1930), 32–4.

consciousness was busy with the toothache, or Hartley's infant ills, or pleasant strollings with the Wordsworths between Nether Stowey and Alfoxden, or what is dreamt of in this or that philosophy—there in the dark moved the phantasm of the fishes and animalcules and serpentine forms of his vicarious voyagings, thrusting out tentacles of association, and interweaving beyond disengagement.' Bald statements like Father Bourzes' reference to fishes which 'made a kind of artificial fire in the water', and Captain Cook's protozoa which 'in the dark . . . had a faint appearance of glowing fire', are born again and born different in the magic of Coleridge's verse:

> *They moved in tracks of shining white,*
> *And when they reared, the elfish light*
> *Fell off in hoary flakes . . .*
>
> *Blue, glossy green, and velvet black,*
> *They coil'd and swam; and every track*
> *Was a flash of golden fire.*

'The creatures of the great deep had become the new creation of a yet deeper deep. And when the flash of inspiration at last came—that leap of association which, like the Angel in the Gospel, stirred to momentary potency the waters of the pool—it was neither fish, nor animalcules, nor snake-like things, nor veritable water-snakes, but these radiant creatures of the subliminal abyss that sported on the face of a sea lit by a moon which had risen from the same abyss. . . . No mortal eye had ever seen them coil or swim—certainly neither Father Bourzes, nor Cook, nor Hawkins, nor Bertram, nor Dampier —in the waters of any earthly sea. They were the birth of that creative deep, which is peculiar to the poet only in degree.'[1]

xix

It is not only the writer who is capable of looking inwardly: the faculty is common to all of us and practised by all according to circumstances, and the circumstances include pressure of experiences and degrees of sensibility. The difference between writer and reader is that the writer can reproduce his subliminal impressions and exhibit them to others, whilst the reader can only exhibit them to himself. The impressions may be equally profound whether the result is a poem or a meditation. The 'phantasms of association'

[1] *Ib.*, 58–9.

which Coleridge distilled from the pages of the books into a 'streaming interplay of images,' and which a reader may summon up and transmute in his own way, are under the influence of the 'creative energy' which is the 'plastic stuff both of life and art'.[1]

There are other ways of stimulating the hidden resources of our lives, but none that is so convenient. Unlike music, the theatre, or pictures, books can be wherever we are. They are the readiest as well as the most influential passports to territories of the mind and the imagination. It would be absurd to argue that they take the place of experience. They do nothing of the sort. What they do is to give, in the first place, experiences to the emotions and the mind which are not otherwise obtainable, and in the second, they augment the quality of living by predisposing the mind and the emotions to the adventure of contemplation, by sharpening the perceptions so that experience may be more vivid and more memorable.

Books may induce that sort of refreshment of the soul which corresponds with religious experience. Without such experiences, however they are obtained, we are not fully alive. 'So long', Amiel wrote in his *Journal*, 'as man is capable of self-renewal he is a living being. . . . If we are to remain among the living there must be a perpetual revival of youth within us, brought about by inward change and by love of the Platonic sort. The soul must be for ever recreating itself, trying all its various modes, vibrating in all its fibres, raising up new interests for itself . . .'[2] Books are one of the most authentic means of such renewal.

It is not suggested that reading should be limited to the promotion of spiritual or intellectual adventures, still less is it intended to belittle the various roles all books are destined to play. Any contributions to personal integrity are acceptable. And although I may have seemed to stress the importance of one kind of reading I am well aware of purposes less recognisable though perhaps not less profound, and in spite of the hint I have given that it is better to live out of a book than in it, there are terms upon which an inward bookishness contributes more to the amenities of the spirit than any measure of objective living. But there is no need to dogmatise since it is better to be good for yourself as well as good for something outside yourself than to limit your goodness to one or the other.

[1] *Ib.*, 92. Lowes explains the difference between art and what is not art by 'the presence or absence of imaginative control'.   [2] 29 : vii : 1871.

Books may serve many purposes. If we are to take sedatives books are better than drugs. If we need respite from ourselves, what better than to take a holiday by becoming someone else? And there is no more economical or convenient refreshment than a book. Indeed it is because all these purposes are beneficial as well as desirable that readers are instinctively disposed to combine them. That need not cause surprise, for the act of reading is co-ordinative, a merging of several faculties and instincts. When we read we endeavour to satisfy desire or whim by perception and comment, and we bring to our aid all the endowments of the mind from the comparatively simple act of observation to the complex activities of creative imagination.

xx

I have emphasised the important part played by memory in the transmission of written expression from mind to mind, because, without memory, reading would be robbed of half its value and much of its excitement. But there is little danger of that loss, for sensitive reading inevitably kindles reverie and contemplation, and most of us have secreted more impressions than we shall ever use. Reading helps us to recall them. From one point of view reading is a process of remembering, and, in certain moods, not the least enjoyable, we sort out our memories, handling the specimens critically in the museum of ourselves. Many of us live as much in the past as in the present, and we may be attracted to books because however much the past is disguised in them it is always present, for in addition to its ostensible theme a book springs memories of allied themes and their associations.

xxi

We differ from one another more by what we have read than by what we have done, for what we have done is often determined by what we have read—or not read. But whether that is true or not, there can be no doubt about the difference between a literate and an illiterate mode of life. Aldous Huxley goes so far as to say that 'If one happens to have received a rather elaborate academic education, it is almost impossible to represent to oneself the mental processes of people who have been taught, for all practical purposes, nothing except the useful arts of day-to-day living. For the educated

mind, all phenomena are interrelated . . . For the uneducated mind
. . . there is no beginning. Each experience is unique, isolated,
related intellectually to nothing else in the world. Between one star
of consciousness and another the only connecting links are the
physiological identity of the person who is conscious and perhaps
some rudimentary system of religious philosophy. The world of the
uneducated is a world of darkness, with a dim little light here and
another there, and between them, invisible, mysterious objects
with which from time to time the benighted traveller comes into
often painful contact, but of which he cannot distinguish the form
or recognise the function.' He sees in this nocturnal world the charm
of a Grand-Guignol thriller.[1]

He was thinking of the uneducated Mexican Indian, who is
beginning to develop a taste for 'reading for reading's sake' and
to believe that the 'printed word is intrinsically magical'. The men
so recently living in a savage state are encouraged, by a Ministry
of Education, by advertisements in the popular press, to read
The Prince of Machiavelli, Rousseau's *Social Contract* and Karl
Marx's *Capital*. Aldous Huxley wonders what will be the effect
of such books on primitive minds. But the primitive as distinct
from the educated mind is becoming extinct, and the contact with
books rarely becomes vital except for those who have been educated
and even then the reaction differs according to the degree and
quality of education. What we call an uneducated man is an inadequately educated man, one, for instance, who has had no
opportunities of education beyond the elementary school, not
one who has received no education at all. It is just this class,
however, which is most likely to be moved or conditioned by
books or newspapers. Education lays the foundations of reading
because it is in itself reading by proxy. When an uncultured reader
comes to read for himself he does not forget what he has been taught
but he adds new memories out of his sub-consciousness to the
intellectual minimum with which he was endowed by his social
condition.

xxii

An author can overshadow his works to their disadvantage, and to
the confusion of the reader. 'The name of a celebrated man often
becomes impregnated with all the impressions aroused by his work,

[1] *Beyond the Mexique Bay* (Albatross Ed. 1936), 240–1.

with the judgments of admiration or disapproval which it has received, and with the greater or lesser degree of the warmth of the said judgments.'[1] We have to contend with this author-legend as well as with the image of the author as revealed in his books plus the image of the book itself on the social screen. Happy the book, the *Bible, Homer, Shakespeare*, which has no author! Every age produces writers whose personal repute becomes so swollen that they are more discussed than read, with the result that when such a literary personality dies his books, no matter how good, pass into a state of suspended animation until Time rescues them from the ironic legacy of the repute of their sire.

Elsewhere in this work I show how literary conditioning affects criticism and, also, how it affects the general attitude towards life, for civilisation is still a product of the printing press whatever influences radio and the cinema may exercise in the not distant future. The average man may read little or nothing, and the little he reads may be useless or even dangerous, but he is none the less conditioned by books. Apart from his own reading he is the product of the reading of others. He sees what he has been taught to see at home and at school, and later by the popular press and the popular novelist. He rarely sees things with his own eyes except when they are within the circumscribed area of his occupation, and even so only the exceptionally sensitised individual observes instinctively what he sees, whether the object be a work of art or a work of nature.

The peculiarity of not being able to see things for yourself, or to think for yourself, is not confined to the average man. Intellectual and cultured people are even more intensively conditioned by the printing press. The outcome for both classes is the development of an artificial method of approaching life. The majority of people see life through the mind rather than through the eyes. They approach things and ideas through a haze of what has been learnt or thought about them rather than by direct observation. Myopia and fixity of idea, not perception, appear to govern the civilised attitude towards life. Every original writer is a challenge to this condition of illusion. The realists were conscious of what they were doing. They were seeing life anew. Flaubert stared at life until he saw it in a new and individual way, and he taught Maupassant to do the same. Perception, not thought, is the origin of originality, and for that reason

---

[1] Benedetto Croce, *European Literature in the Nineteenth Century*, 32.

naïvety and genius are closely allied. It is the eye which should feed the brain, not the brain the eye.[1]

xxiii

Recollections cross-hatch every reading moment so that whatever is read is mingled with what is remembered, and just as every book we read becomes a thread in the texture of life, so every book we read is also woven into the tradition and associations of all books. Books are palimpsests overlaid by the thoughts and feelings of generations of readers. Every new reader contributes something to the life of a book. Yet there are readers who feel that nothing changes but the surface; that change, in essentials, is illusion, and all that has been imagined or observed or thought is preserved in those masterpieces which have conquered time and opinion; so that if there were no more books literature would be complete in the pages of Shakespeare, Montaigne, Plato, Homer, as art is supposed by Whistler to be complete, "broidered with the birds upon the fan of Hokusai at the foot of Fuji-yama.'

So great a concentration is not likely. At all events printing has not only secured the permanence but guaranteed the multiplicity of books, and by so doing imposed upon readers the rewards and penalties of selection. The modern danger to literature is no longer loss by destruction but confusion by overproduction. The difficulties of an unlimited choice are recognised. Many guides appear, real and spurious, but little guidance; neither literary pundit nor book society, publisher or newspaper, has been able to solve the problem of literary selection. They can do little more than start a fashion for a particular book, when for a little while people go about saying to each other 'have you read' this or that new work, which they as readily forget. But fashions cannot give, and are not intended to give, permanent satisfaction, and however useful such methods may be they have little to do with the conception of reading outlined in this work.

[1] See *post*, Chapter v, 'Observation and Reading'.

CHAPTER II

HOW TO READ

'When we confer with masterpieces, exchange, compare our ideas with theirs, we get most out of them, not by absorbing them wholly, or by following them implicitly, but by remaining ourselves in all our traffic with them, only better, fuller, stronger for the association.'—HOLBROOK JACKSON, *The Anatomy of Bibliomania* (1930) i, Pt. 7, Ch. 6, p. 153.

i

Many essays upon reading, especially when they are by authors of pronounced individuality and limited popularity, are oblique, though often unconscious arguments for the reading of their authors' books. They are, in a very real sense, advertisements which may be read with amusement or instruction provided that the reader is aware of the attempt to persuade him to adopt a point of view favourable to the author and his own work. In order that the reader may not be taken in by a disinterestedness which is largely strategic, it is necessary to exercise something more than ordinary judgment. The fit reader will look below the surface and maintain a strict partiality for his own interests, realising, and this is an essential part of his fitness, that creative writers who take the trouble to tell you how to read are persuading you to become one of their own readers. They are building up a public for their own books behind a pose of impartiality. Generalisations on 'how to read' must, therefore, be applied to the books of the author expounding a particular theory of reading and not to all books. The disingenuous-

42

ness of literary advisers who cannot in the nature of things be disinterested, sometimes expresses itself in phrases which pass into the currency of criticism without the author's secret intention being discovered. Stendhal's famous enthronement of his own readers as the 'passionate few', and Meredith conferring upon his readers the equally famous and flattering title of the 'acute but honourable minority,' are familiar examples of this currency without any attempt at disguise.

ii

The habit of disguising egotism, long supported by custom, has made frankness suspect, so that when it appears without disguise, as in Bernard Shaw's Prefaces, it looks blatant. Yet it is natural that an author should want to be read as he would read himself, and Shaw is only a little franker than the others in endeavouring to make you read him in his own way. In doing so he takes the risk of being called a mountebank for his pains, but undeterred he has gone on telling people how to read his plays and novels, and advising other writers to do the same. 'I recommend them', he says, 'to insist on their own merits as an important part of their own business.'[1] Yet even he is conscious of impropriety for he goes out of his way to describe himself as a mountebank for taking his own advice. 'They tell me', he says, in one of the several Prefaces to *Three Plays for Puritans* (1901) 'that so-and-so, who does not write prefaces, is no charlatan. Well, I am . . . I am a natural-born mountebank. I am well aware that the ordinary British citizen requires a profession of shame from all mountebanks by way of homage to the sanctity of the ignoble private life to which he is condemned by his incapacity for public life. Thus Shakespeare, after proclaiming that 'Not marble, nor the gilded monuments of princes, should outlive his powerful rhyme', would apologise, in the approved taste, for making himself 'a motley to the view'; and the British citizen has ever since quoted the apology and ignored the fanfare. . . . I really cannot respond to this demand for mock-modesty. I am ashamed neither of my work nor of the way it is done. I like explaining its merits to the huge majority who don't know good work from bad. It does them good, and it does me good, curing me of nervousness, laziness and snobbishness. I write prefaces as Dryden did, and treatises as Wagner, because I *can*; and I would give half a dozen of Shakespeare's plays for one of the pre-

[1] *John Bull's Other Island and Major Barbara* (1907), 162.

faces he ought to have written. I leave the delicacies of retirement to those who are gentlemen first and literary men afterwards. The cart and trumpet for me.'

It is not usual to think of so self-assertive a genius as an apologetic person but his capacity for self-assertion is unequal to his incapacity for self-deception. He may follow his whims but he always knows what he is doing and never confuses whimseys with reasons. He is convinced of the importance of his writings and is determined to convince others of their value by propaganda even though it means self-advertisement. The process, as we know, was a success, and Shaw ultimately became the best-known and most widely discussed writer of his time, and his ideas, if not accepted in their entirety, have coloured the thoughts of his generation. But he regrets the necessity of these building-up tactics even more directly in 'The Author's Apology' to the first edition of his dramatic criticisms published in 1906. He points out that although the opinions expressed in those essays were the deepest and best things he knew how to say, 'I was', he continues, 'accusing my opponents of failure because they were not doing what I wanted, whereas they were often succeeding very brilliantly in doing what they themselves wanted. I postulated as desirable a certain kind of play in which I was destined ten years later to make my mark as a playwright (as I very well foreknew in the depths of my own unconsciousness); and I brought everybody, authors, actors, managers, to the one test: were they coming my way or staying in the old grooves? . . . I set up my own standard of what the drama should be and how it should be presented; and I used all my art to make every deviation in aiming at this standard, every recalcitrance in approaching it, every refusal to accept it seem ridiculous and old-fashioned. In this', he concludes in a characteristic anti-climax, 'I only did what all critics do who are worth their salt.'

iii

Dryden's prefaces are guides to Dryden without the cart and trumpet; they are written, as Dr. Johnson did not fail to observe, 'to recommend the work upon which he [Dryden] then happened to be employed.'[1] Wordsworth's famous preface to *Lyrical Ballads* is admittedly an exposition of the revolutionary technique of his and

[1] *The Rambler*, 93.

Coleridge's poetry.[1] He believed with Coleridge that 'every great
and original writer, in proportion as he is great and original, must
himself create the taste by which he is to be relished; he must teach
the art by which he is to be seen'.[2] At the same time he is a little
sensitive about expounding his own poetry, feeling that the 'reader
would look coldly' upon his arguments and suspect him 'of having
been principally influenced by the selfish and foolish hope of reasoning him into an approbation' of the poems. Even his widely accepted
recipe for poetry—'emotion remembered in tranquillity', is a better
definition of his own poetry than guide to the poetry of others, for
some poems are clearly the immediate result of turbulent emotional
experiences. To come nearer our own time, Whitman's three Prefaces
to *Leaves of Grass* and his essay on *Poetry To-day in America* are
vigorous pieces of special pleading for the revolution in poetry which
he had attempted. He pitted himself as the poetic he-man of America,
'sounding his barbaric yawp over the roofs of the world,' against the
'accepted notion' of a poet as 'a sort of male odalisque, singing . . ., a
king of spiced ideas, second-hand reminiscences, or toying late hours
at entertainments, in rooms stifling with fashionable scent.'[3] But
more reticent writers are not immune from this kind of self-advertisement, and a brief examination will show that such essays as Pater
on *Style*, Meredith on *The Idea of Comedy*, or Stevenson *On Some
Technical Elements of Style in Literature*, are in varying degrees
instructions on the technique of reading Pater, Meredith and
Stevenson.

iv

It is natural that Pater's essay, and, indeed, several of his essays
on literature, should be pleas for the patient, sensitive and observant
reading which his own style demands, for he took his own advice to
other writers and made time 'to write English more as a learned
language.'[4] His pedagogic concern for the reader is the outcome of
the laborious upbringing of his own art, and it is no surprise to find
him justifying his sensitive and subtly woven prose to himself as
well as to his readers: 'With some strong and leading sense of the
world, the tight hold of which secures true *composition* and not

[1] 'Of the Principles of Poetry and the *Lyrical Ballads* (1798–1802). *Prose
Works of William Wordsworth*, Grosart (1876), ii, 79. [2] Letter to Lady
Beaumont, 21 v: 1807. *Ib.*, ii, 180. [3] 'Poetry To-day in America,' Whit-
man's *Prose Works* (1898), 288. [4] *Essays from the Guardian* (1897).

mere loose accretion, the literary artist, I suppose, goes on consider-
ably, setting joint to joint, sustained by yet restraining the produc-
tive ardour, retracing the negligences of his first sketch, repeating
his steps only that he may give the readers a sense of secure and
restful progress, readjusting mere assonances, even, that they may
soothe the reader, or at least not interrupt him on his way . . .'[1]
And again, the writer with 'a punctilious observance of the proprieties
of his medium will diffuse through all he writes a general air of
sensibility, of refined usage', and 'his appeal . . . is to the scholar,
who has greater experience in literature, and will show no favour to
short-cuts or hackneyed illustration, or an affectation of learning
designed for the unlearned.'[2]

In those words Pater states his own position as a writer, but in
reality he is laying down rules for his reader. This can be seen more
clearly by the expedient of changing a few words in the longer
citation, so as to shift the point of view from author to reader. The
alterations are italicised. 'With some strong and leading sense of the
world, the tight hold of which secures true *concentration* and not
mere loose accretion, the *reader*-artist, I suppose, goes on consider-
ably, setting joint to joint, sustained by yet restraining the *discur-
sive* ardour, retracing the negligences of his first *reading*, repeating
his steps only that he may give *himself* a sense of secure and restful
progress, readjusting mere assonances, even, that they may soothe
him, or at least not interrupt him on his way.'

Pater's method of writing as described by himself, and adapted as
I have suggested for reading, forms an ideal starting place towards a
genuine understanding of that closely integrated and laboriously
welded style of 'a scholar writing for the scholarly', of one who
'insists upon leaving something to the willing intelligence of his
reader'. His style at its best demands effort and the style he advocates
and expounds with apparently impartial eloquence is that which he
himself has perfected. 'To really strenuous minds', he says, 'there is
a pleasurable stimulus in the challenge for a continuous effort on
their part, to be rewarded by securer and more intimate grasp of
the author's sense. Self-restraint, a skilful economy of means,
ascêsis, that too has a beauty of its own; and for the reader supposed
there will be an aesthetic satisfaction in that frugal closeness of style
which makes the most of a word, in the exaction from every sentence
of a precise relief, in the just spacing out of word to thought, in the

---

[1] 'Style', *Appreciations* (1889), 20–1.   [2] *Ib.*, 10.

logically filled space, connected always with the delightful sense of difficulty overcome.'[1]

V

Meredith also believed that he must be content with a select company of readers—an 'acute but honourable minority'. But his essay on *Comedy* and the introductory chapters to *The Egoist* and *Diana of the Crossways* suggest that he had not abandoned hope of extending the number of the elect. He rightly looked upon himself as a maker of comedy-fiction and upheld comedy with its 'thoughtful laughter, nearer a smile', as a civilising agent, rather than a mere entertainment. Like many great novelists he believed in having a purpose and his purpose was to laugh sentimentalism out of countenance, or better to smile it out of countenance, for hearty laugher though he was he had no tolerance for the smack on the back or the dig in the ribs. He kept the guffaw out of his own books, and even the broad humour of Mrs. Berry in *The Ordeal of Richard Feverel* and Master Gammon in *Rhoda Fleming* is toned down as nearly as possible to smiling point. Laughter in Meredith is never uncontrolled.

He placed satire, irony and humour lower than comedy. 'The Comic, which is the perceptive, is the governing spirit, awakening and giving aim to these powers of laughter, but it is not to be confounded with them.'[2] That is a good description of the governing spirit of Meredith's novels. His attitude towards the idea of Comedy is never objective. He is always thinking of himself and his works and in the Prelude to *The Egoist*, which appeared two years later than the essay, it is not difficult to see that he identifies himself with the Comic Spirit. In an oblique but obvious invitation to read *The Egoist* in this spirit of comedy, he says, 'The Comic Spirit concerns a definite situation for a number of characters and rejects all accessories in the exclusive pursuit of them and their speech. For, being a spirit, he hunts the spirit in men; vision and ardour constitute his merit; he has not a thought of persuading you to believe in him. Follow and you will see.' The instruction is for reading mankind, the implication that it is reflected according to that recipe in what follows, and that it is only by fealty to this Comic Spirit that you can benefit by reading him. 'Comedy' he

[1] *Ib.*, 14. [2] *The Idea of Comedy and the Uses of the Comic Spirit* (1897), 80.

47

pronounces 'to be our means of reading swiftly and comprehensively. She it is who proposes the correcting of pretentiousness, of inflation, of dullness, and of the vestiges of rawness and grossness to be found amongst us. She is the ultimate civiliser, the polisher, the sweet cook.' There is oblique flattery here. By reading Meredith thus swiftly and comprehensively (it ought to be comprehendingly) you become a partaker of the finer essences of civilisation. You, in short, become civilised likeMeredith, for 'Sensitiveness to the comic laugh is a step in civilisation'.

The peroration of the lecture on *The Idea of Comedy* is still more clearly a plea for himself compared with those who are 'swelling a plethoric market, in the composition of novels, in pun-manufactories and in journalism':—the remedy for 'forcing perishable matter on a public that swallows voraciously and groans; might, with encouragement, be attending to the study of art in literature'. The critics are not helpful: 'They stipulate for a writer's popularity before they will do much more than take the position of umpires to record his failure or success.' He concludes: 'Now the pig supplies the most popular of dishes, but it is not accounted the most honoured of animals, unless it be by the cottager. Our public might surely be led to try other, perhaps finer, meat. It has good taste in song. It might be taught as justly, on the whole, and the sooner when the cottager's view of the feast shall cease to be the humble one of our literary critics, to extend this capacity for delicate choosing in the direction of the matter arousing laughter.' Which means—Read Meredith!

vi

Stevenson's essay on 'Some Technical Elements of Style'[1] is the best study yet written on the promptings and methods of his own self-conscious and mannered prettiness. It is an exact recipe for that filigree prose which fascinated his readers in the eighteen-eighties. Style for him is a process of fastidiously choosing words and weaving them into a preconceived web or pattern. 'The true business of the literary artist is to plait or weave his meaning, involving it around itself; so that each sentence, by successive phrases, shall first come into a kind of knot, and then, after a moment of suspended meaning, solve and clear itself.' He intends you to be aware of his patterns. The 'knot or hitch' is introduced 'so that (however delicately) we are led to foresee, to expect, and then to welcome the successive

[1] *Essays in the Art of Writing* (1905), 3–43.

phrases'. The pattern is never left to itself, any more than the reader to himself. An 'element of surprise' like the 'knot or hitch' may be introduced to heighten the pleasure, but there must be no descent to 'the common figure of the antithesis', or should you be impelled in that direction, you must be subtle, the antithesis may be 'first suggested and then deftly evaded'.

Stevenson's prose is exhibitionist. It struts and displays itself deliberately. But Stevenson knew precisely what he was doing. In his youth he was obsessed by the music of words and in this essay he treats style as if it were solely the musical quality of literature. Sound is emphasised and a smooth arrangement of sounds advocated. He dislikes 'cacophony', the 'rattle of incongruous consonants', and the 'jaw-breaking hiatus'. When he announces that 'style is synthetic' he is fortifying his own meticulous method and its unsatisfying results, for he must have known that spontaneity played an important part in more robust prose styles. Stevenson's prose never achieved the vigour of his tales. As a story-teller he was masculine and masterly, and at his best—in, say, *Treasure Island* at first, and later in *Weir of Hermiston*—he comes nearest to a robust style, for the reason, doubtless, that his mind was on his theme rather than its presentation.

His ideal is the restrained and modulated voice. Short of being metrical and invading the province of poetry, prose should be charmingly and subtly vocal. 'The task of artfully combining the prime elements of language into phrases that shall be musical in the mouth' is common to both prose and poetry, but the task of 'weaving . . . argument into a texture of committed phrases and of rounded periods' is 'particularly binding in the case of prose'. Finally, and also 'common to both', is the 'choosing of apt, explicit, and communicative words'. To some extent these are the conditions of all writing whether deliberately or spontaneously produced, but with Stevenson they are deliberately fabricated. He was hypersensitive to the intricacies of an ideal of perfection. 'How many faculties, whether of taste or pure reason, must be held upon the stretch to make it,' he exclaims; 'and why, when it is made, it should afford us so complete a pleasure.' Writing for him was an effort and a worry. 'From the arrangement of according letters, which is altogether arabesque and sensual, up to the architecture of the elegant and pregnant sentence, which is a vigorous act of the pure intellect, there is scarce a faculty in man but has been exercised. We need not wonder, then, if perfect sentences are rare, and perfect pages rarer.' Stevenson here justifies his admittedly synthetic style which began by playing the 'sedulous ape' to his predecessors and ended in playing the sedulous ape to himself.

Like most writers he suffered from the usual anxieties incidental to his trade. These anxieties developed into fears, and towards the end of his short life, when his fame was at its height, he had doubts whether the sale of his books would be maintained. The fears were vague and, at the time, unjustified. They were symptoms of an excessive desire to please his readers without relinquishing his ideals as a writer, but they did, in fact, anticipate a recession of his popularity.

vii

Coventry Patmore affords a more recent example of unconscious self-advertisement. There is no more subjective poet, yet he 'deprecated the merely subjective appreciation of books', and 'when he praises the versification of Goldsmith, the diction of Mr. Bridges, the peace of William Barnes, the manners of Mrs. Walford, he is defending the technique of *The Angel in the House*'; and 'into Mr. Bridges' and Thomas Woolner's treatment of the classic myths he reads something of the mysticism of *The Unknown Eros*'.[1]

He has written no direct defence or exposition of his own method as a poet, for although his Essay on *English Metrical Law* covers his own prosody it is a model of objective exposition keeping close to the facts with scientific impartiality and comprehensive scholarship. It is easier to trace the trend of his advocacy in remarks about other writers scattered about his reviews and essays. Nearly all this criticism is unconscious adjustment or defence. His attitude is clearly revealed in his treatment of Goldsmith. It was as natural for the author of *The Angel in the House* to hold 'so lovely and so noble a work' as *The Vicar of Wakefield* 'above criticism', as it was for him to shrug his shoulders over Goldsmith's poetry. 'It is enough to say that the taste and artistic training of the age in which he lived did not admit of any better.'[2] Patmore is no believer in facile expression and his poetry became more and more esoteric. In a review of Aubrey de Vere's *Poems*, he notes with approval that 'the greatest religious poets have, in all ages, expressed themselves in purposely obscured and often playful myths and parables, of which the merely

[1] Frederick Page Pref. *Courage in Politics and Other Essays*, Patmore (1921). [2] 'Goldsmith,' *Ib.*, 61–2.

external sense has sufficient beauty to charm and satisfy the common reader, and to lure him away from their true significance, which is for other ears'.

It is in a grudging notice of Francis Thompson, then 'a new poet', that he gives the clearest exposition of his own more delicate art. The 'masculine intellect' which he recognises as 'the first constituent' of great poetry, he considers, however, too dominant in Thompson's poetry. Thompson is deficient in the 'feminine element, which is as essential to perfect poetry as a crust is to a pie'. The 'new poet' has 'profound thought, and far-fetched splendour of imagery, and nimble-witted discernment of those analogies which are the "roots" of the poet's language, abound; but,' and here we have a catalogue of the attributes of Patmore's muse, 'in the feminine faculties of "taste", of emotion that must have music for its rendering, of shy moderation which never says quite so much as it means, of quickness to "scent the ridiculous from afar", of the dainty conscience which sets "decorum" far above all other duties and knows that in poetry the manner is much more important than the matter, since manner is beautiful in itself, whereas, without it, it is no matter what the matter may be since it fails to express itself with feminine *feeling* and perfection. . . . Even the barest sublimity cannot be adequately rendered in poetry without some measure of the chaste and timid reticence of womanhood. Mr. Thompson throws about him "handfuls of stars", and swings the earth as "a trinket from his wrist"; but these are very cheap sublimities compared with Aeschylus's

Slow is the wrath of gods, but, in the end, not weak.'

Coventry Patmore is the poet of understatement, of mannered diffidence, of longing heightened by the tender refusal, wistfully glanced at by St. Bernard, and of the 'continuous slight novelty' of Aristotle. Few at any time are capable of appreciating so shy, yet so passionate a poet; there were fewer in his time, so he strove to indicate what readers were missing by their devotion to the obvious.

viii

Examples of unconscious propaganda similar to those I have cited could be multiplied, but the reader, having been started, may and should prefer to follow up further trails for himself. Yet before I leave this phase of the art of reading and lest I may have given a wrong idea of my intentions, I should like to make it clear that all I have tried to do in this chapter is to indicate the ineradicably egoistic basis of criticism. No condemnation is meant. The condition is natural and its recognition is essential to fit bookmanship. There is, however, an implication, and it is that all guidance in reading should be treated, if not with suspicion, at least with care. There is no harm in learning from Pater or Stevenson or Patmore how they would have you read Pater and Stevenson and Patmore, but it is obviously harmful to accept their arguments at their face-value and apply them without reserve to all your reading. The fit reader does his own criticising, and he differs from the rank and file of readers by knowing what he is doing, for every reader is a critic however uncritical he may appear to be, and all reading is criticism.

CHAPTER III

READERS AND CRITICS

'The unconscious critical acumen of a reader is both just and severe.'—
ANTHONY TROLLOPE, *Autobiography*, Ed. Sadleir (1923) 218.

---

i

The relationship between author and reader is often confused by professional criticism mainly because of the habit which so many readers have of trusting ready-made opinions instead of exercising their own. It is a curious fact that although both writer and reader may be victimised by criticism, the critic is more frequently challenged by the writer than by the reader. A writer invariably looks upon a frank or unfriendly critic as a saboteur who throws a spanner into machinery that would otherwise maintain communications between him and his readers. Objections of this kind need not be arguments against criticism so much as reasons for examining the relationship between the professed critic and the fit reader.

Whatever justification there may be for enmity between writers and critics there is no real cause for confused relationships between readers and critics. There are long-standing differences of opinion upon such relationships, and as they are likely to continue, circumvention is more probable than cure; but cure can be most readily achieved if the reader becomes his own critic. He can attain that condition not by siding with the writer or by ignoring the critic, but by understanding the nature and meaning of criticism, and learning how to guide himself through the undergrowth of meretricious and ephemeral comment whose only object is to flatter or deceive for commercial or personal reasons, or the heresy hunting and witch burning which belong to propaganda and are only subconsciously associated with legitimate criticism. Having added this useful accompaniment to his equipment, the reader is less likely to be misled or irritated, for he will realise not only that criticism is inevitable but that critics, like readers, can be artists in their own right though the materials of their art are second-hand.

Criticism can be read for the same reasons that we read any other kind of literature—for pleasure, escape, rest, as well as spiritual and aesthetic nourishment. Subtlety of reason and skill of statement can be studied and point of view examined both intrinsically and extrinsically. The only wrong thing to do with criticism is to give way to it, especially to be easily convinced. Critics as well as readers are entitled to their opinions, which should be resisted but not resented. Critics may even act as guides—but not in the direction canvassed—not, that is, unless you wish to go in that direction. If the critic is going your way he may be a useful as well as an agreeable companion, but not necessarily if he takes command of the jaunt. All of which means that you must never permit a critic to come between you and your book. In the long run unadulterated impressions are best. You may sharpen your wits on criticism by opposition where passive acquiescence would only blunt them. To give way is enervating and, if persisted in, would finally destroy judgment altogether. A good dispute justifies any cause.

It is impossible, in fact, to taste the full flavour of a book unless the critical faculty is brought into play, either voluntarily or involuntarily, for criticism is as inseparable from reading as it is from writing. It is no exaggeration to describe reading as informal criticism, but, apart from a condition which is general and largely subconscious, some readers are more critical than others. But whether the reader is more critical or less critical, he must always remember that criticism is as much an attempt on the part of the critic to argue others into liking the things he likes as to appraise for himself or for the sake of appraising, or to re-adjust the relationships of ideas and opinions for the sake of a new point of view, or to do either for the purpose of exercising spleen or malice, or advertising himself. Criticism, in short, is rarely, if ever, disinterested.[1]

[1] 'While a poet is in the initial stages of obscurity, a reader—and in particular, a reviewer—can gain credit for himself by remembering the

There is no fundamental difference between the virtues and defects of criticisms; both are characteristic, and when superficially differentiated they are found to be interdependent. A critic is useful as an individual, as a point of view. His reactions to the arts are phenomena and the more idiosyncratic the better. The worst that can happen to him is that his opinions should be accepted as authoritative and become the nucleus of a school, a movement, or, worse, a fashion. It is not the critic but his followers who are a nuisance.

ii

Books are cosmographies of their period and reflect its manners as well as its moods, and every age has its own characteristic expression, which is rarely new and strange, yet always changing, however slowly. Literature, like life, is never static, and for that reason alone it is necessary for the reader to avoid the kind of criticism which confuses fashion with style. Style is individual and innate, fashion common and imitative. One is the instinct of a person, the other the behaviour of a group. A style may become fashionable, just as a group may have style, but there can be no permanent allegiance between them for as soon as a style becomes fashionable it ceases to be stylish, and when a group, or a class, or a nation, adopts a fashion, it does so at the cost of style, or in the absence of style. The reason for this is that style, being idiosyncratic and peculiar to an individual or a group, changes gradually from inward necessity rather than from external pressure. Group styles, which are not to be confused with fashions, are traditional and generic, expressing the character and quality of all units of the group. Thus a species, or a school, or a regiment, can have style, which is rarely and only temporarily affected by fashion. A group without style has no status; a crowd without style is a mob.

No great work of art can become fashionable for its own sake. There is always an ulterior motive, and it affects books as much as it affects clothes. People are willing to subject themselves to herd-instincts both in dress and art because they fear to be 'out of it'.

obscure name, by spotting a winner. Later, if the young author survives, and publishes a second, third, fourth or fifth book, and becomes known, the reader—still in particular the reviewer—can best gain for himself credit by finding fault; for there is no sphere of life in which practice of "each for himself" is more commonly found than in the review columns.' Kathleen Raine, *Horizon* (Sept. 1942).

But if fashion serves a useful purpose by giving confidence to people who have no tastes or opinions of their own,[1] it also leaves behind blocks of fixed opinion which get in the way of individual thought and expression. It is one of the most useful functions of criticism to sweep those dead leaves from the path of literary appreciation.

There are cycles of criticism reflecting the major mental changes of civilisation, when all fashions and conventions have been revalued: what Nietzsche called a transvaluation of values. Nietzsche himself advocated such a readjustment in relation to his own conception of the will-to-power and the evolution of superman. Most periods have their own critical backgrounds against which readers as well as writers are forced to play their parts. The past continues into the present, and is being welded into the future so far as mankind is concerned by adjustment of contemporary attitude towards natural phenomena as reflected and interpreted by works of art. 'The specific character of a work of art', says Salvador de Madariaga, 'that which separates it not merely from formless matter but from works achieved without inspiration, is that it lives.'[2] But a book is much nearer to us than a picture or a statue or perhaps any other work of art except a song or a sonata. It is true, as Madariaga points out, that 'for us, children of the twentieth century, *Westminster Abbey*, *Hamlet*, Beethoven's *Ninth Symphony*, Michelangelo's *Moses*, are not what they were for the coevals of their respective creators, for they have since then assimilated centuries of mankind's spiritual growth. . . '. Works of art not only live: like all living things they change if only for the reason that we change, for change is also an illusion. *Hamlet* has changed by assimilating more of mankind's growth than any of the works of art named because he is closer to us. He is also the mirror of our spiritual maladies. We look into the soul of Hamlet and see ourselves, and this capacity for adjustment to contemporary needs is one of the tests of what is enduring in literature.

Even the most original of writers is largely conditioned by the characteristics of his own age.[3] He is an unconscious plagiarist of the *Zeitgeist*, and his readers value him or devalue him according to the ideas and standards they have unconsciously absorbed with the moods and manners of the moment. Every reader is both debtor and

[1] 'But your sensibility is too poignant, and too natural, to sink, palsied, beneath the touch of that torpedo to real excellence, fashion.' Anna Seward, *Letters* (1811), iv, 222. [2] *Don Quixote, An Introductory Essay in Psychology*, Salvador de Madariaga (1935.) [3] See Notes.

creditor to his period. He reflects as much of it as of himself without knowing it, and more of his criticism than he would care to admit is inspired and directed by the age in which he lives. The Victorian era, for instance, insisted upon literature being didactic in tone or purpose; our own era denies literature that privilege. The Reformation imposed a critical re-adjustment which changed Western Civilisation, and later the acceptance of the theory of evolution brought about world-wide adjustments. In our own period criticism is being reconstructed according to the theories of physicists like Einstein and Eddington, psychologists like Freud and Jung, and more deliberately, the 'ideologies' of Communist and Fascist.[1]

iii

The function of criticism in general is continuously in dispute and there are many stock weapons in this indeterminate warfare. One of them (generally put forward by artists) is that the artist is the best critic of works of art. Stripped of its bias the idea is based upon the assumption that excellence of technique and validity of appraisal are invariably associated. Such an assumption is at least plausible. It seems so reasonable that it ought to be true, but, as a matter of fact, it is disproved by history and experience. This is inevitable because criticism is more of an art than a science and is least reliable in its scientific escapades. Scientific method can be applied to a work of art, but only if it is treated as a phenomenon, and not as a work of art. Analysis and inference, or references to precedent or even fact, cannot assess the quality of a book or a picture, nor can artistic status be determined by such processes. A poet or a painter or a musician may be a good critic of poems or pictures or symphonies, not because he is an artist in words or pigments or tones, but because he is also an artist in opinion. Opinion is the quintessence of criticism when it is the result of an experience: the contact of two minds or temperaments.

The position is not altered when it is recalled that all artists are self-critics, and the best of them are more ruthless with their own work than any outsider could be. But self-criticism is largely subconscious and few artists are able or think it worth-while to convey

---

[1] The idea of the critical background is elucidated in F. R. G. Duckworth's *Browning: Background and Conflict* (1931) in which he shows the poet against backgrounds of the eighteen-fifties, the eighteen-nineties, and the nineteen-twenties.

their critical method to others in formal essays. Their opinions must in the main be sought in letters or other personal records, and they rarely attempt and never achieve the impartiality of science. A distinguished and self-opinionated artist, Charles Ricketts, said that 'the attitude of artists towards their art is more stimulating than the actual value of their opinions'.[1] Individual artists with the gift of verbal expression may contribute invaluable opinions upon their own work, as Wordsworth, Wagner, Rodin, and Whistler have done, but judgments of artists, like those of critics, are often prejudiced by self-interest, jealousy, and even malice, when they approach the works of other artists, especially their contemporaries.

Much negative criticism is based upon inward and often unconscious or half-conscious likes or dislikes, but approvals as well as disapprovals refer back to self rather than to standards or principles. 'Every man imputes himself', said Tennyson, 'no man can see further than his moral eyes will allow him.'[2] A writer turned critic will mark for praise or blame the characteristics which approximate to what he admires or attempts in his own works. 'Critics, like the rest of mankind, are frequently misled by interest,' said Dr. Johnson, and he reminds us of the 'treachery of the human heart', and the readiness with which we 'gratify our own pride or envy under the appearance of contending for elegance and propriety'. Addison, for instance, was 'suspected to have denied the expediency of poetical justice, because his own *Cato* was condemned to perish in a good cause'.[3]

Not even the greatest of poets have been immune from this kind of treachery. A classic instance is to be found in the records of Wordsworth who was poetically rich enough to scatter praise with both hands. The incident occurred at a meeting of several poets, among them James Hogg, 'The Ettrick Shepherd', who, impressed by the sight of so many bards, remarked to Wordsworth: 'Lord, keep us a', there's nae want of poets here the day at ony rate!' Wordsworth replied: 'Poets,Mr. Hogg? Pray, where are they, Sir?'[4] Southey tried to convince himself that his antagonist Jeffrey was 'utterly feeble in intellect' and a mere child in 'taste and learning', and that the 'whole corps of Edinburgh reviewers' were 'miserably puny' to one who had 'been accustomed to live with strong men'.[5]

[1] *Self-Portrait of Charles Ricketts, R.A.* Ed. T. Sturge Moore and Cecil Lewis (1939), 60. [2] *Alfred, Lord Tennyson* by his Son (1897), ii, 76. [3] *The Rambler*, 93. [4] See *Noctes Ambrosianae*, No. xvii *Blackwood*, xvi, 592. [5] *Southey's Letters* (World's Classics). Ed. 104.

iv

The subjective character of criticism comes out clearly in literary conversation or in the reviewing of books and plays. It often finds expression in a greater inclination on the part of writers to praise the failures rather than the successes among authors in their own line of business. Lockhart observed this tendency in Wordsworth, who 'said Shelley was a greater genius than Byron (i.e. a less successful one)'.[1] An amusing comment on the egoism of Wordsworth also occurs in a letter from Lockhart to his wife after a visit to the poet, in 1825. Lockhart was 'continually quoting Wordsworth's poetry and Wordsworth ditto' but 'the great Laker never uttered a syllable by which it might have been intimated to a stranger that your Papa [Sir Walter Scott] had ever written a line of verse or prose since he was born'.[2] Even an honest reviewer can be dishonest malgré lui. Macaulay was asked by Macvey Napier to review *Martin Chuzzlewit* for the *Quarterly*. Macaulay read it and found it 'frivolous and dull'. He could not therefore praise it, neither would he 'cut it up'. He would not attack it, 'First, because I have broken salt with Dickens; secondly, because he is a good man, and a man of real talent; thirdly, he hates slavery as heartily as I do; and, fourthly, because I wish to see him enrolled in our blue-and-yellow[3] corps, where he may do excellent service as a skirmisher and sharp-shooter.'[4]

The tendency to read self into a dramatic theme was recognised by A. B. Walkley, who was doubtless thinking of his own method. He described ideas as a godsend to the dramatic critic, they enable him to 'pass in review all the possible formulations and combinations of the problem presented'. Not apparently to expound the author so much as himself. 'The result is apt to be a little deceptive about the play itself, because it suits the critic to travel further afield in the region of ideas than the playwright. Nor is it merely a question of the intellectual area covered; the need for logical symmetry, for strict form, in analysis will often have tempted the critic to assume these qualities in the play when they are not, in fact there. . . . Hence the playgoer is often disappointed when he goes to see the play for himself. Half the ideas he had read about are not there, and

---

[1] Qt. Trevelyan, *Macaulay* (1876), ii, 109. [2] Qt. in *Familiar Letters of Sir Walter Scott* (1894), ii, 34. [3] *The Quarterly Review*. [4] *Life*, Trevelyan (1876), ii, 109.

those that are there are not so shipshape. I doubt . . . if there is so much in *Hamlet*, the actual play, seen within the four walls of the theatre, as the vast "Hamlet literature" which has grown out of it would have us believe.'[1]

v

Approvals are often self-praise. E. M. Forster says that the citizen who survives the ordeal of *Ulysses* and gets to the end of that novel 'is naturally filled with admiration at his own achievement, and is apt to say that here is a great book' when 'he really means that he is a great reader'.[2] Much of the more violent kind of disapproval is in the nature of self-contest. The critic is quarrelling with some internal maladjustment which he can't straighten out, and if he protests too much it is probable that he is uncertain of his case. Criticism of this kind is invariably a defence of the critic rather than an appraisal of the criticised. Any form of distress or frustration is likely to determine a critical attitude. Dr. Johnson allowed himself to belittle blank verse, not because there was anything wrong with it but because he was musically defective, having 'no ear for the subtleties of the musical cadenza.'[3]

When Henry James censured Tolstoy for his failure to select adequately from his massive material, he was doubtless thinking of the defects in his own powers of selection. Flaubert consoled himself for lack of appreciation of his works by announcing that criticism was dying out and that popular education was ruining the nation. Being a pioneer in literary method he resented the historical and ideological attitudes of Sainte-Beuve and Taine which, he thought, placed his own works at a disadvantage, and demanded that all works of art should be assessed on their 'intrinsic value' alone.[4] George Moore 'often became particularly disputatious and overbearing when he was trying to convince himself on a matter about which he was not himself sure'.[5] He devoted, in fact, a life of dis-

---

[1] Qt. James Agate, *Ego* 3 (1938), 315–6.   [2] Qt. Rose Macaulay *The Writings of E. M. Forster* (1938), 216.   [3] Sir Walter Raleigh, *Six Essays on Johnson* (1910), 13.   [4] *The George Sand-Gustave Flaubert Letters.* Trans. Aimee L. McKenzie (1922), 228. George Sand had no illusions about the subjectivity of criticism in Flaubert or anyone else. 'Criticism', she said, 'always starts from a personal point of view, the authority of which the artist does not recognise.' *Ib.,* 322.   [5] Joseph Hone *Life of George Moore* (1936), 231.

putation, masquerading as candour, to the creation of that integrity which was so admirably revealed in his later books, but his opinions and attitudes were always defensive actions and generally within the frontiers of his own personality.

This internecine warfare is often precipitated by a feeling of incompetence. The would-be creator becomes a captious critic or a mere grouser. He feels that those who have done what he has failed to do have 'jumped his claim', and his criticism becomes an act of revenge or a reprisal. Some writers, like their less gifted fellows, take a delight in disparagement, especially of the first-rate. But although the resentment of the impotent is a well-known phenomenon, irascibility is not peculiar to the perverse or the impotent, and apparently disinterested criticism (there is really no such thing as disinterested criticism) can be as misleading as that which is involuntarily inspired by envy or jealousy. Irascibility of each kind is often found lurking among the opinions of writers of repute. 'What plagues us', the Goncourts admitted at the height of their fame, 'is an insatiable and rankling literary ambition, the galling bitterness of the specific literary vanity. That critic who fails to mention you, wounds you; and he who mentions other writers casts you into the depths of despair.'[1]

This state of mind is not a modern neurosis, it exists in all times and places. When the American publisher, George Ticknor, was a guest of the *Saturday Night Club* at Leigh Hunt's house, he was most impressed by the cattiness of the distinguished authors he met there. He noted 'Lamb's gentle humour, Hunt's passion, and Curran's volubility, Hazlitt's sharpness and point, and Godwin's great head full of cold brains, all coming into contact and conflict, and agreeing in nothing but their common hatred of everything that has been more successful than their own works.'[2] Stephen Spender has detected a sub-species of jealousy in the criticism of so self-sufficient a writer as T. S. Eliot, where he finds 'a note almost of personal irritation with writers whom he is criticising, so strongly does he feel that they oughtn't to be doing something which they do, but something quite different'.[3] There may be little or no resentment in such irritation, and it has nothing to do with literary impotence, but it is none the less subjective: a literary form of self-righteousness.

[1] Edmund and Jules de Goncourt, 9th April, 1864. *Journals.* Trans. Galantière (1937), 178. [2] Qt. Birkbeck Hill *Talks About Autographs* (1896), 153. [3] *The Destructive Element in Criticism* (1935), 163.

vi

Literary criticism often travels backwards, yet it never catches up to the facts of history because it is impossible for the critic to put himself precisely into the place of a contemporary observer and commentator. For that reason critics and readers of books often misrepresent the past. And apart from lack of precision in point of view, commentators, whether historians or their readers, have preconceptions of what was, is, or should be, with the result that, willy-nilly, they are generally adding to already existing legends, and at best rarely do more than interpret. History resembles translation, for just as you can't translate one language into another, so you can't translate one period into another.

An author is rarely if ever appreciated by succeeding generations of readers in the same way or even for the same reason.[1] When, for example, we think of the early days of the nineteenth century we think of Keats and Shelley as dominant poets, but whilst they lived they were known to few. Recognition came much later. The average reader in their day knew as little of Keats and Shelley as the average reader of today knows of Auden or Day Lewis. Byron and Rogers were the popular contemporary poets, and the majority of those who had heard of Keats or Shelley treated them with amusement or contempt as the revolutionary protégés of the fantastic and rather bolshie Leigh Hunt. The relationship of Byron to Shelley might be compared with that of Kipling and Eliot in our own time. If you asked the average Kipling enthusiast what he thought of Eliot he would reply either that he had never heard of him or that he did not know George Eliot wrote poetry. His prototype a hundred years ago who read his Byron would dimly recall Shelley, if the name meant anything to him at all, as the youthful pamphleteer of atheism and vegetarianism, who had an affair with a girl who drowned herself.

It is not only point of view but appreciation of style which changes. The rhetoric of Marlowe and the conceits of Lyly were enjoyed in their own time by cultured people who would be bored by them now;

---

[1] 'Perhaps it would be no exaggeration to say that Richardson was most appreciated in his own times for the very characteristics we most decry in ours.' Sheila Kaye-Smith, *Samuel Richardson*, Intro. 27. 'The merit of Trollope has of late years been somewhat exaggerated. For a generation he was almost forgotten, and when he was re-discovered, having in the interval acquired the charm of a period piece, greater praise was awarded him than he deserved.' W. Somerset Maugham, *Books and You*, xiii.

and even the ordinary reader so lately entertained by Ella Wheeler Willcox and Laurence Hope could summon up nothing but a superior sense of amusement if by chance he were reminded of the verses of Eliza Cook or Mrs. Hemans, much as the generation which appreciated Sir Edwin Arnold and Sir Lewis Morris despised that which would have placed Martin Tupper among the immortals. We are apt also to forget that so popular a poet as Tennyson was considered difficult until he wrote *Maud*, the *Idylls of the King* and *The Princess*, and that it is upon those early lyrics and their successors which puzzled his early critics that his present fame rests.[1] In most periods, however, there are shrewd judges who see through popular enthusiasms and passing fads; fastidious appraisers like Edward FitzGerald, who was one of the first to forecast the status of Tennyson as he now stands. 'I think', he wrote in 1876, 'Tennyson might have stopped after 1842, leaving Princesses, Ardens, Idylls, etc., all unborn: all except the Northern Farmer, which makes me cry . . .'

The rise and fall of literary appreciation reflects the mind of the reader more than that of the professional critic. If 'Shelley, today, is by no means the poetic angel he was thirty years ago',[2] it is because the conditions of appreciation have changed. But the change has not been sudden. It was implied in Matthew Arnold's 'beautiful but ineffectual angel beating in the void his luminous wings in vain'. The notorious phrase may have helped to depreciate Shelley's angelic stock but this does not mean that Shelley is out-moded or that Matthew Arnold's belittlement of the poet inaugurated a neo-classical era. Shelley's reputation has always aroused controversy. It was his realism rather than his romanticism which excited the wrath of his contemporaries. He was a poet with a mission and his teaching cut across the religion and politics of his time. The offence was aggravated because he was a gentleman born, and it was expected that a gentleman would leave subversive ideas to low-down fellows like William Cobbett and Tom Paine. But the wheel of time has had many turns since then, and Shelley, the accepted composer of a handful of undying poems, has swung into place once more as a prophet of freedom. His appreciators can afford to be amused at the vagaries of criticism, for such a poet is not likely to be forgotten. His reputation may be swayed by fashion, or readjusted

---

[1] *Letters* (1889), 391. [2] E. M. W. Tillyard, *Poetry Direct and Oblique* (1934), 163.

to meet new social or intellectual conditions, but like those delicately poised rocks found in some parts of Yorkshire, he will not fall. Parallels could be multiplied from every age.

vii

The effect of reading upon the mind is elusive. A simple test may be made by opening a book in which you have marked passages which at one time you thought were memorable. Turning them up again you may find that they have lost their savour, and you will probably wonder why you marked them. The reverse is also true. We may have known an essay, a story, or a poem for years without being deeply moved, but, suddenly, on some re-reading under special circumstances (not necessarily apprehended) the work strikes a neglected chord which harmonises us with the whole of life. 'I have, at intervals, read and found *Emerson's Poems* very exquisite and distinguished,' wrote Anne Douglas Sedgwick, 'but only in the last few days has he simply intoxicated me—an ethereal intoxication.'[1] The explanation is that the books did not lack meaning at the time, but that the impression they made was peculiar to that moment, and the circumstances which governed it, and the passages would remain dormant until touched into life by a renewal of the old circumstances which made them important, or by a rearrangement of circumstances which gave to the old word or phrase a new meaning.[2]

viii

Literature varies with time, place and mood and a book goes on changing from its conception until it is laid in limbo. It never ceases from being subject to the intimidations of caprice, fashion, editors, censors, printers, and time. But apart from the conditions imposed upon a reader by his period and the domestic, educational, and vocational conditioning to which we are all subject, every reader is subject to his own literary tradition and its laws. The two sets of influences are individual but inseparable. No one can escape the circumstances which have made him what he is, and no reader can form an opinion which does not refer back, knowingly or unknowingly, to the unwritten but very persuasive laws formulated by the processes and experiences of past reading.

[1] *Anne Douglas Sedgwick: A Portrait in Letters* chosen by Basil de Selincourt (1936), 70-1. [2] See *Post*, iv., 78-80.

Every time you read a book, even though the intervening periods are short, changes have taken place in your consciousness so that the work, or parts of it, seems to have changed, and not always for the better. We may grow out of as well as into a book. Coleridge found *Pilgrim's Progress* one of the few books which could be read repeatedly at different times and 'each time with a new pleasure'. He himself read it 'once as a theologian . . . once with devotional feelings . . . and once as a poet'.[1] Every time Mark Rutherford took up Carlyle, a 'new' and 'greater' Carlyle was revealed to him.[2]

There is no such thing as an absolute book, any more than there is a final criticism or opinion. The greater the book the more relative and the more adaptable it becomes. Ideas, records, reputations gather accretions of other ideas and records and reputations as a ship or an oyster gathers barnacles, and since these accretions begin at birth and continue indefinitely, impressions of them are in a constant state of flux. Writers are thus always tempted to revise, amplify, cancel every new edition of their own works, and editors of established works do not hesitate to give them the twist of their own approval or interpretation. The danger is even greater when literary records such as letters and diaries are edited by relatives or executors of a deceased author; the path of biography is strewn with the devastations and distortions of well-meaning suppressions and misrepresentations.

ix

Even during the writing of a book an author will allow an opinionated friend, wife or other critic on the hearth to crab his style. Both Nathaniel Hawthorne and Mark Twain suffered from a conjugal censorship which left scars upon their works, not apparently serious on Hawthorne's but disastrous to those of Mark Twain. The feminisation of Hawthorne can only be inferred from what happened to his notebooks. Memoranda of this kind are of first importance in the study of a writer's work, and the preservation of their integrity should be an axiom for those responsible for their care. Hawthorne's notebooks are particularly precious because they are interesting as literature, as records of his friendships, and as the raw material of many of his novels and tales. In 1868, four years after his death, Mrs. Hawthorne published *Passages from the American Note-Books*. There were no indications that the manu-

[1] *Table Talk* (1874), 88. [2] *Letters to Three Friends* (1924), 66.

script had been tampered with. Two years later she published *Passages from the English Note-Books*, this time contributing a preface which seemed to refer to both series of *Passages*. If it did, the statement that 'The Editor has transcribed the manuscripts just as they were left . . . merely omitting some passages, and being careful to preserve whatever could throw any light' on Hawthorne's 'character', is certainly untrue. An examination of the original manuscripts now in the Pierpont Morgan Library, New York, proves this beyond doubt. The new editor is 'surprised to find, upon comparing the published passages with the manuscripts', that his predecessor not only omitted portions which throw important light on Hawthorne's character, but also revised the notebooks to such an extent that the published version seriously misrepresents his character and literary genius'.[1] Mrs. Hawthorne did more than edit the notebooks, she edited her husband by substituting her own attitude towards life for his. But any tampering with such personal documents destroys their validity, and this editing did not stop at grammatical corrections, it went on from grammatical reconstructions to the alteration of style, expression, and opinion. Hawthorne appears to have led a blameless life and nothing he wrote resembled what used to be called 'coarse', but his widow was not content. She wished to endow him in the eyes of posterity with her own ladylike conception of a literary husband.

X

The case of Mark Twain was more serious, for his wife began to make him respectable as a man and genteel as an author from the day of their marriage. His manners too often recalled the pioneer days in Nevada and California and the heartiness of the Mississippi pilot for the bourgeois society in which he was now destined to move; and there were too many echoes of those early masculine experiences in his vocabulary—spoken as well as written. But Olivia Clemens saw to all that: with unwearied patience she adjusted him to the new conditions, censored his vocabulary, edited his prose, and even suppressed his stories. This Delilah on the hearth had literary views of her own which did not correspond with those of the husband who wrote masterpieces like *Tom Sawyer* and *Huckleberry*

[1] *The American Note-Books of Nathaniel Hawthorne*, edited by Randall Stewart (1932).

Finn, and in the domestic battle of the books which began, Delilah was the victor. Mark Twain settled down to writing potboilers and bestsellers, soothing his outraged genius with ironical comments upon the human species.

He rarely complained openly, and even then his protests took the half-mocking tone of one who was reconciled to his fate. 'I was a mighty rough, coarse, unpromising subject when Livy took charge of me', he told W. D. Howells, 'and I may *still* be to the rest of the world, but not to her. She has made a very creditable job of me.'[1] But he gets nearer to his real feelings when he confesses that he 'never saw a woman so hard to please about things she doesn't know anything about'.[2] And he has left a playful but illuminating record of the remarks which passed between husband and wife when she was overhauling the proofs of *Following the Equator*. She objected to the word 'stench', he thought it 'a noble, good word', but out it went. She disliked a reference to his father lashing a slave boy. 'It's out', he complied, 'and my father is white-washed.' She shied at 'breech-clout' and 'offal' which she would like to have taken 'out of the language'. 'You', protested the decontaminated author, 'are steadily weakening the English tongue, Livy.'[3] The result was that the real genius of Mark Twain never reached the full splendour of its early promise. The weakness was evidently innate, for he had compromised his integrity as an artist, for commercial reasons, before meeting Olivia. His marriage completed the rout to such an extent that, in the words of Van Wyck Brooks, 'quite literally, as a man of letters, his honour rooted in dishonour stood, and faith unfaithful kept him falsely true.'[4]

xi

Again, criticism may be 'wishful thinking'. When Aubrey de Vere, who was a Roman Catholic, complains that Shelley 'seems to have a lack of reverence quite extraordinary in a man of genius— for high genius seems to be commonly as quick as mere vulgar talent is slow, in recognising the greatness of the things above us',[5] he is doing no more than express his disappointment that so admirable a poet did not share his own reverences. Shelley was ir-

---

[1] Qt. Van Wyck Brooks, *The Ordeal of Mark Twain* (1922), 119. [2] Qt. *Ib.*, 183. [3] Qt. *Ib.*, 122. [4] This theme is considered from another point of view in the next chapter. [5] *Aubrey de Vere: A Memoir*, Wilfrid Ward (1904), 333.

reverent because Aubrey de Vere could not see the wood for trees. A rationalist would take the opposite view, and be equally wrong. Poets are not to be pigeonholed in this way, or only temporarily, for an impressive prig or a persuasive propagandist may delay wiser appreciation. Some authors even have to fight snobbery. If, as Herbert Read has pointed out,[1] you create the impression that to admire a writer is bad form or a mark of inferior taste, you will set up a 'fashionable inhibition' so powerful in its effect and range that a poet's reputation will die of neglect.

All serious writers are aware of the obstacles which stand between them and their readers. Wordsworth's reply to a correspondent, who urged that nothing was fit for poetry which did not please, reveals a consciousness of many of the more obvious of these difficulties. 'Please whom?' he asks, for 'some have little knowledge of natural imagery . . . some cannot tolerate a poem with a ghost or any supernatural agency in it; others would shrink from an animated description of the pleasures of love, as from a thing carnal and libidinous; some cannot bear to see delicate and refined feelings ascribed to men in low conditions of society, because their vanity and self-love tell them that these belong only to themselves and men like themselves in dress, station, and way of life; others are disgusted with the naked language of some of the most interesting passions of men, because either it is indelicate, or gross, or vulgar. . . . Then there are professional and national jealousies forevermore. Some take no interest in the description of a particular passion or quality, as love of solitariness . . . genial activity of fancy, love of nature, religion, and so forth, because they have (little or) nothing of it in themselves. . . .'[2] Yet, in spite of this clairvoyance, Wordsworth himself was subject to a whole range of prejudices and taboos which differed less in kind than in quality from those he has enumerated. He was as quick to shrink from what he felt to be an indelicacy as he was to resent any new tendency in poetry which departed from the trail he so patiently blazed for his own muse.

xii

There is also a difficulty, perhaps inherent, in the approach of the reader of an older generation to the books of the new. The result often leads to misunderstandings which sometimes descend into

[1] *In Defence of Shelley* (1936), 4. [2] *Early Letters of William and Dorothy Wordsworth*, ed. E. de Selincourt (1935), 294–5.

mutual contempt. It is assumed, too readily I think, that there are fundamental differences between crabbed age and youth. That is true of the physique but not of the mind. There are differences of opinion, but they are not fundamental. It may be easier for the young to shake off old intellectual garments and put on new, but that is not always an advantage. New ideas are sometimes no more than fads or fashions, and the advantage in the long run may be with those who hasten slowly. There is a challenge on both sides. Age has as much right to cry 'Who goes there?' as youth to bawl: 'Get out of the way!' It is obvious that youth is the time for adventure and experiment, but Oscar Wilde observed that not even the youngest of us is immune from error. And whether we are young or old we are all actors on the same stage and surrounded by the same old properties. We spend most of our time between inverted commas. Advanced and reactionary ideas tend to meet, and thoughts are often the result of environment. We are all, at any time, contemporaries of the same intellectual conditions. We play our parts against the backcloth of other people's thoughts. 'I wish that I knew the poetry of the twentieth century better than I do, that is only to wish myself younger than I am, for I cannot know it by reading it, but only by being in it and of it.'[1] If Professor Garrod feels that way, others may take heart, although it is not always necessary to be a member of a movement before you can read in it.

xiii

A certain tolerance is as necessary in criticism as in other faculties. Exactitude in the last resort is relative. It is rare in letters. For that reason logic-chopping robs reading of many of its subtleties. Scientific exactitude is so rare in imaginative literature that we are surprised when we come across it. Shakespeare is full of anachronisms and misstatements, even bad grammar, but he gets there all the same. Dickens is often a gate-crasher in the Palace of Truth, and austere John Milton would rather mix his evidence than his metaphors. Keats is, if possible, a greater offender. He made the gods of Greece dance to his own tune and composed immortal odes out of terminological inexactitudes. William Michael Rossetti has shown that the 'Ode to a Nightingale' is a tangle of inaccuracies—yet it remains a noble poem.[2] So it is with the rest. You may catalogue the

[1] H. W. Garrod, *Poetry and the Criticism of Life* (1931), 21.   [2] See Notes.

inadequacies of Shakespeare and Dickens without shaking the foundations of their works, and if you had a logical enough mind you could man-handle almost any poem as Dr. Johnson man-handled *Lycidas*. But however incisively you may expose a poet's inconsistencies and equivocations, you can neither dissect nor disintegrate the essential qualities of his poetry. For all Dr. Johnson's ruthlessness, *Lycidas* remains one of the few great English Threnodies secure in the affections, and admiration of all who can read and feel great poetry.

CHAPTER IV

INTERACTION OF AUTHOR
AND READER

'Literature always anticipates life. It does not copy it, but moulds it to its purpose.'—OSCAR WILDE, 'The Decay of Lying,' *Intentions* (1891).

'Every considerable book, in literature or science, is an engine whereby mind operates on mind.'—SIR WALTER RALEIGH, *Six Essays on Johnson* (1910), 28.

---

i

Books are necessary to authors and readers for much the same reasons. Whether we read them or write them they are means of expression. We may read the author behind the words, but that is not always our object. We often, perhaps generally, read ourselves into the words, often unknowingly. It may be that we only find in a book what we seek, and it is a common experience that our own ideas tend to find immediate support in every subsequent book we take up, or, if not support, stimulating (and easily overcome) opposition. One of the reasons is that authors write as readers read. The one projects himself into an idea or an image, the other into the book in which the idea of the image is recorded. Tennyson must have felt this when he dedicated the *Idylls of the King* to the Prince Consort:

> *These to his memory*
> *Since he held them dear,*
> *Perchance in finding there unconsciously*
> *Some image of himself,*

I dedicate, I dedicate,
I consecrate with tears,
These idylls.

ii

The difference between the mental and emotional processes of writing and reading is not so great as is sometimes supposed. It is widely believed that a writer lives in his writing more intensely than a reader can possibly live in his reading. I doubt it, although there is little evidence to the contrary for the reason that even fit readers are less articulate and less communicative than writers. But we have sufficient evidence of what is called the 'influence of books' to support the conclusion that when the experience of reading is profound, it is for the same reason that the experience of writing is profound, namely, a capacity for profundity in both reader and writer.

Writers generally enjoy reading, just as readers often feel that they might have been writers. It is rare, however, for a writer to admit that reading may be a more eventful experience than writing. One such instance occurs in a letter of Anne Douglas Sedgwick who told George Moore that she put more of herself into reading than into writing. 'I read Turgenieff, but I divert myself in writing about pleasant imaginary people, whom I realise more or less acutely, and whose doings interest me mildly.'[1]

The release of pent-up emotions by writing or talking (writing is written talk) has its counterpart in reading. A reader relieves his feelings by reading in the same way as a writer by writing. The difference is in technique not function. The reader has the advantage of the writer in several respects because he has more freedom of expression. He need not consider the feelings of others, and he is not bound to associate his thoughts with the best (or the worst) thoughts of the writer. He can, in short, indulge in self-criticism, self-mockery, self-appreciation, and their opposites, without fear of rebuke or challenge.

It is useless, therefore, to lay down hard and fast rules, or to set one of these intellectual processes above the other. 'One is inclined to feel', said Sir Hugh Walpole, 'that no book is written by its author, or rather that an author merely collects notes for a certain

[1] *Anne Douglas Sedgwick: A Portrait in Letters*, chosen by Basil de Selincourt (1936), 4.

72

suggested work and that every reader then writes the book for himself.'[1] The making of literature and the appreciation of literature are thus two sides of the same medal. Literature achieves its final purpose when it becomes an act of collaboration between writer and reader. The writer expresses himself in a book, the reader through a book.[2] Reading at its most intense becomes writing by proxy. 'Not in Montaigne, but in myself I find all that I see in him,' said Pascal.

iii

The reading of drama or fiction resembles acting. When we read Shakespeare and Homer, Cervantes and Fielding, Sterne and Dickens, we play, involuntarily, the parts of Falstaff and Hamlet, Odysseus and Don Quixote, Parson Adams or Uncle Toby, Pickwick or Micawber, as their authors did when creating them. Both reading and writing are dramatisations. The Princess Mathilde told the Goncourts that she only enjoyed those novels of which she would have liked to be the heroine. The Goncourts thought that was a feminine characteristic,[3] and it may be, but it is not confined to women. Miss Rose Macaulay holds that readers are most ready to identify themselves with the sensitive, amiable, unlucky types, such as Rickie, in E. M. Forster's *The Longest Journey*, 'since practically every reader knows himself to be sensitive and weak.'[4] In some reminiscences of his early reading of fiction Sir Hugh Walpole gives an explanation of this phenomenon. 'I was not myself,' he says, 'an especially cruel little boy, being for the most part timid and sycophantic, but from the very earliest age it gave me pleasure to hear of others in distress, because it made my own misfortunes seem less terrible, and this pleasure in the misfortunes of others is one of the earliest self-gratifications we obtain from reading.'[5] But true as these observations may be, identifications of the kind are as varied as human character and temperament, and projection into the strong and ruthless is often equally soothing to the weak and sensitive. That shrewd valuer of popular opinion, Anthony Trollope, strove to represent to his readers 'characters like themselves—or to which they might liken themselves.'[6]

---

[1] *Reading* (1926), 78–9. [2] See Notes. [3] *Journals*, 4th March, 1868.
[4] *The Writings of E. M. Forster* (1938), 55. [5] *Reading* (1926), 19.
[6] *Autobiography*, ed. Sadleir (1923), 135.

iv

Long ago Whistler and Oscar Wilde caused amusement and indignation by defending the paradox that nature imitated art. They both drew their examples from pictures. Whistler's famous saying about nature catching up to art, with reference to a tendency of sunsets to imitate Turner, is still recalled with mild amusement; but Wilde's argument that Holbein and Vandyck brought their types to England and 'life with her keen imitative faculty set herself to supply the master with models', supported by reference to the contemporary appearance in public places of 'a certain curious and fascinating type of beauty' created by Rossetti and Burne Jones, no longer appears to be extravagant. Wilde went further than Whistler and followed the idea into the varied realm of fiction.[1]

He begins with the well-established example of the influence of crook stories on small boys, an 'interesting phenomenon, which always occurs after the appearance of a new edition' of *Jack Shepperd* or *Dick Turpin*, and he goes on to point out how Hamlet invented the pessimistic philosophy of Schopenhauer, how Turgenev invented and Dostoievski completed the type of Nihilist; how the nineteenth century was largely the invention of Balzac, and he continues with examples from Thackeray, Walter Besant and Robert Louis Stevenson. Some of his arguments are whimsically exaggerated.

The only one I shall consider is that of the Nihilist, because the facts of the widespread reincarnation of Turgenev's Bazarov are well known, and it is probable that, by giving Nihilism a local habitation and a name, Turgenev crystallized the spiritual unrest which ultimately brought about the Russian Revolution of our time. Whether the influence went so far or not, the readiness with which Bazarov was accepted as a model by revolutionists began immediately after Turgenev had invented him, in 1862. Bazarovs began to appear all over Russia and they adopted the word 'Nihilist', which Turgenev had invented to describe the type, as the badge of their movement. 'It was a new method as well as a new type I introduced—that of realising instead of Idealising,' Turgenev explained. No other character in fiction has had such a power over love and hate. Bazarov was denounced and upheld but he was necessary to the time-spirit and so manifested himself in life.

Alexander Herzen was one of the first to recognise the birth of this

[1] 'The Decay of Lying,' *Intentions* (1891).

new anti-romantic type who became the intellectual grandfather of Lenin. Bazarov had been defended by the critic, Pisarev, and Herzen who had less sympathy with the oncoming rush of ideas represented by Turgenev's creation, remarked that 'among the admirers of Bazarov there will doubtless be some who will be delighted with his rude manners . . . and will imitate those manners, which are in any case a defect and not a virtue'. In a footnote added later Herzen says, 'The prophecy has now been fulfilled,' and he reflects on the curious fact of 'the mutual interaction of men on books, and books on men', noting how at one time all young Germans resembled *Werther*, and the 'young ladies', Charlotte, and how later they changed into Schilleresque 'Robbers'. 'The young Russians who have come on the scene since 1862 are almost all derived from *What Is to be Done?* with the addition of a few Bazarov features.'[1]

v

Projection is not confined to fiction or drama. It is much the same in the literature of ideas. Just as we are capable of projecting ourselves into all manner of folk so we are capable of absorbing and sometimes of digesting all kinds of ideas as though they were our own, the reason being that reading startles into life those parts of us which might otherwise have remained dormant. It reminds us of something we knew but did not know we knew. The reader takes from a book what he needs at the moment, much as Shakespeare took what he needed from older books, and transmutes it into himself. He does not become the author, the author becomes a part of him. Such transmutations are not always taking place. The need must be there, the moment opportune. 'One's liking for a book depends in large measure upon the time when one reads it,' says Anne Douglas Sedgwick; 'further, it must form a link with something that has gone before, answer some unanswered thoughts, open some closed door before which one has been helplessly standing.' It was William James who did that for her, but 'perhaps the year before and perhaps next year he would have meant nothing to me', she says, concluding that it is the 'environment of thought into which one takes a book' that determines its final effect.[2]

[1] *Memoirs of Alexander Herzen*, Trans. Constance Garnett (1927), vi, 193. [2] *Anne Douglas Sedgwick: A Portrait in Letters*, chosen by Basil de Selincourt (1936), 18.

vi

Books do not minister only to our culture or our comfort, they feed our fears and passions. John Bunyan was scared into 'grace' by the terror of the eternal damnation which he extracted from religious books. He read little, but every word affected him like a powerful drug. The *Bible*, says Edward Dowden, 'is like a world of living agencies to him: a text leaps out upon him and grapples him as if it were an angel or a demon.'[1] Books startle the mind into closer and more vivid contact with its own culture, or send it adventuring in strange places. 'When one takes a sentence of Coleridge into the mind it explodes and gives birth to all kinds of other ideas.'[2] Unless in some way or at some time words, sentences, or books explode thus beneficently and creatively, not only revealing life but showing us how to live, reading is a waste of time. Emerson was not concerned about how a book affects us; so long as it moves us in some measure, it does not matter whether it is by contradiction or approval, or whether it enrages, edifies, or inspires: 'a good indignation brings out all one's powers.'[3] Wonder is not enough. Many other things could serve better the purpose of living than books which merely foster our spiritual impotence.

The process can be demonstrated from the recorded experiences of Keats as a reader and H. G. Wells as a writer. Keats readily transposed himself into the condition of what he read so that by turning a page he could be with Achilles in the trenches or with Theocritus in the Vales of Sicily, and, he wrote, 'When man has arrived at a certain ripeness in intellect any one grand and spiritual passage serves him as a starting-post towards all "the two-and-twenty Palaces".' In writing a story Wells found that, 'taking almost anything as a starting-point and letting my thoughts play about it, there would presently come out of the darkness, in a manner quite inexplicable, some absurd or vivid little incident more or less relevant to that initial nucleus. Little men in canoes upon sunlit oceans would come floating out of nothingness, incubating the eggs of prehistoric monsters unawares; violent conflicts would break out amidst the flower-beds of suburban gardens; I would discover I was peering into remote and mysterious worlds ruled by an order logical indeed but other than our common sanity.'[4]

[1] *Fragments from Old Letters* (1914), 132. [2] Virginia Woolf, *A Room of One's Own* (1929), 153. [3] *Journal*, vi, 99. [4] Intro. to *The Country of the Blind and Other Stories*, iv.

Such experiences are not the privilege of the creative genius alone, they must be common to all readers not entirely insensitive or devoid of imagination. They were frequent with Edward Dowden, who may possibly be remembered as a greater reader than writer. One occurred to him after reading the story of the Swiss patriot who opened a passage into the Austrian ranks by making his own body a target for the enemies' spears. 'I went over this achievement in imagination', he says, 'until it became an involuntary reflex act of the imagination, and I still remember the almost bodily sensation of anguish, and the intense joy of spirit as I would gather the armful of spears and drive them into their place home.'[1]

vii

The two methods of expression facing the same problem are examined by William Empson in *Seven Types of Ambiguity*. 'There is a preliminary stage in reading poetry', he says, 'when the grammar is still being settled, and the words have not all been given their due weight; you have a broad impression of what it is all about, but there are various incidental impressions wandering about in your mind; these may not be a part of the final meaning arrived at by the judgment, but tend to be fixed in it as part of its colour. In the same way, there is a preliminary stage in writing poetry, when not all the grammar, but the grammar at crucial points of contact between different ideas, is liable to be often changed.' The inward processes correspond. The author escapes through the characters he has created or the ideas he has expressed, and so does the reader. Both writer and reader experience that relief which follows the release of suppressed forces and their revitalised entry into the stream of consciousness. No book is complete until it has found a reader, not alone because books are written to be read, but because an author can only express a part of himself. The reader completes the circle of expression by transmuting art into life again.

A book is thus not complete at its birth. One of the tests of a great book is that it grows in depth and power over long periods. Some books, perhaps the greatest, are always contemporary. They seem to possess the faculty of adapting themselves to the needs of different ages. Others may be overlooked at birth to be discovered and acclaimed by the next generation or by future ages. Katherine Mansfield believed that Jane Austen was 'one of those writers who

[1] *Letters* (1914), 128.

seem not only to improve by keeping but to develop entirely new and adorable quality'.[1] Whether that is true or not, it is certain that time can ripen a book of the right vintage, but the test of literary excellence is not time but use. Reading is the great preservative of literature. The best books improve by reading, because they possess depths of experience which cannot be read dry. 'With every added year of age,' said George Gissing, 'Shakespeare becomes greater to one, and fuller of intelligent meaning.'[2]

viii

Even trivial reading has significance for the reader; and it is not only bad books which put ideas into people's heads, a reason against reading which was popular in the last century and is now as popularly used to whip the cinema. But trivial reading, like idle chatter, soothes rather than changes. The popularity of the vamp and the gangster in fiction suggests the existence of a large class of readers who are physically and acquisitively repressed, just as light reading may be a compensation for light living. Sexually starved readers are soothed by stories of vamps and lecherous he-men, as men who would like to be crooks but daren't, and those, more numerous, who have crookedness in their sub-conscious but are not likely to allow it to come to the surface, revel in tales about crooks.[3]

ix

Neither technical perfection nor the pervasion of genius can alter a condition in which the reader makes the fate of books as much by adjusting the author to himself as by adjusting himself to the author.[4] The confusion is liable to be intensified because the qualities of a book are often latent, sometimes even fortuitous, to be revealed only by time, as the images on a photographic plate are developed by chemicals. What ultimately appears depends upon the loyalty and veracity of the reader to himself as well as to the author, and neither of them is always under his control. However much he may desire to listen to the author, he cannot avoid listening to himself as well,

[1] *Letters* (Albatross Ed.), 354.　[2] *Letters to Members of his Family* (1926), 138.　[3] See Notes.　[4] 'A good poem has many possible interpretations, and an intellectual scheme may be useful to some readers even though it is not the scheme which the poet himself would expound.' Michael Roberts, *Critique of Poetry* (1934), 11.

and sometimes he finds himself listening to himself and the author simultaneously. Nor is the way clear when acceptance of an author seems easy and loyalty inevitable, for the tendency of the disciple is to outstep the master. It is only by rigorous attention that the principles laid down by a teacher can be maintained in their original purity. Even then the slow erosions and penetrations of the years are out-manoeuvring the watchmen, and long after its purpose has gone into limbo a book may enter upon a fresh career of usefulness or mischief which would astonish no one so much as the author.

Nor can we be certain that we admire in ancient authors what would have pleased their contemporaries, or dislike what they disliked. The prose of many a seventeenth century sermon has survived its theological content like an exquisite shell which remains beautiful after its inmate is forgotten, and its theology changes with the variation of spiritual values. Theologies, and philosophies and sciences as well, not only vary with time, they come to an end, worn out, and live on only as curiosities, derelicts stranded like those fossil beaches which we find upon tops of mountains hundreds of miles from the sea.

If literature is not static neither is the past: it changes as we change. The past, which depends so largely upon books, reflects us as much as if not more than itself. Histories and biographies are constantly being re-written so that they always seem to cheat or challenge established or popular opinion. Nowadays the process is called 'debunking', but it is new only in name, and operates also in reverse, sometimes with the regularity of a pendulum. Writers, as I have shown on another page, are continuously being enthroned and dethroned, so that rebunking may be expected to follow debunking as an inevitable part of the process of literary continuity. History and the philosophy of history are always changing because a man or a nation exists only as he or it is seen at a given time. There is no absolute, no finality. The past is as variable as the present; every historian tries to make it static, to give it his own fixation; but he can rarely if ever escape from the influence of the present which is always guiding his hand and whispering irrelevancies into his ear. The author of Lytton Strachey's *Queen Victoria* was not Lytton Strachey but the period in which and for which Strachey wrote, just as Hume's or Green's or Trevelyan's histories of England are the peculiar inspirations and expressions of the times in which those historians lived and wrote. A contemporary historian of equal genius who gave us a history of Rome would differ from Mommsen as Mommsen did from Gibbon. The idea of an objective past is an illusion which persists although succeeding historians and scientists are constantly, and, not seldom, unconsciously, exploding it.

x

Taste also varies with time. Even the differences between youth and age in one lifetime are revolutionary. What inspires boyhood leaves manhood cold. We are puzzled as we grow older at the sort of books which thrilled us in our youth. Yet those early enthusiasms were genuine aesthetic experiences commensurate with our years. Every reader could summon instances out of his own life. Arthur Machen remembers stories read long ago which produced emotions recognised afterwards as 'purely aesthetic', and he recalls how 'the sorriest pirate, the most wretchedly concealed treasure, poor Captain Mayne Reid at his boldest' gave him sensations which he now searches for in the *Odyssey*, and years afterwards he wonders how he managed 'to penetrate into "faery lands forlorn" through such miserable stucco portals'.[1]

It was perhaps such obstacles as these that Henri de Regnier had in mind when he reflected that 'an understanding between the reader and the writer can only come about slowly; one has some chance of being understood by tradition', but, he concludes less surely, 'one has never been understood except by oneself.'[2] Even that is doubtful for it is true also that the subjectivity of authors is often a confession of failure to understand themselves, and the projection of themselves into fiction is an attempt to remedy the defect. Disraeli, according to André Maurois, wrote *Vivian Grey* 'to create a hero under whose name he could explain himself to himself',[3] and Jung recognises Nietzsche's 'peculiar need to back himself up by a revivified Zarathustra as a kind of secondary personality, a sort of alter-ego, with whom he often identifies himself in his great tragedy'.[4] The device is familiar and in some instances it is admitted ('Madame Bovary, c'est moi!' said Flaubert), and in many more it is a transparent disguise as in Stendhal's Lisio and Salviali, Tolstoy's Nekhlyudov, Anatole France's Bergeret, Pater's Marius, Maurice Barres' Philippe (in *Le Jardin de Bérénice*),

[1] *Hieroglyphics* (1902), 95. [2] Qt. Havelock Ellis' *Rousseau to Proust* (1936), 341. [3] *Disraeli*, André Maurois (Penguin Ed. 1937), 37. [4] *Psychology and Religion*, C. G. Jung (1938), 103.

Paul Valéry's Teste, James Joyce's Daedalus, and Georges Duhamel's Salavin. Such characters have been deliberately created by their authors as media for ideas and opinions of which they are fully conscious, but which they can express more frankly when free from the tyranny of what is subjective and contemporary.

An attempted objective characterisation of what is fundamentally personal is also a vital part of the reader's equipment. When a reader is reading he is trying to understand himself, and whatever the author may have meant the reader will transmute it into his own meaning. It is inevitable that unexpressed wishes and desires will come into play and transmute acceptable passages to their own advantage, stimulating mind and imagination, and, under favourable conditions, reaching appropriate expression in modes of living. But even when the logical sequence is not so complete, the transmission of meaning from writer to reader is never more than partial. Books rarely if ever put anything into the mind of a reader which is not already there. The primary effect of reading is awakening not informing: it is a process of reminding. The fit reader does not take the form or colour of the book he is reading, but the form and colour of himself even when he is helping himself to the writer's meaning, his aim being the intensification, not the dilution, of what is peculiar to his own personality.[1] The processes governing the interaction of writer and reader are still obscure and therefore controversial, but enough is known about them to say that cause and effect in reading are never simple and direct, and that they are reciprocal only when writer and reader happen to be going the same way.[2]

[1] '... almost anything suffices to set Baring off on one of those disquisitions—sometimes genial, sometimes undisguisedly frivolous, sometimes merely a certain juxtaposition of words—that touch a deep-lying spirit of thought in the reader and transport him into the heart of some vivid experience of his own.' Ethel Smyth, *Maurice Baring* (1928), 166.
[2] See Notes.

CHAPTER V

OBSERVATION AND READING

'Crafty men condemn Studies, Simple men admire them, and wise men use them: For they teach not their own use, but that is a Wisdom without them, and above them, won by Observation.'—FRANCIS BACON, 'Of Studies,' *Essays* (1625).

'I see, and sing, by my own eyes inspired.'—JOHN KEATS, 'Ode to Psyche' (1819).

'Nothing changes from generation to generation except the things seen, and that makes a composition.'—GERTRUDE STEIN, *Composition as Explanation* (1926), 6.

'Truth in and for poetry is given by the report of the senses. Poetry begins in the free surrender of ourselves to the impressions of the senses. To be poets, we must trust our senses; and we must speak the language of the senses, and not the conventional language of Reason . . . the cardinal dogma is that the only knowledge worth having (worth having for the poet) comes from the senses.'—H. W. GARROD, *Keats* (1926), 123.

---

i

Art is called romantic or realist, symbolist or naturalist, according to whether it is going to or coming from the world of external things, but it never goes the whole way in either direction. Every work of art is composed of spirit as well as matter, and perhaps the only difference between masterpieces is one of density. Whether that is so or not the finer and unseen essences, feelings, emotions, thoughts, imaginings, can only function through the senses in material substances, or effects, such as pigments, minerals, timber, plastics, words, sounds. These materials of the arts are called natural as distinct from super-natural, but again the division, though convenient, is illusory, for nothing can be outside or above nature—not even the super-natural. Even the arts and artificiality are natural and it is natural, also, to look to nature for guidance in ideas and forms. The 'return to nature' is not only a romantic protest against excessive sophistication, it is the traditional remedy for the ills of art. Weary of mode and habit we turn to nature medicinally as cats eat grass. But looking at nature is not confined to botanising, bird-watching or those other operations of the field-naturalist so fondly featured by our nature-poets.

Genius looks at life frankly and freshly with no more regard for the conventions of art or morals than is necessary to express what is seen. The life to be observed for the purposes of art is not a specially selected phase or feature, 'picturesque' or 'poetical'; it is a personal and timely selection from the whole of life, beautiful or ugly, good or bad. Life is people, animals, phenomena, things. We can only sense life through natural things or things made by man. You can't see life as life, you can only see the actual or 'factual' expressions of life made by 'nature' or by man. You can think about life as an idea, but you can no more look at life than you can look at abstract ideas like truth, goodness, or beauty. All art refers back to the concrete. Phenomena, not ideas, are the artist's 'terms of reference', and only what you see for yourself is your own. Sensibility is the source of the arts.

It is for this reason that observation plays so important a part in the creation of works of art, and particularly in the many-faceted art of writing. Whatever happens to the raw materials of art in their progress towards formal expression their origin is sensory. Milton's famous definition of poetry as being 'simple, sensuous, passionate', applies to all literature. Conrad, who was not blind to the forces of imagination, or even of inspiration if dissociated from superstition, recognised the dependence of the art of fiction upon these primitive functions. The appeal of fiction is to temperament and must be made through the senses 'if its high desire is to reach to secret springs of responsive emotions'. As an artist he was trying 'by the power of the written word, to make you hear, to make you feel . . . before all, to make you *see*!' The ultimate aim is to invoke 'in the hearts of the beholders that feeling of unavoidable solidarity . . . which binds men to each other and all mankind to the visible world', and to do so by arresting 'for the space of a breath, the hands busy about the work of the earth', and so to 'compel men entranced by the sight of distant goals to glance for a moment at the surrounding vision of form and colour, sunshine and shadows'. The task is difficult, but once accomplished 'behold! all the truth of life is there'.[1]

ii

Observation precedes perception and leads to it, the one complementing the other. The difference is between seeing with and through the eye. The so-called non-sensuous operations of an art, those associated with visions, dreams and imaginings, are determined and brought to light by perceptive processes which refine and amalgamate observed phenomena. Observation sees things; perception sees analogies—the relationship between things and idea, it is observation plus comment, and as much the comment of the emotions as of the mind.[2] Observation is sensuous, perception includes mind as well as matter,[3] it is allied on the one part with observation, and on the other with contemplation, which is inward-looking observation, what Siegfried Sassoon calls 'mind-sight' and defines as the faculty which 'eliminates what is inessential, and achieves breadth and intensity by transmuting perception'.[4] But such commonplaces of criticism as 'mind's eye' and 'inward-looking eye ' are rarely defined and nearly always used so loosely that they only succeed in perpetuating a general fogginess, which would not matter if it did not sanction the illusion that inspiration is independent of observation. It is necessary to look inwardly as well as outwardly, but unless you look outwardly with some sort of precision the 'mind's eye' will have little to contemplate and perception less to perceive. Skill in each of these faculties demands experience but artists are invariably born with sensibilities well adapted for taking advantage of what they see—which often requires courage. A genius might be defined as one who believes what he perceives in the face of all opposition, and a work of art as an

[1] Pref. *The Nigger of the Narcissus* (1897). [2] 'Where there is true emotional reaction to the objects of the external world, there is also a keen sensuous perception; and the vividness of the perception is warrant of the genuineness of the emotion.' J. Middleton Murry, *The Problem of Style* (1922), 100. [3] Even the word 'observation' has contracted a double meaning which adjusts it to this interpretation of literary function. It is commonly used as a synonym of 'perception' and also for the double process of seeing and believing. You may make as well as take observations. [4] *On Poetry* (1939), 25.

attempt to perpetuate what is seen plus the accompanying temperamental responses.[1]

iii

In an essay on Robert Bridges, Coventry Patmore refers to what
he calls the 'synthetic perception' of that poet. The phrase is useful
and could be attributed equally to reader and writer, for reading, no
less than writing, is a synthesis of several faculties focussed by
perception. The facets and depths of a book which are the con-
stituents of its meanings, yield their secrets to the exact observer, they
'unveil themselves', in Patmore's words, 'in proportion to the deserts
and the capacity of the beholder.' Patmore is dealing specifically
with Robert Bridges apropos of *Prometheus the Firegiver*, and with
a poet's perception of what is needed for the reading of poetry he
points out that those who have eyes to see with Bridges 'may
discover fire within fire—from that which consumes the heap of
sticks upon the altar, through the fires of the senses, the affections,
and the will, up to the last ardour of intellectual light'.[2] For many
years Patmore's poetry suffered from just this lack of perception on
the part of critics who mistook superficial simplicity for lack of depth.

This attitude persisted throughout Patmore's life and is occasionally met with even now. As late as the year 1886 when the number
of the poet's intelligent readers was considerable, so respectable
a critic as Edmund Gosse, reviewing the newly issued Collected
Edition of the poems, is puzzled by a feeling that there is more than
meets the eye in these well-mannered poems, but he is unable to
define what it is. 'It is difficult for those who do not look at human
affairs from Mr. Patmore's dogged outpost not to be angry with him
or to misunderstand him. So admirable an artist has rarely been
content to do so little with his art; so brilliant and pungent a thinker
has perhaps never been content so long to dwell on the very border-
land of insipidity. Born with a gift which we believe would have
enabled him to adorn a wide circle of themes, he has almost
obstinately confined himself to the embroidery of one. Dowered

[1] 'Art, like life, perpetuates itself by contact. The "abstract artist" (to
use a contradiction in terms) by abjuring the evidence of his senses, cuts
himself off from the sources of creation and, in the immunity of a philosophical vacuum, assumes an air of expressionless beatitude, strongly suggestive of the condition known to alienists as *Dementia Praecox.*' Augustus
John, *Fragment of an Autobiograhy. Horizon* (Jan. 1943). [2] *Courage in
Politics and Other Essays* (1921), 145–6.

with a rare ear for metrical effect, educated in all the niceties of metrical science, he has of set purpose chosen the most sing-song of English metres as the almost exclusive vehicle of his ideas. The laureate of the tea-table, with his humdrum stories of girls that smell of bread and butter, is in his inmost heart the most arrogant and visionary of mystics. There is no figure more interesting or more difficult to analyse on the poetic stage of our generation.'[1]

It is obvious now that Gosse's ear and eye were so attuned to the observation of conventional poetic sound and sense that he missed the novelty and daring of Patmore's metrics as well as the depths and subtle variations of his themes. He mistook 'the splendour of perception to which nothing is common,'[2] for commonplace at a time when he ought to have perceived that poetic diction was once more undergoing one of its periodic changes of front. The movement from pomposity and rotundity towards a slender and disarming shyness and reticence was well advanced but poetry was attempting to say more, not less. Patmore was not always unaware of his own intentions. It was his boast that his work had 'none of those airs of profundity which those poets who are not so profound so easily assume', and he was right in further assuming that the 'arbiters of poetic fashion' looked upon *The Angel in the House* 'as unworthy of serious notice because all mere pretence of profundity has been so carefully avoided, and the truths that form the granite foundations of life are expressed with such clear simplicity and polish that the profundity and the labour are both obscured by their completeness.'[3]

iv

Literary genius (and also the genius which uses other art-forms) is a balance between perception and expression, and although it has been convenient to stress visual observation and perception in this chapter, the arguments hold for any process of sensuous observation. Seeing is the dominant sense in all the arts except music, but literature, more than any other art, is capable of taking tribute from each of what Sir Thomas Browne called the 'five ports of knowledge'. This is not possible with music, painting, or sculpture. Music depends mainly upon hearing, painting and sculpture upon seeing, and except under the strictest supervision of the imagination,

[1] *The Athenaeum*, 12th June, 1886. Qt. *Further Letters of Gerard Manley Hopkins* (1938), 290.   [2] Coventry Patmore, *Courage in Politics and Other Essays* (1921), 170.   [3] Letter to Hopkins, 11th May, 1888. *Op. cit.* 243.

intellectual pressure is intolerable. Literature at its richest is the emotional and imaginative expression of what a writer has observed by sight, hearing, smell, taste and touch. The writer who observes nothing has nothing to express. Creation in art is sensuous perception transmuted and transcended by what we should now call a process of sublimation,[1] not, as Coleridge foresaw, 'from the sensuous impression, but from the imaginative reflex.'[2] Even contemplation is a form of perception.[3] In the creation of a work of art, observation, perception, contemplation and reflection are interlocked with emotion and imagination. And although the literary artist is the point at which all the senses become sharply receptive to external influences it is probable that the sense of sight is the most active of them all.

It has never been sufficiently realised that the artist sees more than the average man because he has the gift of looking at things freshly without the encumbrance of habit or convention. He looks at things steadily and sees them not necessarily whole but new. One of his greatest assets is this freshness of vision. It is said that Corot's daily prayer was that he might see and draw with the eyes of a child. But that wish did not encourage Corot to pose as a child. Freshness of vision in an adult is not a reversion to childishness so much as a looking upon things with an eye which has been disengaged as far as possible from preconceptions. The artist is like a child in so far as he sees things for the first time. But no child remains for long in a state of wonder. Children are realists, not artists, and soon weary of the latest wonderment. 'To carry on the feelings of childhood into the powers of manhood; to combine the child's sense of wonder and novelty with the appearances, which every day for perhaps forty years had rendered familiar ... this is the character of genius.'[4] By such achievements artists blaze new trails for the consciousness and the senses.

[1] 'The storyteller ... has taught himself to observe. He wants, for the purpose of his craft, to develop to the highest possible pitch his own senses, to constantly see more, hear more, feel more. . . . The Imagination must constantly feed upon reality or starve.' Sherwood Anderson, 'Man and his Imagination,' *The Intent of the Artist*, ed. Augusto Centeno (1941), 40, 67. [2] 'The sense of sublimity arises, not from the sight of an outward object, but from the beholder's reflection upon it; not from the sensuous impression, but from the imaginative reflex.' S. T. Coleridge, *Lectures and Notes on Shakespeare*. Bohn Ed. 345. [3] 'Observation, investigation, inspection, become, in certain circumstances, *introspection*.' P. Mansell Jones, *French Introspectives* (1937), 100. [4] S. T. Coleridge, Qt. Stephen Potter, *Coleridge and S. T. C.* (1935), 81.

Without art few people would see anything beyond what they had been in the habit of seeing. To take a familiar example, the novelist is popular because he forces us to notice characters which would otherwise pass unnoticed.[1] He records what he observes, that is, he assembles his people out of the details of the moment by inspired perception. Dickens did not invent Mr. Micawber any more than Turgenev invented Bazarov. Literature provides many examples of this kind of 'creation' but in each instance it is the result of discovery or singularity of observation, not occult power.[2] Joseph Conrad advised the artist to 'mature the strength of his imagination amongst the things of this earth, which it is his business to cherish and know, and refrain from calling down his inspiration ready-made from some heaven of perfections of which he knows nothing'. He believed that mental power depended upon the enlargement of sympathies by 'patient and loving observation'.[3] Characters in fiction are designated rather than created out of some such attitude towards life. Conrad calls it, 'rescue work,' the 'snatching of vanishing phases of turbulence, disguised in fair words, out of the native obscurity into a light where the struggling forms may be seen, seized upon, endowed with the only possible form of permanence in this world of relative values—the permanence of memory'. And when the reader demands that the writer should take him out of himself, he means out of his 'perishable activity into the light of imperishable consciousness'.[4]

Sometimes the character thus created reveals a new type, as in the case of Bazarov, but more often fresh emphasis or sharper definition is given to types already known: climbers like Kipps or Babbitt, or adventuresses like Becky Sharp, or minxes like Proust's Gilberte and Albertine, or degenerates like Huysmans' des Esseintes in *À Rebours*, or Charlus again in Proust. It is not only the unusual or remarkable types which are revealed by the novelist, and the

---

[1] George Moore 'had an extraordinary capacity for observing the simple truths that other men pass by'. Charles Morgan, *Epitaph for George Moore* (1935), 49. [2] '... scarce a character or action ... which I have not taken from my own observation and experience.' Henry Fielding, Intro. *Joseph Andrews* (1724). 'I rarely write save from the suggestion of something actually observed.' George Meredith, 1861, *Letters* (1912), i, 45. He is referring to his poetry but the statement applies equally to his prose. 'I had an acute power of observation and it seemed to me that I could see a great many things that other people missed.' W. Somerset Maugham, *The Summing-up* (1938). [3] *Notes on Life and Letters* (1921), 11–12. [4] *Notes on Life and Letters* (1921), 15–16.

reader is equally and perhaps even more interested in the revelation
of the familiar. Henry James indicates two kinds of taste in the
appreciation of imaginative literature, 'the taste for emotions of
surprise and the taste for emotions of recognition'.[1] It is significant
that this classification occurs in an essay on Anthony Trollope who
was and remains our greatest master of the emotions of recognition.
It may be that the novel has been established on such a firm basis of
popular appreciation because it is an infallible aid to recognition,
thus adding surprise to what is already known.

The effect of the emergence of fictional types resembles the effect
of those verbal recognitions which are familiar to all readers. A word
assumes undue prominence on the page. It may not be an unusual
word, but the circumstances under which it is now seen give to it
the emphasis of novelty or discovery. The word is thus impressed
upon the mind. But no effort is needed to remember it for it immediately begins to appear in book, periodical, or conversation as though
by magic. This is called coincidence, and whatever it may be, it is
more closely connected with observation than with creativeness.
What we have observed was there all the time. All that has happened
is that it has been thrown into relief.[2]

Characters and types exist and novelists teach us to see them both
as people and as ideas, much as Rousseau gave being, in the person
of Madame de Warens, to what we now meet everywhere as the
'mother-principle' in sex. Jean Jacques was a novelist in the
Confessions and an autobiographer in *Émile*. Flaubert looked at
things until he saw their unique characteristics and those only were
recorded. Guy de Maupassant who was Flaubert's pupil outdid the
master, by deliberately making observation the foundation of his
art. He did not, however, try to organise and record all the facts, as
Zola did, but only essentials: thus detail in his stories and novels is
always integrated with action or plot. In the preface to *Pierre et Jean*
he says: 'The thing is to look at anything one wants to describe long
and clearly enough to discover in it an aspect which nobody else has
seen or reported. There is the unexplored in everything because we
are accustomed to use our eyes with the remembrance of what
people before us have thought about the thing we are contemplating.
The smallest thing contains something that is not known.' We can
pick out the results of this method not only in the works of Flaubert,
Maupassant, and their realist followers in France, but in most of the

[1] *Partial Portraits* (1888), 133.   [2] See Notes.

novels and stories of the western world; in the work of Tchekov no less than in that of Joseph Conrad, in Dickens, Meredith, and Hardy; in Rudyard Kipling and O. Henry; in Somerset Maugham, Aldous Huxley, and D. H. Lawrence; in Sinclair Lewis, William Faulkner, Ernest Hemingway and John dos Passos. In the works of all these writers visual and other sensuous observations show up like objects that have come into the range of a powerful searchlight.

v

The practice of direct observation which is so conspicuous in contemporary poetry and fiction has been encouraged by the example of scientists and technicians. At the same time, and in spite of much clear seeing, many modern writers observe intellectually rather than visually. Intellectual concepts terminating in 'ism', and ideological attitudes, like Fascism or Communism, are allowed to predispose the verdict of the senses. D. H. Lawrence tried to see clearly and to record frankly. He observed human beings who were under the influence of sexual excitement with the object of discovering its significance, but even he came to his task with a preconceived notion which often blurred his observation. His own shibboleths were always getting in the way, and he often lacked wisdom or courage to interfere. He convinced himself that the human race was doomed to extinction if civilised man refused to readjust his sexual habits in accordance with a theory which recalls, in a more specialised form, the romantic idea of the Return to Nature.[1] The result was *Lady Chatterley's Lover*, which is as frankly didactic as Tolstoy's *Kreuzer Sonata* and in the nature of an affirmative reply to the negations of that pamphlet in the form of fiction.

In America it was the custom to look at life through European eyes long even after Walt Whitman had inaugurated a national point of view. But long before Whitman sought to give America a local consciousness and a native culture, Emerson and Thoreau were alive to the importance of a more direct observation of the phenomena of American life and ideas. Emerson saw the close

---

[1] 'We are perishing for lack of fulfilment of our greater needs, we are cut off from the great sources of our inward nourishment and renewal, sources which flow eternally in the universe. Virtually the human race is dying. It is like a great uprooted tree, with its roots in the air. We must plant ourselves again in the universe.' D. H. Lawrence, *A Propos of Lady Chatterley's Lover* (1930), 52–3.

relationship between criticism and observation, and the importance of looking at things was constantly in his mind and frequently noted in his journals. 'Culture', he writes, 'is to cherish a certain susceptibility, to turn the man into eyes, but as the eye can see only that which is eye-form, or of its own state, we tumble on our walls in every part of the universe, and must take such luck as we find, and be thankful. Let us deserve to see.'[1] A little later:[2] 'My life is optical, not practical,' and again,[3] 'I admire perception wherever it appears. That is the one eternal miracle . . . Perception makes.' Nevertheless, Emerson corrected what he saw by what he thought, as Thoreau corrected what he thought by what he saw, and it is probable that he realised more exactly than Emerson the difference between perception and observation. Observation for Thoreau is seeing without compromise and it is quintessential in his practical philosophy. 'How to observe is how to behave.'[4] 'We are as much as we see.'[5] And his whole attitude towards life emphasises the importance of first-sight or freshness of vision. 'The most poetic and truest account of objects is generally given by those who first observe them, or the discoverers of them.'[6]

vi

Wordsworth was more sharply conscious of the power and place of observation in poetry than any other poet of his time,[7] or of any time, and in this respect he is master of all modern English poets, and the most original of all poets who have used the English language. He wished to substitute an imaginative use of common language based upon an exact observation of nature for an outworn 'poetic diction' based upon epithets and ideas.[8] We are often reminded of his definition of poetry as 'emotion remembered in tranquillity', but commentators who are fond of this phrase are apt to forget that Wordsworth lays equal stress, both in the same essay and in various poems, on the part played by observation in the making of a poem. It was the business of the poet to gather

> *The harvest of a quiet eye,*
> *That broods and sleeps on his own heart*

[1] *Journals* (1914), vi, 56. [2] *Ib.*, vi, 158. [3] *Ib.*, ix, 299. [4] *Journal: Spring*, 240. [5] *Ib.*, 344. [6] *Journal: Winter*, 269. [7] He preceded Flaubert and the French realists by half a century, as Constable among painters had anticipated by a century the visualisations of the French Impressionists. [8] 'The *Lyrical Ballads*, are . . . before all else, a revindication in poetry of the life of the senses.' H. W. Garrod, *Keats* (1926), 123.

91

and it is only when he relies solely upon

> *That inward eye*
> *Which is the bliss of solitude,*

that he ceases to be a poet.

Remembrance of emotion in tranquillity is the last operation of a process which began with an act of visual sensibility combined with vivid feeling. He is at pains to make it clear that invention or creation out of nothing is none of his business. Nor is observation confined solely to the eye: 'The objects of the Poet's thoughts are everywhere; though the eyes and senses of man are, it is true, his favourite guides, yet he will follow wheresoever he can find an atmosphere of sensation in which to move his wings.' Imagination follows observation. The 'principal object' of his poems was 'to choose incidents and situations from common life, and to relate or describe them, throughout, as far as was possible in a selection of language really used by men, and, at the same time, to throw over them a certain colouring of imagination, whereby ordinary things should be presented to the mind in an unusual aspect; and, further, and above all, to make these incidents and situations interesting by tracing in them, truly though not ostentatiously, the primary laws of our nature; chiefly, as far as regards the manner in which we associate ideas in a state of excitement'.

It was this contact with nature which determined him to break with the tradition of accepted 'poetic diction' based as it was upon convention or fashion rather than upon vivid feeling and clear seeing. 'Without being culpably particular', he says, 'I do not know how to give my Reader a more exact notion of the style in which it was my wish and intention to write, than by informing him that I have at all times endeavoured to look steadily at my subject; consequently, there is I hope in these Poems little falsehood of description, and my ideas are expressed in language fitted to their respective importance. Something must have been gained by this practice, as it is friendly to one property of all good poetry, namely, good sense: but it has necessarily cut me off from a large portion of phrases and figures of speech which from father to son have long been regarded as the common inheritance of Poets.'

If Wordsworth succeeded in breaking down the adhesions of 'poetic' words and phrases which had cramped the freedom of genuine poetic expression, the vocabulary selected from the 'real language of men in a state of vivid sensation' was successful because it served the purpose of his genius rather than because it reproduced the character of common speech. The words were common enough, so familiar, indeed, that they sometimes formed clichés which were only saved from the bathos into which his verses were too often allowed to lapse, by passionate reinforcement from a creative memory.

I have described the well-known Wordsworthian discrepancies as 'lapses' and so in effect they were, yet they were neither accidental nor callous, but the inevitable result of a method of which the poet was aware. He took the risk knowing as he did that a poet cannot be continuously inspired. He might have waited for inspiration, but he was a teacher as well as a poet and his moral and purposeful nature convinced him that what he had to say was worth saying—poetic or not. In addition to that he did not succeed in realising his ambition of writing poetry as 'a man speaking to men', because he recognised also, and rightly, that a poet was a man 'endowed with more lively sensibility, more enthusiasm and tenderness, who has a greater knowledge of human nature, and a more comprehensive soul, than are supposed to be common among mankind; a man pleased with his own passions and volitions, and who rejoices more than other men in the spirit of life that is in him; delighting to contemplate similar volitions and passions as manifested in the goings-on in the Universe, and habitually impelled to create them where he does not find them.' There are other differences, largely intensifications of similarities, which I need not enumerate. So long as he was content to report the 'goings-on' of his Lakeland Universe, in that impassioned language which is unmistakably and solely his own, all was well.[1]

In his inspired moments Wordsworth welds visual and other sense-impressions into inevitable words and cadences by a transmutation at its best so perfect that the finished poem is not so much a reflection or imitation as a part of nature. All evidence of technique has gone; there is no obvious trace of the processes of artistry; the legitimate, the natural artificiality of poetry is forgotten. Wordsworth's poems at their best are as artless as the design of a fish or the architecture of a bird's nest.

Often it was his sister Dorothy who saw first what William turned into poetry. 'It is in her peculiar ability', says Mark Rutherford, 'to get so much out of the common world that Dorothy is remark-

[1] The citations are from Wordsworth's essay 'Of the Principles of Poetry', prefaced to the *Lyrical Ballads* (1798-1802).

able. The reason why she can get so much from it is that she can look long and steadily, and is free from any conscious desire to do more than look.'[1] The best passages in her diaries reveal a genius for looking at natural objects, which are recorded with such verisimilitude that they played an important part in giving a new and indigenous quality to English poetry.

vii

The artist observes and makes observations on what he has experienced through the senses, by a process of exfoliation which involves the paradox of accepting and denying the evidence of the senses simultaneously. That is probably what Coleridge meant when he said that 'To emancipate the mind from the despotism of the eye is a first step towards its emancipation from the influence and intrusion of the senses, sensations and passions generally. Thus most effectually is the power of abstracting to be called forth strengthened and familiarised.'[2] In a letter to Thomas Poole (16th October, 1797) he makes an even bigger gap between inward and outward looking: 'I never regarded *my senses* in any way as the criteria of my belief. I regulated all my creeds by my conceptions, not by my *sight*.' He is referring specifically to the reading of romances relating to giants, magicians, and genii, in which he sees the best way of 'giving the mind a love of the Great and the Whole', and he adds that 'those who have been led to the same truths step by step, through the testimony of their senses, seem to me to want a sense which I possess. They contemplate nothing but *parts*, and all *parts* are necessarily little. And the universe to them is a mass of little things'. This was an early opinion and although modified or otherwise varied from time to time, as though he felt the attitude was not fully justified, it was never entirely abandoned, and, finally, dominated his attitude towards life.

A note in *Anima Poetae* (233) proves that he is aware of the true relation between observation and contemplation. He is telling himself that men of genius place things in a new light, and goes on to say that 'the poet not only displays what, though often seen in its unfolded mass, had never been opened out, but he likewise adds something, namely, light and relations. Who has not seen a rose or

[1] *Last Pages from a Journal* (1915), 240. [2] Qt. Potter, *Coleridge and S. T. C.* (1935), 198.

sprig of jasmine or myrtle? But behold those same flowers in a posy or flower-pot, painted by a man of genius, or assorted by the hand of a woman of fine taste and instinctive sense of beauty!' The thing must be seen by the eye, and then given a new relation or significance by the inward eye, the extra sense which he possessed. Coleridge's notebooks and letters prove that he did realise the importance of sensuous observation, but was only interested in seeing and knowing in so far as they were aids to being, and many of his inconsistencies and obscurities fade away when they are related to this preoccupation with a theory of life. In spite of a life-long interest in style and diction, his main object was not how to write poetry or prose, but how to live, and in the last resort he was more metaphysician than artist, or, perhaps, an attempted combination of the two. His notebooks reflect this evolution. In his earlier and happier period, when he was content to share the aesthetic experiences of the Wordsworths, he records many glimpses of nature for future poetic use. But as time passes the notes become more abstract until in the end the outer world has no place in his records.

Coleridge's apparent inconsistencies were the result of an impulse to run away from life, or, rather, to escape from the coarser manifestation or more painful incidents of common physical affairs. His two chief means of escape were introspection and drugs. He appreciated the importance of observation, as we have seen, but observation, being an extrovert process, becomes suspect as his tendency to introversion develops. A note on Samuel Richardson in *Anima Poetae* throws an oblique ray on this anomaly. Coleridge is reflecting once more on the unending conflict between his ideas and experiences, this time apropos of a clash between aesthetics and ethics. He confesses that it costs his philosophy 'some exertion' that he must admire, even 'greatly admire', Richardson's novels. As a writer and a critic he realises the importance of those novels, but as a moralist he deplores the attitude of their author towards life. Richardson has created notable fictions, but Richardson's mind is 'so very vile a mind, so oozy, hypocritical, praise-mad, canting, envious, concupiscent!' Coleridge was often bewildered by his own duality but he was always honest, and in this dilemma he exhorts himself to charity and calmness: 'a heart fixed on the good part, though the understanding is surveying all.' He consoles himself with the thought that Richardson behaves uncharitably towards his rival, Fielding, 'a trick', he adds, 'often played, though not exclusively by contemporaries.' Fielding's talent was observation, not meditation, but

'Richardson was not philosopher enough to know the difference', or, he hastens to correct himself, 'to understand and develop it.' Coleridge certainly felt that it was better to be a good observer than a bad philosopher, but that observation at its best was inferior to meditation. As a matter of fact neither Fielding nor Richardson was a philosopher. They were both observers of genius with a passion for moral reflection. Richardson's powers of observation are often overlaid by his self-righteousness, but as observer and analyst of social sensibilities he is a pioneer of the fictional method which reached florescence in Henry James and Marcel Proust.

The complex problem of Coleridge's poetic downfall is perhaps more closely connected with certain changes in his attitude towards the faculty of observation than the commentators have fully understood. A defect in character coupled with a tendency to ill-health was the fundamental cause, and the chance of complete recovery seems to have passed away when he lost his faith in the visible world and abandoned his genius to introspection. The cause need not be considered here but whatever explanation is given it was brought to a crisis by the collapse of his home life, the final break of his friendship with the Wordsworths and the repudiation of his early faith in Nature, all of which came about at the same time and are closely connected. If orderly and happy domestic relations had been possible for a man of Coleridge's wandering temperament many of his difficulties might have been smoothed out. But the chances of a favourable arrangement with the incompatibility that existed between him and his wife were remote. Collapse was temperamentally inevitable. Coleridge gave many explanations of his domestic troubles but none so illuminating as that contained in the surviving fragment of a letter to his wife written in 1802. He analyses their two characters showing clearly that the differences are between what we should now call extrovert and introvert, with the implication that they were neither of them capable of modifying their temperaments by the exercise of reasonable give and take. The fragment concludes with words which seem like a rebuke and bear significantly upon Coleridge's determination to escape from the world of the senses. 'So', he concludes, after explaining his own inward-dwelling, 'you on the contrary exist almost wholly in the world *without* you— the Eye and the Ear are your great organs, and you depend upon the eyes and ears of others for a great part of your pleasures.'[1]

[1] *Unpublished Letters*, ed. E. L. Griggs (1932), i, 190–1.

Coleridge was not the only loser by the changed relations with the Wordsworths, for although Wordsworth was saved from moral collapse by possession of a harder core to his character, he ultimately came to a bad poetic end, but not before he had created a body of verse which placed him high in the front rank of English poets. Coleridge was aware of the consequences of these trials, particularly in relation to the transference of his outlook upon life from the concrete to the abstract, and he has recorded his feelings in the ode called 'Dejection', originally addressed to Wordsworth in 1802, when the happiest chapter in his life closed. The poem is, among other things, a lament for the loss of the inspiration which came from contemplation of natural phenomena:

> *I see the old Moon . . . foretelling*
> *The coming-on of rain and squally blast.*
> *And Oh! that even now the gust were swelling,*
> *And the slant night-shower driving loud and fast!*
> *Those sounds which oft have raised me, whilst they awed*
> *And sent my soul abroad,*
> *Might now perhaps their wonted impulse give,*
> *Might startle this dull pain, and make it move and live.*

Perhaps his exotic imagination with its preference for the remote in time and place was never really anchored, as Wordsworth's was, in what was near and present. He helped Wordsworth to come into harbour but himself he could not pilot, nor could Wordsworth return the service—though Dorothy Wordsworth might have done so. There is no indication of firm belief in the indwelling law which he is now to pursue, and although he is convinced that he

> *. . . may not hope from outward forms to win*
> *The passion and the life, whose fountains are within,*

he still looks outward, towards Wordsworth happy in his nearness to earth and the tender consolations of an inspired observation of common things. This attitude, though clear enough in the ode as printed in his works, is made clearer in the poignant lines as they originally appeared in a letter to his friend William Sotheby (19th July, 1802),

> *Calm steadfast spirit, guided from above,*
> *O Wordsworth! friend of my devoutest choice,*
> *Great son of genius, full of light and love*
> *Thus, thus dost thou rejoice ;*

> *To thee do all things live from pole to pole,*
> *Their life the eddying of thy soul,*
> *Brother and friend of my devoted choice*
> *Thus may'st thou ever, evermore rejoice.*

But for himself he has little hope. He looks out on the 'things which live from pole to pole' but with 'how blank an eye!'

> *I see them all so excellently fair,*
> *I see, not feel, how beautiful they are!*

viii

English poets, even before Wordsworth, had never for long neglected the calm visualisation of objects. Chaucer had the gift of seeing things and so had Shakespeare—greatly as both of them relied upon books for the machinery of their fictions. The greater the writer the greater the faculty of observation.[1] Herrick and most of the Elizabethan lyric poets had flashes of outsight as well as insight. In the seventeenth century poets were equally gifted, despite their engagements with religious and political controversy, and it is the observed even more than the thought in their works which survives.

When, in middle age, Milton lost his sight—'that one talent which is death to hide,' he had observed life so variously that his well-stored mind provided him as we know with abundance of material for the completion of an unsurpassed life-work. The consolatory climax of the sonnet 'On his Blindness',

> *They also serve who only stand and wait,*

thus becomes little more than a pious thought. The man who occupied the blind half of his life with the creation of *Paradise Lost*, *Paradise Regained* and *Samson Agonistes*, did not stand and wait. His inward riches nourished him, and, far from acting as a drag on the wheel, the curtailment of his physical activities stimulated a genius which could feed

> *. . . on thoughts that voluntarie move,*
> *Harmonious numbers; as the wakeful Bird*
> *Sings darkling, and in shadiest covert hid*
> *Tunes her nocturnal note.*

[1] 'Shakespeare had the finest faculty of observation of all men that ever breathed.' Gerard Manley Hopkins, *Correspondence* (1935), ii, 140. See Notes.

And if he was cut off by 'ever-enduring dark' from the 'cheerful ways of men', and robbed of such joys as

> ... *the sweet approach of Ev'n or Morn,*
> *Or sight of vernal bloom, or Summer's Rose,*
> *Or flocks, or herds, or human face divine,*

he was not without compensations. There is evidence that his hearing was as sensitive as his sight, and there are some well-known lines in *Comus*, written before he became blind, which suggest that he was aware of this faculty:

> ... *I was all ear,*
> *And took in strains that might create a soul*
> *under the ribs of death.*[1]

It may be presumed that the sense of hearing became more acute as his sight declined, adding a new power to his artistry. But although he was always alive to sensuous impressions which might have been condemned in the Puritan age of which he was the finest flower, his mind habitually worked inwardly. But when he invokes the 'Celestial Light' it is in terms of ordinary sight:

> *So much the rather thou Celestial light*
> *Shine inward, and the mind through all her powers*
> *Irradiate, there plant eyes, all mist from thence*
> *Purge and disperse, that I may see and tell*
> *Of things invisible to mortal sight.*[2]

ix

The poets of the eighteenth century observed men and manners rather than nature, until the arrival of Collins, Thompson and Burns; thence and throughout the nineteenth century observation, particularly of nature, played an increasing part in our literature. The idea, however, that imagination was more or less independent of external impressions was still prevalent.[3] Thomas Moore noted as though it were unusual that Byron 'could not describe anything which he had not actually under his eyes, and that he did it on the

---

[1] *Comus* (1634), 560–2. [2] Milton, 'Light.' [3] 'Shelley was an inferior poet because he did not qualify his dogmas with observation.' Louis Macneice, *Modern Poetry* (1938), 202.

spot or immediately after'.[1] But while the century was in its teens
the faculty of looking at life freshly and steadily was reborn. Poets
under the general but indirect inspiration of Wordsworth, even
when they were as far removed from that influence as Keats was,
were introducing the results of an almost scientific observation of
nature into their verse. But, with the exception of Wordsworth, they
did little more than intensify a traditional practice which goes back
to Chaucer and Shakespeare and forward to Tennyson and Matthew
Arnold.

Much of what is characteristic and excellent in Keats's poetry is the
sublimation of his delight in sensuous experiences. This is particularly evident in passages derived from memories of country sights
and sounds, which are always recorded for the pleasure they have
given him and not, as so often happens in the poetry of Wordsworth,
as pegs upon which to hang philosophical or ethical ideas. The
process of sublimation reaches maturity in the poetic romances and
the five odes, in such perfect transmutations as the opening verse of
The Eve of St. Agnes:

> *St. Agnes' Eve—Ah, bitter chill it was!*
> *The owl, for all his feathers, was a-cold;*
> *The hare limp'd trembling through the frozen grass,*
> *And silent was the flock in woolly fold:*
> *Numb were the Beadsman's fingers, while he told*
> *His rosary, and while his frosted breath,*
> *Like pious incense from a censer old,*
> *Seem'd taking flight for heaven, without a death,*
> *Past the sweet Virgin's picture, while his prayer he saith.*

Or the third verse of the ode 'To Autumn':

> *Where are the songs of Spring? Ay, where are they?*
> *Think not of them, thou hast thy music too,—*
> *While barred clouds bloom the soft-dying day,*
> *And touch the stubble plains with rosy hue;*
> *Then in a wailful choir the small gnats mourn*
> *Among the river sallows borne aloft*

[1] *Memoirs* (1853), ii, 2–8. It is worth remembering that when Byron's
observation failed he borrowed from books. In a letter to John Murray he
says 'Almost all *Don Juan* is *real* life, either my own, or from people I
knew;' and he repeats that he 'told Mr. Hobhouse, years ago, that there
was not a *single circumstance* of it not taken from fact. He goes, however,
to Tully's *Tripoli* for 'description of the furniture'. 23, viii, 1821.

Or sinking as the light wind lives or dies;
And full-grown lambs loud bleat from hilly bourn;
Hedge-crickets sing; and now with treble soft
The red-breast whistles from a garden croft;
And gathering swallows twitter in the skies.

But the habit of observation is revealed in earlier poems, notably in the lines beginning 'I stood tiptoe upon a little hill', where he demands a wide margin

for the greediest eye,
To peer about upon variety,

and in another passage he shows us some of the results of this peering:

Linger awhile upon some bending planks
That lean against a streamlet's rushy banks . . .
Where swarms of minnows show their little heads,
Staying their wavy bodies 'gainst the streams,
To taste the luxury of sunny beams
Temper'd with coolness. How they ever wrestle
With their own sweet delight, and ever nestle
Their silver bellies on the pebbly sand.
If you but scantily hold out a hand,
That very instant not one will remain;
But turn your eye, and they are there again.

Keats is more consistent here as observer than as poet—although it would be unfair to expect complete mastery in an experimental piece of the kind, the description of the minnows

Staying their wavy bodies 'gainst the streams,
To taste the luxury of sunny beams
Temper'd with coolness

is an anticipation of the welding of observation and imagination in his later work.

x

The poets of the eighteen nineties were better observers of their own moods than of those of nature. They contemplated themselves in various attitudes, always sophisticated, and they wished to luxuriate in a vague melancholy induced by their own waywardness and its subsequent weariness. Books and art were the sources of their

101

inspiration, except when they turned their eyes upon the common objects of the town. Some of the most characteristic poems of the period, notably those of John Davidson and Arthur Symons, record impressions of music halls, public-houses, and street scenes in the East End. W. B. Yeats saw inwardly more clearly than outwardly. He was a seer in the mystic sense, but although it is true, as Stephen Spender has pointed out, that 'the visual experiences of his whole life which have found their way into his poetry could probably be counted on the fingers of both hands',[1] his finest poems contain many passages which illustrate keen observation.

Rudyard Kipling and A. E. Housman had what a commentator on Housman (Miss Gundred Ellen Savory, *Birmingham Post*, 22nd June, 1957) called a sense of place. Rudyard Kipling not only makes you see places, he makes you smell them. Housman, on the other hand, was not one of the conspicuous observers among poets. He saw the outer world in flashes which broke only occasionally into the continuity of his brooding mind. The impressions, though intermittent, were so vivid that they took poetic form naturally. He was more deeply concerned with his own feelings and the study of books: his studies were peculiarly subjective and always steeped in emotion. Life seems to have been something which happened to him long ago. Even his poetry is incidental and although original in content is surprisingly synthetic in detail. You can often read him as you read a pastiche. This is possible because his undisputed scholarship was based upon an unprecedented sense of textual precision. He brought to the observation of living things the same sort of precision which he applied to the scrutiny of a Latin text. And as poetic truth is not the same as scientific truth it is surprising that such precision should end in poetry instead of in science or topography: but as the writer of the *Times* memoir said, 'The future will have no excuse for supposing that Housman's poetry is a cold exercise of scholarship, or that his simplicity is the affectation of an over-subtle brain. His simplicity in the simplest feeling is genuine; but it has passed through his impeccable mind to come out on the far side a purer simplicity, the perfect product of head and heart together.'

It is probable that Housman's sense of smell was more active than his sense of sight. Whether this was so or not, he enjoyed using that sense. 'He absorbed the look and scent of flowers with a vivid perception that visibly moved him. Maybe it was this sense that after-

---

[1] *The Destructive Element* (1935), 125.

wards made him a connoisseur of wines.'[1] 'Like Robert Bridges, he had a peculiar fondness for the scent of flowers and herbs. I have seen the former, when well past eighty, flop onto the ground a dozen times in as many minutes to smell the flowers at his feet. Housman, with more sobriety and less regard for pernickety propriety, would trample a border to get at any flowers which promised the desired whiff on unbending terms.'[2]

Kipling's sense of sound was pronounced but he was not moved by subtle sounds—little noiseless noises—but by obvious and familiar sounds which everyone has heard without observing. He appreciated the clanging of hammers, the purring of engines. He makes words imitate the tramp of soldiers on the march, he notes the calls of workmen and animals, the chant of lascars during the passage from India, and the mewing of otters in an English river; he tries to reproduce the sound of musical instruments like the banjo, and one of his soldiers brags that he has heard the 'revelly' round the world 'from Bir to Barelli, from Leeds to Lahore'. When he wants to impress us with the glamour of the Eastern sky he makes the dawn come 'up like thunder outer China 'crost the Bay'.[3]

xi

Among contemporary poets few of the older generation show transcendent powers of observation. The perceptions of the Georgian poets are intellectual or emotional: they think and feel rather than see. Walter de la Mare seems to be listening to the unheard melodies of a fanciful world of his own, rather than noting the common affairs of this world. He differentiates between the poetic and the intellectual imagination, and believes that imagination is 'essential to the poetic', but not 'exactitude of observation to imagination'.[4] W. H. Davies on the other hand was a romantic with flashes of realism who made a profession of looking at things:

> *What is this life, if full of care,*
> *We have no time to stand and stare.*[5]

He comes nearest among moderns to seeing things as a child might see them, but his inquisitive range was limited, and latterly he

[1] Mrs. E. W. Symons, *The Bromsgrovian* (1936). [2] Percy Withers, *New Statesman*, 9th May, 1936. [3] Hearing and literature are expounded in the next chapter. [4] Walter de la Mare, *Pleasures and Speculations* (1940), 218. [5] W. H. Davies, 'Leisure,' *Songs of Joy and Others* (1911), 15.

was content to make poems out of remembered and already exploited observations. Ralph Hodgson is a better observer than either of them. His verses often suggest the enthusiasm of the field-naturalist, and the experienced eye of the bird-watcher has clearly supplied him with material for poetic imagery. Siegfried Sassoon is conscious of this introspective habit, and in his lecture *On Poetry* (1939) he reveals the interplay of outward and inward looking in his own method and the predominance of insight. 'I have taught myself to write', he says, 'not so much by the study of verse technology as by trusting my own ear . . . the faculty of inward vision. . . . Thinking in pictures is my natural method of self-expression. I have always been a submissively visual writer.' But Rupert Brooke alone among his contemporaries possessed that unconditional delight in sensuous impressions which we associate on a grander scale with Shakespeare and Keats. He tasted life with all his senses alert, and when it came to looking at things he was not afraid of reality in its uglier forms. 'If, unlike Methuselah, he did not live long enough to see life whole, he at least confronted it with a remarkably steady and disconcerting stare.'[1]

More recent poets have so far broken with the English tradition as to give wild nature the coldshoulder, and to apply the poetic sense to the changing habits of a mechanistic era. The modern poet is on strike against the immediate past and an embittered critic of the present. He is more of an anthropologist than an archæologist. The only past which interests him is the remote past; not what is merely old, but what is archaic, primitive, barbaric. He sees clearly and disapproves passionately and is as obsessed with ideologies and technics as his forbears of the seventeenth century were obsessed with metaphysics and politics. Neither would feel out of place in the other's era, and each, although addicted to fantastic analogy and experiments in form would agree with Hulme's axiom that 'accurate description is a legitimate object of verse',[2] but they might use 'statement' for 'description'.

<h2 style="text-align:center">xii</h2>

Modern poets are all lively and often aggressive controversialists, and they have produced a considerable literature expounding their

[1] Walter de la Mare, *Rupert Brooke and the Intellectual Imagination* (1919), 18. [2] *Speculations* (1936), 127.

aims and technique. Edith Sitwell has stated clearly and frankly the attitude towards sensuous impressions. She attributes one of the difficulties in the appreciation of modernist poetry to the necessity of exercising 'a new and heightened consciousness of life' which it has brought into being. This new consciousness is based upon a 'fresh perception of natural objects', and she claims that contemporary poets are doing for the common life of to-day what Words-worth did for his day. This new range of observation (for natural objects with modernist poets included organisations and machines, and the mass movements of an increasingly technical civilisation), comes 'as a shock' to people who are inured to second-hand impressions, and whose senses are blunted through lack of use. 'The result of this is that there is no connection between their senses and their brain. The modern poet's brain is becoming a central sense, interpreting and controlling the other five senses; for he has learned the truth uttered by Blake, that "Man has no body distinct from his soul, for that called body is a portion of soul discerned by the five senses, the chief inlet of soul in this age". His senses have become broadened and cosmopolitanised; they are no longer little islands, speaking their own narrow language, living their sleepy life alone. When the speech of one sense is insufficient to convey his entire meaning, he uses the language of another. He knows, too, that every sight, touch, sound, smell of the world we live in has its meaning; and it is the poet's duty to interpret those meanings.'[1]

xiii

Visual observation, as I understand it, is a peculiarly human faculty and closely allied with those contemplative characteristics which distinguish human beings from the other animals.[2] We are the self-regarding species and what begins as observation and ends as art is a means of giving permanence to self-expression, for, in the words of the proverb 'the eye is not satisfied with seeing or the ear with hearing'. Looking and seeing are necessary to thinking and imagining. To observe first, then to describe what is observed in the light of what is felt or remembered. According to Leonardo da

[1] *Poetry and Criticism* (1925), 17–18. [2] This theory has been investigated by Prof. Wood Jones who speaks of the 'association areas between the auditory and the visual, and between the visual and sensory fields which, enlarging in the arboreal Primates, become the distinctive features of the human brain.' *Arboreal Man* (1918), 174–9.

Vinci the eye is the 'lord of the senses'. This over-lordship has the power of turning sight into an accessory of the art of life as well as of the arts. The arts may help us to enjoy living by teaching us how to look at life. There can be little doubt that Dr. Johnson had some such idea in mind when he pointed out that all original and native excellence 'proceeds from vigilance of observation'.[1] The ethical value of vigilant observation, often emphasised during the nineteenth century, had no greater advocate than Ruskin. His genius was augmented by an infinite capacity for seeing things intensely and exactly. He stared at pictures and buildings, at flowers and minerals, until he saw more in them than anyone had seen before. His theories were elaborations of what he had observed, not of what he had read, and he was convinced that his mission in life was to teach people to see.

xiv

Observation need not be confined, however, to material things. There is an observation of the less substantial life, both internal and external. We can and do observe the behaviour of our own emotions as well as those of others. Unless novelists did so they would not be novelists. Edward Hallett Carr points out that Dostoievski 'works not by observation, but by imagination and introspection'. No characters in fiction are 'so difficult to visualise, to imagine as being of flesh and blood' as Dostoievski's. 'The concern of their creator is not with their bodies but with their souls and with the relations between mankind and the dark unknown reality beyond.'[2] This is the opposite to Tolstoy, who 'is first and foremost an artist of the visible world'.

The processes of observation are affected by purpose as well as by culture. In the first place, you see what you are looking for, that is, what profoundly interests you. The entomologist and the ornithologist, for instance, see more insects or birds in a wood than the unspecialised observer, just as the skilled proof-reader will spot typographical faults quicker and oftener than the ordinary reader, who tends to read with the inward rather than the outward eye. In the second place, the general background of culture and experience forces us to see things differently from those which stand outside our usual experience.[3]

There are as many differences between readers as between writers,

[1] Qt. Logan Pearsall Smith, *On Reading Shakespeare* (1933), 119. [2] *Dostoievski* (1931), 297. [3] See Notes.

and those differences are due as much to professional experience or
class distinction as to culture and sensibility. The man of science or
the lawyer, the philosopher or the poet may each observe identical
phenomena, but rarely if ever in the same way. It is impossible for
anyone wholly to dodge the impact of the external world upon his
own mental bias. Every record or interpretation of things or events
is determined by the conditional sensitiveness of the perceiver. A
description of a scene or an incident is inevitably coloured by the
physical and emotional condition of the writer. It will be good or
bad according to whether he was in good or bad health at the time,
or whether he was happy or sad. And these temporary and accidental
conditions add further to the subtle differences imposed by training,
habits, or associations. But the variations of perception do not end
there: they continue until the original impression is turned into
prose or poetry, drama or fiction, when, in the pages of books, they
begin a new life and thus reincarnated enable future generations to
experience the sensations produced by the original impact between
the writer and reality with variations according to the temperament,
condition and individuality of the reader.

Some novelists make a point of emphasising the inner dreaming of
the soul or imagination, and there is a vast and mysterious dream-
land which is yet to be explored and mapped. Forrest Reid makes a
distinction between invented and observed fiction. 'One knows . . .
when one invents a story or a character, and one knows when these
are the products of direct observation.' But neither of these methods
is to be mistaken for that use of dreams which he has made his own.
'Where', he asks, 'did my Moon-worshipper come from? He was not
consciously invented, certainly not observed. He was created by a
collaborator working beneath consciousness.'[1] Such experiences do
not supplant observation and they would, in fact, be less effective if
the writer were not an observer during his normal hours. Dreams
are made up of the materials observed and memorised during keen
wakefulness, the difference is that the materials are more vividly or
more fantastically arranged. A dream is unconscious fiction. In the
last chapter of *Private Road* Forrest Reid tells how his novel, *The
Retreat*, was inspired by a dream which had not sufficient impetus
until he visited one of those familiar London churchyards which
have been turned into miniature parks. Here, as in others, some of
the ancient and broken tombstones remained. They were ranged

---

[1] *Private Road* (1940), 85–6.

along one side and on the top of each was a cat. It was twilight, and this picture in the fading autumn light 'seemed drenched in sorcery', which created 'an immediate response' to his imagination, so that he was able to go on with the novel which had hitherto hung fire. Here observation was the catalytic to the material of his dreams.[1]

xv

Observation is as necessary to the reader as it is to the writer; for a book has depths as well as facets: inner and outer meanings. The more profound the writer the closer the observation required of the reader. The reason is put well by Coleridge in a note on Milton: 'The reader of Milton must always be on his duty: he is surrounded with sense; it rises in every line; every word is to the purpose. There are no lazy intervals; all has been considered and demands and merits observation.'[2]

The boundaries of books are broadened and deepened when those who write and those who read bring to the service of their writing or their reading more than one sense, or in other words, stimulate the mind or excite the imagination by a variety of sensations instead of one. Most people, for instance, bring the sense of sight into play upon what they read or write, fewer observe the sounds of words or the music of their arrangement except in the more obvious of verse-tunes. Still fewer are capable of responding to any but the coarser smells[3]—whether pleasant or unpleasant, and fewer still are sensitive to the subtleties of taste or touch.[4]

Unless your perceptions are sharpened by the constant exercise of the power of observation you see nothing. 'It is our noticing them that puts things in a room', says Marcel Proust, 'our growing used to them takes them away again.'[5] It is also our noticing the shapes and patterns as well as sounds and rhythms of sentences that puts us in touch with a writer and his intention.[6] The observation of design

[1] 'Imagination is *based* upon experience: experience is its taking-off ground: and the more solid this basis—the stronger and deeper the poet's understanding of reality—the further the leap.' L. A. G. Strong, *Common Sense about Poetry* (1932). 74. [2] *Coleridge*, Potter (1933), 414. [3] See Notes. [4] See Notes [5] *Within a Budding Grove*, trans. Moncrieff (1929) ii, 342. [6] 'Every good prose will reveal at a heedful reading a marked tendency in its sentence and paragraph construction towards a loosely measurable sequence of a variable pattern, occupying so much time, and therefore its equivalent of sensuous and mental activity—as in a grave and ceremonious minuet.' Walter de la Mare, *Pleasures and Speculations* (1940), 102–3.

in literature is as necessary to good reading as the capacity to share in the spirit of the author. The two must go together for the one is the complement of the other. The reader may follow the writer's process with a running commentary based on his own observations, but he will soon find that a writer recalls impressions which have been seen but not observed by the reader, or which have been observed and forgotten. Anything in a book that has been well and freshly observed has its own special value if it does no more than help the reader to recall and perpetuate useful or happy memories which might otherwise sink into sub-conscious limbo without hope of resurrection.

CHAPTER VI

LISTENING TO LITERATURE

'All who have consciously practised the art of writing know what endless and painful vigilance is needed for the avoidance of the unfit or untuneful phrase, how the meaning must be tossed from expression to expression, mutilated and deceived, ere it can find rest in words.'—SIR WALTER RALEIGH, *Style* (1898), 16.

---

i

You read with your ears as well as your eyes. Reading resembles conversation, not only as a direct means of communicating ideas or images, but as an oblique means of approach for more subtle intimations. Vowels and consonants; words, phrases and sentences, apart from the more obvious rhymes and rhythms of verse, have sound-values as well as sense-values which augment meaning and illuminate understanding. Looking and listening are thus related and interdependent.

You listen for cadence which is the gesture of the written word as you look for gesture which plays a large part in the style of talking. Two people may converse and although they do not supply each other with tangible information or definite opinions they create in each other a state of consciousness not attainable by other means. They create feelings of well-being, as well as anger or gloom, by an interchange of words which depend upon sound rather than sense. When such exchanges of sounds are the results of excitement or passion they are presumed to be natural, but in other directions we

110

pretend to be contemptuous of the ordinary small-talk in which we are all ready to indulge. It is only 'idle chatter' and when indulged in by others we adopt a superior attitude and wonder what the chatterers have to say to each other, much as we wonder at that kind of after-dinner speaker who contrives to expend the maximum of words on the minimum of meaning without trying the patience of the majority of his hearers. But idle chatter cannot be as idle as it is supposed to be, otherwise it would not be so widely popular. The belittlement it so often receives is due, probably, to the false assumption that speech is solely a means of communicating information or reporting concepts or ideas when, as a matter of fact, it is equally engaged in communalising feelings or emotions which refuse to be fitted with words. At times the idlest chatter might serve as an expression of unpremeditated art aspiring to the condition of music which Pater believed to be the destiny of all artistic endeavour. When it has a more definite purpose it is like the twittering of birds seeking points of contact or recognition and advising the participants that they belong to the same class, or warning them if they don't.[1]

ii

Long before the invention of psycho-analysis, Oliver Wendell Holmes observed that six persons took part in all conversations between a man and a woman:—He as he thinks he is; and, as he thinks she thinks he is; and, as he is. And, she as she thinks she is; and, as she thinks he thinks she is; and, as she is. The complexity is here increased by the clash of sex, but there is a similar complexity in all conversation. Much the same sort of reflex action takes place in the traffic between author and reader, and just as communications between persons are maintained by sound as well as sense, so the unheard melodies of the human voice evoke responses through the printed word.[2]

There are reasons why this should be so for if literature 'has

[1] 'As a rule the exchange seems to consist of ideas which are necessarily common to the two speakers and are known to be so by each. The process, however, is none the less satisfactory for this; indeed, it seems even to derive its satisfactoriness therefrom. The interchange of the conventional lead and return is obviously very far from being tedious or meaningless to the interlocutors. They can, however, have derived nothing from it but the confirmation to one another of their sympathy and of the class or classes to which they belong.' Wilfred Potter, *Instincts of the Herd in Peace and War* (1916), 109–110. [2] See Notes.

favoured rather the way of the ear and has given itself zealously to the tuneful ordering of sounds', it is because sense was conveyed by sound before words were invented, and this most primitive form of literature still survives in life as well as in letters.[1] It survives even more persistently in those phases of life which may or may not be dependent upon letters as well as in those phases which are: 'What is sung or articulated in the most solemn or the most critical moments of life: what we hear in a liturgy; what is murmured or groaned in the extremity of passion; what calms a child or the afflicted; what attests the truth of an oath—these are words of a particular tone and expression which cannot be resolved into clear ideas ... such words incite us to *become*, rather than excite us to *understand*.'[2] And we all know that attempts to translate such sounds into sense end in silliness.

iii

At all times there has existed a literature of nonsense (as distinct from silliness) and it is not confined to books for the young. Probably nonsense verse is more widely appreciated by adults than by children, because it is an attempt to recapture something of the inconsequence of youth. Much of it dispenses entirely with 'dictionary words'. The popular songs of generation after generation of adults have often depended for their final effect on words which are not words, and nonsense choruses of the kind possess character and meaning which normally-worded verses lack. The Elizabethans knew the value of such jingles as 'Hey, nonny, nonny', and anyone who has taken part in choruses with a 'Fa-la-la' or a 'Bumpsey-bumpsey-bay-ri-tooral-looral-laddy', must have enjoyed the ebullition of feeling which they evoked. Nor are these choruses otherwise useless. There was a challenge in 'Lilli bullero bullen a la!' now welded into the history of freedom, and a practical purpose in the lullabies which soothed our infancy.

Nonsense is not an outmoded method of expression. It is probably the earliest specimen of applied song, and is thus as old as mankind, but it has maintained its morning freshness in spite of repetition, and without special advocacy. No era is exempt from nonsense songs and stories. The most matter-of-fact of centuries produced Edward Lear and Lewis Carroll, and every new crop of music hall ditties has its nonsense offshoots, which appeal to all tastes and classes most

[1] Sir Walter Raleigh, *Style* (1898), 9. [2] Paul Valèry, Qt. Herbert Read in *The Defence of Shelley and Other Essays* (1936), 157–8.

112

of us having either joined in such choruses as 'Ta-ra-ra-boom-de-aye!' and 'Yip-i-addi-i-ay!' or if we have had no opportunity of singing in chorus we have hummed the tunes to ourselves with secret delight. Such rhythms are the lullabies of grown-up children, inducing not sleep but oblivion.

iv

What we call nonsense is probably primitive expression, language feeling its way. Modern writers like James Joyce and Gertrude Stein use a new language to express a new understanding of life, and perhaps a new phase of consciousness. In *Finnigan's Wake* Joyce 'has tried to make his hero express directly in words, again, states of mind which do not usually in reality make use of words at all—for the subconscious has no language—the dreaming mind does not usually speak—and when it does, it is more likely to express itself in the looking-glass language of "Jabberwocky', than in anything resembling ordinary speech'.[1]

It is curious, and doubtless significant, that this kind of rhythmical utterance has hitherto reached its most complete, but not its most profound, expression in primitive verse-form, and that in nearly every instance these verse-forms are functional, or applied to some definite purpose, generally associated with the relief of emotional reserve or stress. Nonsense-choruses either lull or soothe or cheer. The very word 'lullaby' is a lullaby, and cradle-choruses are often no more (and could be no better) than a reproduction of its soothing sounds or sounds which resemble them as:

> *Ba-loo, my lammie,*
> *My lammie, ba-loo.*

Convivial choruses soothe and cheer in much the same way. Such jingles as:

> *Fal-lal-la-fal-lal-lay,*

when sung in chorus are solvents and produce the same effect as the lullaby. They lull anxieties like wine or an opiate.

v

Action-choruses again play upon the same chords. They are lullabies in reverse. Soldiers on the march keep up their spirits as well as their speed by thus harmonising their emotions, which is a

[1] Edmund Wilson, *Axel's Castle* (1932), 227.

process of sublimating their actions. Rhythm is a solvent whether it flatters or taunts. 'Lillibulero' is said to have been more powerful than the eloquence of a commander with the tongue of a Demosthenes or a Cicero, when it was used as a taunt during the religious wars in Ireland at the close of the seventeenth century. The *esprit de corps* of the hunt is equally stimulated by primitive sounds, like 'yoicks!' and 'halloo!' which have often been recorded in traditional songs:

> *Hey Frola, trola!*
> *There boys, there!*
> *Hoicka, hoick, whoop!*
> *Cry there they go.*
> *They are at fault.*
> *Boy, wind the horn!*
> *Sing tive, tive tive now in full cry!*
> *With yeeble, yabble, gibble, gabble, hey!*

It is likely that all spoken language tends to revert to the primitive by approximating either to music or to nonsense, much as the street calls of itinerant merchants like milkmen, coalies, and newsvendors have long since become inchoate but communicative noises. Edward Lear is a good example of the reversion of a writer to a primitive mental state. He stretched the bounds of nonsense into a new kind of sense, relying instinctively upon primitive noises when creating the soothing atmosphere generated by his verses. In a famous chorus his pelicans behave as human beings do when they fortify themselves with song:

> *Ploffskin, Pluffskin, Pelican jee!*
> *We think no bird so happy as we!*
> *Plumpkin, Ploshkin, Pelican jill!*
> *We think so then, and we thought so still!*[1]

vi

If it be true, therefore, that the reading or repetition of nonsense-words and jingles produces emotional, imaginative, or even intel-

---

[1] In a recent lecture T. S. Eliot expressed the opinion that the nonsense of Edward Lear was 'not vacuity of sense' but rather a 'parody of sense'. 'The Jumblies' thus becomes an expression of 'nostalgia for the romance of foreign voyage and exploration' and 'The Yongy-Bongy Bo' and 'The Dong with the Luminous Nose' are poems of unrequited passion—'blues' in fact. *The Music of Poetry* (1942), 14.

lectual repercussions, how much more certain is it that the reading of normal poetry and prose will evoke similar but more complex changes. Professor Whitehead maintains that 'the whole basis of the art of literature' is 'that the emotions and feelings directly excited by the words should fitly intensify our emotions and feelings arising from contemplation of the meaning'.[1] But meaning in its intellectual form is often of secondary importance in communication by sound-symbols. Literature not only affects the mind of the reader by what it says or by how it says it, it affects the mind of the reader by the sound of the words, their rhythms and rhymes. I am not here referring to the familiar trick of onomatopœia by which words are forced to reproduce significant sounds, as in the lines from *Paradise Lost* (ii, 879–83) admired for that quality by Tennyson:

> *On a sudden open fly*
> *With impetuous recoil and jarring sound*
> *The infernal doors, and on their hinges grate*
> *Harsh thunder, that the lowest bottom shook*
> *Of Erebus,*

or in the more obvious and more familiar example of the concluding couplet of Tennyson's own lyric 'Come down, O maid, from yonder mountain height':

> *The moan of doves in immemorial elms,*
> *And murmuring of innumerable bees.*

There are other and more subtle sounds which suggest rather than represent, which express meanings and feelings beyond what can be sensed or verbally expounded. These harmonies are a bridge between words and music, and their relationship to ordinary lilt and rhyme is about as close as that between, say, a gavotte by Gluck and a fugue by Bach. Such harmonies evoke memorable feeling without desire for further recognition still less for actual meaning. Milton abounds in them, and many of his more familiar passages have achieved familiarity by that quality alone:

> *Thick as autumnal leaves that strow the brooks*
> *In Vallombrosa, where th' Etrurian shades*
> *High over-arch'd embower.*[2]

The rhythm in those well-known lines is more important than the sense. It is not the picture, sharp as it is, which etches itself upon the

[1] *Symbolism: Its Meaning and Effect* (1928), 98. [2] *Paradise Lost*, i, 292–4.

memory, but the tonal value of the words, which convey something deeper or more remote than their exact meaning.[1] Every poet bemuses himself and his readers by rhythms which tell more than the words:

> *Not poppy, nor mandragora,*
> *Nor all the drowsy syrups of the world,*
> *Shall ever medicine thee to that sweet sleep*
> *Which thou owedst yesterday.*[2]

That climacteric aside of Iago, a crude and melodramatic incident in itself, is tuned by the fugue-like arrangement of vowels and consonants into high tragedy.

vii

Poets at all times have been sensitive to the sub-harmonics of language. They have listened for the sound of the human voice in their own written words as though they longed to recapture some of the spoken music which was associated with poetry before the days of printing. W. B. Yeats went further when he advocated the restoration of spoken verse and worked out a system of chanting a sort of plain-song to an accompaniment on the psaltery. Yeats looked upon plainsung verse as the natural method of rendering poetry. 'If I were a wise man', he said, 'and could persuade a few people to learn the art I would never open a book of verse again'.[3] But few of those who are sensitive to hidden music in literature would go so far, they are content with an inward appreciation, heightened by a closer attention to the nuance of sound which is an important ingredient of prose as well as verse.

viii

Gerard Manley Hopkins was so fond of tonal effects that he often resembled a musician using words instead of sounds. He was a

---

[1] The sound of a line from Virgil 'Claudite iam rivos, pueri; sat prata biberunt', can hurry us 'away from mere human accident to some deeper realms of experience'. It is 'an innocent line enough yet how much meaning lurks in the rhythm. An ineffable sadness pervades it, as if to suggest that though the fields are at rest, having drunk their fill, men cannot be so easily satisfied.' And in this writer's opinion it is 'a perfect case of rhythm suggesting something quite beyond or alien to what the words state'. E. M. W. Tillyard, *Poetry: Direct and Oblique* (1934), 155–6.
[2] *Othello*, iii, 3. [3] 'Speaking to the Psaltery' (1902), *Essays* (1924), 15.

student and composer of music so came to the subject of word-music with technical experience. 'My verse', he told Robert Bridges, 'is less to be read than heard . . . it is oratorical, that is the rhythm is so.'[1] He was more than usually sensitive to musical parallaxis in Greek drama and in passages of the tragic dramatists he found ('usually' though not 'always') two counterpointed strains. He called one the 'overthought' which is 'conveyed chiefly in the choice of metaphors etc. used and often only half realised by the poet himself, not necessarily having any connection with the subject in hand but usually having a connection and suggested by some circumstance of the scene or story'. The opposite, or 'underthought', is 'an echo or shadow of the overthought, something like canons and repetitions in music, treated in a different manner, but that sometimes it may be independent of it'.[2] Counterpointed strains are so widely distributed throughout literature that a book may be compared with a musical score and its comprehension may require a similar kind of attention if it is to be fully experienced, and even then, as in reading a musical score, the experience is not likely to be more than an approximation to that of the author.[3] This applies even more to prose for the musical notations of poetry are expected and, in their more superficial aspects, they are obvious to all.

The rhythms of both prose and poetry approximate also to the cadences of the normal human voice. Robert Bridges believed that 'all verse derives its beauty mainly from its speech rhythms',[4] and Edward FitzGerald thought that the sound of the writer's voice was the 'sign of a good book'.[5] Some stylists have deliberately introduced the tonal quality of talk into their arrangement of words and sentences. The oral characteristics of literature make it necessary for readers as well as writers to have a good ear in addition to a

---

[1] *Letters of Gerard Manley Hopkins to Robert Bridges* (1935), i, 46. [2] See Notes by Robert Bridges to Hopkins' *Poems* (1930). [3] 'There are possibilities for verse which bear some analogy to the development of a theme by different groups of instruments; there are possibilities of transitions in a poem comparable to the different movements of a symphony or a quartet; there are possibilities of contrapuntal arrangements of subject-matter. It is in the concert room, rather than the opera house, that the germ of a poem may be quickened. T. S. Eliot *The Music of Poetry* (1942), 28. [4] Qt. Walter de la Mare, *Pleasures and Speculations* (1940), 114. [5] 'A night or two ago I was reading old Thackeray's Roundabouts; and (sign of a good book) heard him talking to me.' Edward FitzGerald to W. F. Pollock, 1871, *Letters*, ed. William Aldis Wright (1889), 332. 'I have been, and am, reading Borrow's *Wild Wales* which *I* like well, because I can hear him talking it.' Edward FitzGerald to George Crabbe, 10th December, 1862. *Ib.*, 289.

good eye, and it is probable that writers are more sensitive to hearing than to seeing, even if the results are not so obvious. The sensitiveness of the ear may limit its creativeness. Writers are often so irritated by sounds that in trying to avoid them they reduce the power of oral perception, sounds being registered as annoyances rather than phenomena. This is not true of all writers although the protests of some of the more famous of them are so loud as to give them an exaggerated importance, and the advocacy of those who seem to like noises is so defiant as to suggest protests in reverse, attempts to create an impression of stoical calm or masculine toughness.

ix

Many distinguished men of letters, Carlyle in England, Flaubert in France, and Schopenhauer in Germany, were noisy objectors to noises. Carlyle particularly disliked the crowing of cocks and the barking of dogs, common sounds in Chelsea in his day, and amusing stories are told of the philosopher's attempts to quell these noises by various protests and gesticulations, and throughout his work there are passionate advocacies of silence and quietness indicating a sensitiveness to external sounds which was probably pathological.

Flaubert sought seclusion from all normal activities, and he was an early opponent of mechanical noises. One of them was the grating of the chains of the tugboats as they went up and down the Seine before the windows of his Normandy retreat at Croisset. He complained bitterly of these disturbers of the rural peace in letters to his gregarious and hearty friend, George Sand, who revelled in noises of all kinds. Her bantering reply throws a light upon her own attitude as well as on that of her more neurotic correspondent. 'I love everything that makes up a *milieu*,' she wrote, 'the rolling of carriages and the noises of workmen in Paris, the cries of a thousand birds in the country, movement of ships on the water; I love also absolute and profound silence, and in short, I love everything that is around me, no matter where I am.' But even she found it necessary to apologise for this attitude by calling it a new variety of *'auditory idiocy'*.[1]

Schopenhauer objected to a variety of noises: hammering, door-slamming, the crying of children, and most of all to the cracking of

[1] *21st June, 1868. The George Sand-Gustave Flaubert Letters.* Trans. Aimee L. McKenzie (1922), 94. 'C'est de l'idiotisme auditif, varieté nouvelle.' *Correspondence entre George Sand et Gustave Flaubert,* 120.

whips. 'Your only genuine assassin of thought is the crack of a whip.' But being a philosopher he was not content to protest. He substantiated his sensitiveness by arguing that dislike of noise was the prerogative of intellectual people because it interfered with the rhythm of thought and imagination: 'Noise is the most impertinent of all forms of interruption. It is not only interruption, but also disruption of thought. Of course, where there is nothing to interrupt, noise will not be so particularly objectionable.'[1]

X

Listening with most writers is necessary to the technique of experience and expression. They would probably sympathise with George Sand and look upon sounds of all kinds as among the materials of their art. Responses vary and if the more blatant annoy and the gentler and sweeter soothe and inspire, every noise has its laureate. With Wordsworth it is a means of that communion with nature which is the underlying principle of all his poetry:

> *and she shall lean her ear*
> *In many a secret place*
> *Where rivulets dance their wayward round,*
> *And beauty born of murmuring sound*
> *Shall pass into her face.*

Keats refined even upon this attitude by invoking the music of silence:

> *Heard melodies are sweet but those unheard*
> *Are sweeter . . .*

and although he is inspired by the song of the nightingale, he can listen enraptured for

> *A little noiseless noise among the leaves,*
> *Born of the very sigh that silence heaves.*

And at the other end of the poetic scale, we have Rudyard Kipling enjoying the mechanical sounds which distracted Flaubert:

> *See the shaking funnels roar, with the Peter at the fore,*
> *And the fenders grind and heave,*
> *And the derricks clack and grate, as the tackle hooks the crate*
> *And the fall-rope whines through the sheave.*

[1] 'On Noise,' *Studies in Pessimism*. Trans. T. Bailey Saunders (1891), 128–9.

Thoreau, who was for a time a professional recluse and always something of a curmudgeon, never wearied of bragging about his enjoyment of unpopular noises such as the crowing of cocks (he kept a cock 'for the sake of its music' at Walden Pond), the sighing of the wind through telegraph wires, the 'booming' of ice, and the barking of dogs. 'I drink in a wonderful health, a cordial, in sound,' he says. 'The effect of the slightest tinkling in the horizon measures my own soundness. I thank God for sound. It always mounts and makes me mount. I think I will not trouble myself for any wealth when I can be so cheaply enriched. Here I contemplate to drudge that I may own a farm, and may have such a limitless estate for the listening.'[1] He frequently refers to the music of the 'telegraph harp' as he calls the telegraph wires which run alongside the railway. It makes him long to read the Greek poets, and recalls 'brighter colour, red, or blue, or green, where all was dull white or black'. It is the 'poetry of the railroad' prophesying 'finer senses, a finer life, a golden age'. Or maybe it is 'the Gods expressing their delight at this invention'.[2] Many a time has he 'lain awake at night to think of the barking of a dog' and he compares the experience to that of 'a frequenter of the opera' lying awake to remember the music he has heard.[3]

xi

The music of words has been expounded by many writers, and few readers or writers with any claim to fitness for their art will disagree with Walter de la Mare when he says that a good writer in addition to writing 'efficiently and effectively' must pay 'attention to the arrangement of verbal sounds'. This characteristic of good writing is the result of 'a natural taste and impulse', bringing into play 'two sensuous activities, speech and hearing'. He points out that in English there is an 'inexhaustible variety' of verbal sounds 'since each such sound either in prose or verse has not only its relative accent, stress or emphasis, or lack of them, but also its quality, volume, and pitch—its intonation—and is affected by those of its more or less immediate neighbours'.[4]

To what extent sound and meaning or sound and aesthetic intention are related cannot be estimated since capacity to adjust sound to meaning either in the making or in the appreciation of literature

---

[1] *Journal: Spring* (1885), 48.   [2] *Ib.*, 94.   [3] *Journal: Winter* (1884), 41.
[4] *Pleasures and Speculations*, Walter de la Mare (1940), 87–8.

depends upon sensibilities which vary from writer to writer and reader to reader. Sound in words, like music, is liable to fitful and casual interpretation, even when the intention of the author is deliberate and precise. It is doubtful whether even the fit reader will always grasp Edith Sitwell's aim when she combines 'high screaming e's', with 'dulled o's' to make the lines of a verse 'toss up and down violently', and 'an arrangement of soft s's, and their slightly firmer counterpart the ch's' to give a feeling of rotting flesh.[1] But sensitiveness to verbal sounds is often unconscious or semi-conscious: we feel almost without hearing the melody as the diapason is felt and blended with the wider and more detailed enjoyment of a symphony. Attentive listening is essential to creative reading and the finer degrees and subtleties of words are heard only when the sensibilities are refined by much practice. This faculty is so essential that Walter de la Mare places the reader on a level with the writer when he says that making these sounds may certainly be no *less* an aesthetic pleasure than listening to them. 'Indeed', he continues, 'whether pleasant or otherwise, their effects at least as closely concern the vocal organs as they do the ear. Both sensuous and mental, pleasurable or otherwise, they cannot be avoided. Leagues away from poetry, the most artless speech exhibits them. And although in childhood we had to learn our mother tongue . . . any delight we may find in verbal melody, no less than a delight in colour or form, or for that matter in the savoury or the sweet, or even in kisses or crumpets, was ours from birth.'[2]

---

[1] Edith Sitwell, 'Some Notes on my Own Poetry,' *Selected Poems* (1936), 49. [2] *Pleasures and Speculations*, Walter de la Mare (1940), 87–8.

CHAPTER VII

GETTING BEHIND THE WORDS

'Among those who have endeavoured to promote learning, and rectify judgment, it has been long customary to complain of the abuse of words which are often admitted to signify things so different, that, instead of assisting the understanding as vehicles of knowledge, they produce error, dissension, and perplexity, because what is affirmed in one sense, is received in another.'—DR. JOHNSON, *The Rambler* (1752), 202.

'There are those who seem to understand everything till one puts it into words.'—F. H. BRADLEY, *Aphorisms* (1930), 30.

'It is not pathetic messages that make us shed our best tears, but the miracle of a word in the right place.'—JEAN COCTEAU, *A Call to Order*. Trans. Rollo H. Myers (1936), 153.

---

i

When the fit reader has battered his way through the barricades of style, convention, fashion, eccentricity, reticence, subterfuge and exhibitionism, he has still to fight his last and perhaps his greatest battle with words. Every word may be a barrier or a pitfall because each has a life of its own which in turn, like a book, has been coloured and conditioned by its own experiences and the experiences of others. This mutability alone makes sensitiveness to word-values as necessary to the reader as it is to the writer, and reading a perpetual adventure.

Words are commonly looked upon as the raw material of literature, but they are far more than that: they are keys with which we unlock doors of imagination and knowledge, and if writers use the wrong, or the misshapen word, or readers misinterpret the right word, the keys will not function and may even break the lock! Bad writing is marked not only by a loose or shallow handling of words, but by the use of faded words, woolly abstract nouns and work-shy verbs, or words which have a literary instead of a functional recognition. Slang is more reliable than genteel jargon, but much depends upon the user, words, like colours, being affected by the company they keep. The desire to be correct, polite, respectable is more likely to achieve vulgarity than the acceptance of what is strong, coarse and of common usage. But if the vulgarisation of words means the devaluation or watering of language, their technical appreciation can be so over-emphasised as to destroy vitality as well as charm. The corrective is to add affection to observation, for words, like people or animals, respond to personal devotion, they reward care and friendship with richer meanings and so move us with deeper pleasure and finer attachments.

At the same time, words remain and will always remain adventurous symbols of expression, because they are the most intractable of the raw materials of an art, and with the exception of those which are purely functional words such as prepositions, conjunctions, and the definite and indefinite articles, they rarely, if ever, retain their objectivity for long. They have wills of their own and a habit of breaking away from their families and striking out for themselves. They are as moody as prima donnas and as plastic as putty, and cannot be relied upon to mean the same thing at different times or to different people at the same time, and they vary not only in meaning but in construction and pronunciation. They 'move and change, they wax and wane, they wither and burgeon; from age to age, from place to place, from mouth to mouth, they are never at a stay. They take on colour, intensity, and vivacity from infection of neighbourhood; the same word is of several shapes and diverse imports in one and the same sentence; they depend on the building they compose for the very chemistry of the stuff that composes them.'[1] This innate mutability exposes them to the vagaries of fashion and plays up to the fickle whims of a restless age so that familiar vocabularies can scarcely be relied upon to stay put from one season to another.

This is a general condition expressing the mass mind, but meaning

[1] Sir Walter Raleigh, *Style* (1896), 25–6.

125

is also adjusted to meet the needs of particular and often purely personal experiences. Individuals, sometimes shyly, sometimes blatantly, use words to exercise passing whims and idiosyncrasies, and not content with the normal possibilities of confusion there are others who take an impish delight in giving strange meanings to old words, or even to dropping new words into the sanctuaries of old ideas with cat-in-dovecot consequences. On the other hand, and at all times, there have been professional and technical writers for whom precision in expression is essential. They have to walk delicately through what J. M. Robertson called 'the scoriae of unsmelted speech',[1] or resort, as in the past, to the more static etymology of a dead language, or, in the present, to the comparative safety of a jargon familiar only to members of a particular craft or profession.

ii

Words also have esoteric as well as exoteric meanings. Remy de Gourmont reminds us that 'Words, which are signs, are almost always ciphers as well. The unconscious conventional language is very much in use, and there are even matters where it is the only one employed. But cipher implies deciphering. It is not easy to understand even the sincerest writing, and the author himself often goes astray because the meaning of words varies not only from one man to another, but from moment to moment, in the case of the same man. Language is thus a great cause of deception.'[2] Even simple people who might seem to be inoculated by press and cinema against individual observation and deduction can put their own private construction upon words. The virus of propaganda has not yet succeeded in immunising the herd against an outbreak of personal understanding. No amount of education has entirely succeeded in doping the popular mind into complete uniformity, for however uniform the doped minds of the masses may appear to be, somewhere lurks the undefeated and non-gregarious ego waiting a chance of 'breaking through' and asserting itself. Often the last kick of indomitable individuality is against the accepted meaning of words, it is none the less a kick even if it misses its mark like the legendary old lady who had always been under the impression that Cherubim and Seraphim were 'man and wife like Sodom and Gomorrah'.

[1] 'Concerning Preciosity,' *The Yellow Book*, April 1897.　[2] *Decadence and Other Essays*, trans. W. A. Bradley (1922), 26–27.

iii

It is a curious thing that although the mutability of words is so widely recognised contemporary changes cause irritation and even anxiety among normal readers as much as to grammarians and pedants. It is one of the functions of scholarship to police our vocabularies, for although words, like the stars in William Watson's poem, are free because in amplitude of liberty their joy is to obey the laws, some ignore those ample laws. Only the more dogmatic of Anarchists would resent the admonitions of the ever readable Archbishop Trench, or Sir Edward Cook's urbane rebukes, or still more the wise commentaries of that witty watchman of our liberties, A. P. Herbert. But there is a vast difference between liberty and licence and although writers of this kind would not unduly seek to curb one in order to save us from the other, it is well to remind ourselves occasionally that there are legitimate variations.

Language as well as law may grow from 'precedent to precedent' but even a precedent must have had a revolutionist in its ancestry. Yet, if it is wise to scrutinise carefully all such attempts to insert the thin end of the wedge, it would be unjust and shortsighted to scrap a useful word because it has not taken the precaution of providing itself with a precedent. Verbal legitimacy in the last resort is a matter of opinion, and verbal changes are natural and justifiable when they aid meaning or convenience. It is as pedantic to reject new applications of old words as it is to suspect words which are brand-new, and it is as snobbish to refuse to admit self-made words (that is slang-words) into literature as it is to refuse to admit self-made men into society—provided that they know how to behave. The two general attitudes were illustrated by Anthony Trollope over eighty years ago, in a conversation between the sisters, Bell and Lily Dale, in *The Small House at Allington*: ' "I don't like those slang words, Lily." "What slang words?" "You know what you called Bernard's friend." "Oh; a swell. I fancy I do like slang. I think it's awfully jolly, to talk about things being jolly. Only that I was afraid of your nerves I should have called him stunning. It's so slow, you know, to use nothing but words out of a dictionary." "I don't think its nice in talking of gentlemen." '[1]

Slang is an industrious climber and never happier than when pushing its way into polite conversation. At the present time it is

[1] *The Small House at Allington* (1864), Bohn Ed. ii, 16–17.

encouraged in intellectual circles. In the search for a robust and masculine style, low-down words are given a leg-up by poets of the Left much as minor poets talked music-hall in the Nineties and pubs in the early Nineteen Hundreds. The change probably began in France during the reign of that king of word-fanciers, Edmond de Goncourt, who was never so happy as when he had 'found a word in the street that he could stick in a book'.[1] But there is good slang as well as bad slang. 'Perfect slang has a cunning brevity that braces you. It should taste sweet and keen, like a nut. If it does, it will make its way yet into that holy of holies where "literary" English lives in state.'[2] Those words from the master of a delicate prose-style are encouraging because resistance to slang is often priggish when it is not pedantic. Both forms of resistance are objectionable but if a choice had to be made the prig might be preferred to the pedant because he is moved by a sensitiveness for style, often misplaced, but there none the less. The choice of words is an operation in the making of literary style, and style is the legitimate concern of its devotees: they have the right to get excited about it, especially if they are not merely negative. Prigs are often silly, but they are not always negative. Pedants are seldom silly but nearly always negative, especially about words. But slang is no respecter of theories or opinions, and has therefore become the stamping-ground of both prigs and pedants who, however, and it is a commendable inconsistency, are ready to recognise slang-words when, in spite of obstacles, they have managed to climb into the language.

iv

Languages die hard, and never from indiscriminate breeding or from foreign invasions.[3] English is the best of all examples, for despite the fears of purists and pedants it has increased and prospered until, in one or another of its forms, it has become a universal means of communication. And it has done so by living dangerously. The English language, like the English people, is strong and practical because it is elastic in structure and adaptable in use. It is the most adventurous of all languages, coming from anywhere and going

[1] *The George Sand—Gustave Flaubert Letters*, trans. Aimee L. McKenzie (1922), 349. [2] C. E. Montague, *A Writer's Notes on his Trade* (1930), 22. [3] Classical Latin and Greek are often called 'dead languages' but it is the ancient Greeks and Romans who are dead. Their languages have gone on living.

everywhere, whilst paying so little homage to rules that it seems to risk destruction by indiscriminate breeding and uncontrolled immigration. If foreign words are needed for any of its numerous purposes it does not hesitate to commandeer them any more than to set some dusty old word to a new job of work, to press into its service the jargon of science, or to adopt a low-born waif of slang. A comparison between the population of, say, Dr. Johnson's *Dictionary* and the *Oxford Dictionary* proves that the English language is as prolific as it is promiscuous.

No wonder that purists live in a continuum of anxiety, nor, as many too hastily think, is this anxiety a modern development. If we are to believe the experts it would seem that the English language has always been falling to pieces—much as England has always been disintegrating. Swift, to go no further back, demanded an annual *Index Expurgatorius* to 'expunge all words and phrases that are offensive to good sense'. Dr. Johnson feared the invasion of *Gallicisms* and 'rarely admitted' into the close corporation of his dictionary 'words not authorised by former writers', for he believed that 'whoever knows the English tongue in its present extent will be able to express his thoughts without further help from other nations'. Lord Morley in our day believed that the language had 'never been so exposed to such dangers as those which beset it'. Nor are these hygienic warnings offered only by professed scholars. Frequent discussions in the correspondence column of *The Times* reveal a concern for the right use of words as widespread as it is various. Yet in spite of these periodical scares our language goes its madcap way, multiplying and prospering and proving its virility by the immemorial methods of exuberance and audacity.

The truth is that it is rare for anything quite new to happen to language, and few words are inappropriate or inadequate in themselves. Everything that can happen has happened in one form or another so that what looks like novelty is seldom more than acceleration of some innate but undeveloped characteristic. Students of words, indeed, most thoughtful users of words, call upon precedent to reduce novel incursions into familiar usage. But all may be debased by cheap or incompetent use. Words that are bad in themselves should be withdrawn from currency. But if that were accomplished we should still be faced with the difficulty of preventing the misuse of new words or old words with new meanings, just as we are faced with the eternal comedy (or tragedy) of the misuse of good money by foolish or incompetent spenders. But there are reliable precedents on the side of the interlopers, and languages like races survive as much by infiltration of new blood as by conservation of what is worth saving in the old. Yet the loud vulgarities of the parvenu are not a valid argument against mild and scholarly reticence, or even well-mannered opulence or luxury. There are, in fact, no golden rules for verbal righteousness, and the English language has survived not by circumspection but by kicking over the traces!

v

Unconscious interpretation governs much of our verbal understanding. Words may have a meaning which is comprehended more or less clearly, but in the very act of reading and understanding them we are re-reading them in the light of half-suspected memories. 'For a sensitive reader', says Georges Duhamel, 'each word changes its quality and its resonance and perhaps its meaning according to whether it is used by a poet or a prose-writer, a master or an apprentice, a shy man or an aggressive one, a soft-hearted man or a hard one.'[1] Observation of any kind can never be insulated from memory; even if that were possible it could never escape the comments of the unconscious, and some writers believe that words are more adequate vehicles of thought and knowledge when they are invested with a large variety of associations. The adequacy here depends upon the intended application of the thought; it is obvious that where precise expression is demanded the fewer associations the better; for that reason scientists and technicians invent new words to define new processes and incorporate them in a jargon which is the acknowledged means of communication between members of their craft, much as scholars surmounted the language bar by the use of Latin up to the middle of the eighteenth century. Even then it is not certain that a word will maintain its purity. Corruption, which in this case is the accumulation of associations, begins at birth. A word never retains its simple clarity for long because it is used by changing persons in changing circumstances. It is subject to the common flux, and if it cannot adapt itself to new conditions is soon scrapped. The dictionaries have as many words which have become obsolete by remaining pure as those which have changed their habits and saved their lives. It may be presumed that a word begins its life with only one meaning, but.

[1] *In Defence of Letters*, trans. Bozman (1938), 179.

as soon as it sets up in business on its own account it accumulates meanings to accommodate the needs and whims of a large variety of users. These natural and inevitable mutations make it certain that if you insist upon using words with only their original meaning or pronunciation no one will understand you.

In spite of their apparent inevitability variations in the use and meaning of words are often challenged by purists. Coleridge looked upon such changes as perversions of the truth, due in his day to a 'prevailing laxity in the use of terms' tending 'to the misapplication of words, and to the corruption of language'. His examples are, *indorsed*, which had been 'strained from its true signification, as given by Milton in the expression—"And elephants *indorsed* with towers" '; and *virtue*, which had been ' equally perverted: originally it signified merely strength; it then became strength of mind and valour', and it had later been changed to 'the class term for moral excellence in all its various species'. His remedy was precision of thought and expression, rather than a 'pedantic niceness in the choice of language' which would only 'render conversation stiff and stilted', as over insistence upon nothing but the 'properest word' made Dr. Johnson 'laborious where he ought to have been light, and formal where he ought to have been familiar'.[1] But Coleridge's insistence upon precision was not disinterested. He only paid lip-homage to the objectivity of words for as soon as he began to use them he packed them with meaning peculiar to himself. 'The printed word for Coleridge has a depth dimension, a root, so that his distinctions, for instance, are less than any other writer's merely verbal. He will take a word like "reason" or "idea", and create into it the meaning of an individual experience, really using the word, not letting it use him, giving the word itself life (tending to choose dead, sapless words for his purpose), so that instead of confining meaning, fixing it, he implants a seed of meaning capable of growth.'[2] The process would have had the opposite result to that supported by him in his advocacy of changeless precision. The success of his advocacy would have been a curb upon his own genius, for one of his outstanding distinctions is a use of words based upon an attitude towards life and ideas which was peculiarly his own.

Coleridge's fears are not generally upheld even by poets, who would be seriously handicapped if words lost their plasticity, and in

[1] *Lectures and Notes on Shakespeare and other English Poets*, Bohn. Ed. (1914), 44–45. [2] Stephen Potter, *Coleridge and S. T. C.* (1935), 129.

our own day Walter de la Mare has put the case for mutability with insight as well as a sense of responsibility: 'Like all such objects, words gather with age a curious flavour, look, mien, and reference. The bloom—if at times only a mildew—of sentiment creeps over them. The process is obvious. The neologism subsides into the colloquial, the colloquial may attain to the literary (the Promised Land), or to the poetic (a sort of Nirvana), or it may lapse into disuse. In the last resort it becomes, first *passé*, then old-fashioned, then antique, then archaic, then a mere relic. But even if, unlike flowers and insects, words are man-made, a certain respect for them should be theirs even when they are in the sere, and a more curious appearance of hidden energy may be manifest the older they grow. There the old thing lies in its shroud—a verbal Methuselah: yet but one instant's imaginative use of it may restore its voice, its character, its energy, and its personality. It is, too, seldom the words of infrequent and fastidious usage that utterly perish: only the miserably and heedlessly over-worked. For antique words, on which Time has scattered her poppy, lulling them to an agelong but terminable sleep, awaiting only their Prince Charming.'[1]

vi

Although a vocabulary is common to all, each of us has one of his own which has been inherited from family or school, or acquired by contact with particular groups of associates in either office or workshop[2] or political, religious, literary, scientific, or almost any other circle of thinking and talking people. If you are a Christian Scientist or a member of the R.A.F., a Communist, a Fascist, or a member of the Smart Set of the moment, you will add to your normal vocabulary a lingo common to your associates. Personal vocabularies with a common idiom may have a family likeness yet each of them contains words peculiar to the individual user. We attract to our service words which express our purpose or need, or, what is equally or even more important to the observer of language and its behaviour, our character. The process is in the main unconscious, particularly when selection is personal rather than functional. The act of selection, whether conscious or unconscious, reveals mental and other qualities. You can not only tell from his vocabulary whether a man comes from north or south of the Tweed or east or west of the

---

[1] Walter de la Mare, *Pleasures and Speculations* (1940), 332.   [2] See Notes.

Severn, from Yorkshire or Hampshire, you can tell his social class
and his intellectual status. This is true of the common man and it is
doubly true of the man of letters. And so inevitably every writer has
his own vocabulary. It would be easy to make a selection of characteristic words from pronounced stylists like Carlyle, Meredith or
Pater, and not very difficult to do the same from the unobvious or
more classical styles of Swift, Landor or Bernard Shaw.

Writers invent or re-invent words as well as select them; they
play with words as jugglers play with the properties of their art, and
in the process of manipulation they instil new meanings and discover original contexts. With the help of the *Oxford Dictionary* it is
now possible to attribute a very large number of English words to
their originators. Logan Pearsall Smith has shown how words have
been invented or revived by writers to express theme and purpose;
and although verbal inventions and revivals are generally deliberate,
it would seem as if they were sometimes spontaneous, and although
Dr. Johnson declared that he rarely used a word without the
authority of a previous writer, he was as inconsistent in this respect
as Coleridge, for, as Logan Pearsall Smith has pointed out, he has
'added a considerable number of learned words to the language'.
Many of them, such as *irascibility* and *acrimonious*, are typically
Johnsonian. 'When', he continues, 'we find words like these, with
the exclamation *fiddledeedee*, traced by the *Oxford Dictionary* to
Dr. Johnson; *etiquette*, *friseur*, *picnic* and *persiflage* to Lord
Chesterfield, *bored* and *blasé* to Byron, *propriety* in its modern use
appropriately to Miss Burney, and *idealism* in its non-philosophical
sense to Shelley, it begins to seem as if writers had a desire to invent
or import, or at least to use first in print, words descriptive of their
own characteristics.'[1] But the new word is not always new either in
structure or context. Great writers recharge ordinary words with
fuller and richer meaning so that a new light is thrown upon
common things, rather than a new word into the melting pot of
common speech.

vii

Words even of lowly and sometimes of dubious origin often dig
themselves into the language so successfully that their descent can
be traced in masterpieces of prose and poetry, which have been
strengthened by an infusion of idiom or a dash of slang. Yet the

[1] *The English Language* (1912), 119.

right of common words to go about doing good is still challenged. Newcomers are interlopers and must still fight for their place in the sun, but when they prosper none dare call them parvenus. On the other hand, nature and artifice being what they are, language might degenerate if words had no longer to fight for their lives. Even English would not be the powerful and sensitive instrument it is if it had not experienced the conscientious objections of Samuel Johnson and his kind. It is necessary to challenge everything from time to time, even the truth, to prove that it continues to be true. Dr. Johnson called the bluff of enthroned cant and vulgarity, and if it is necessary to call his bluff in turn, it only proves that the process is beneficial. What we must never forget is that language suffers as much from the use of dead words as from the misuse of live ones. The important thing is that words should be alive and effective and that cannot be unless they are fully charged with meaning, in the sense that Wordsworth's words always meant 'the whole of their possible meaning'.[1]

Nothing is more curious than the consistency with which words, condemned at birth, have muscled their way into the language. Dr. Johnson doubted the legitimacy of so useful a word as *humiliating*, and Boswell, who had an instinct for the right and a liking for the new word, and did not always agree with his distinguished friend's dogmas, was this time on the Doctor's side, although he rightly contested the wisdom of dethroning *civilisation* in favour of *civility*. 'With great deference to him', Boswell 'thought *civilisation*, from to *civilise*, better in the sense opposed to *barbarity*, than *civility*; as it is better to have a distinct word for each sense, than one word with two senses, which *civility* is, in his way of using it.' Dr. Johnson was the defender of precision; as a lexicographer (and here I must apologise to his august shade) he was a methodist: 'To make money is to coin it, you should say *get* money.' As might have been expected, John Wesley, so like his compatriot in many ways as to be his theological counterpart, became thoroughly Johnsonian when faced with new words and expressions. Words like *sentimental*, or *continental*, now commonplaces, wrought him up to a fine frenzy of indignation. 'I casually took a volume of what is called *A Sentimental Journey through France and Italy. Sentimental!* What is that? It is not English: he might as well say, *continental*. It is not sense. It conveys no determinate idea; yet one fool makes many.

[1] S. T. Coleridge to Robert Southey, 14th August, 1803. *Unpublished Letters of S. T. Coleridge.* Ed. E. L. Griggs (1932), i, 272.

And this nonsensical word (who would believe it?) is become a fashionable one! However,' he consoles himself, 'the book agrees full well with the title; for one is as queer as the other. For oddity, uncouthness, and unlikeness to all the world beside, I suppose, the writer is without a rival.' And, nearer our own time, Edward FitzGerald is almost as vehement about words now in common use, like *realistic*—'a d—d word.' *Individual* (for person) and *locality*, he complained, are always 'cropping up' and marring the 'authenticity' of Borrow's *Wild Wales*. These words are stigmatised as vile together with 'this vulgar young Ladyism, "The scenery was beautiful *to a Degree*". *What* Degree?' he complains. 'When did this vile Phrase arise?"[1]

viii

Scholarly men, however tolerant, have blind spots and under their influence new words, especially of unlearned origin, are challenged as a matter of course. But in so adventurous an age as our own when word-makers have the maximum of freedom, and word-making has become a common craft, no scholarly efforts can hope to check the influx of verbal novelties. Objections are loud and frequent, but they are curiously uniform. In the main they show a genuine concern for integrity but based upon the illusion of a static language. Thus attacks are still made upon foreign verbal invasions. In addition there are always academical objectors who resent slang and jargon, however much these upstarts may add to the strength, precision, and elasticity of the language. Examples of such objections are as numerous as they are instructive, and they occur at all times.

Mrs. Piozzi fancies Madame D'Arblay must live much with foreigners because she 'talks of *demanding* and *according* in a way English people never talk; and of *descending* to breakfast, and says one sister *aided* another to *rise*, or *lye* down, as English people never do. We say *ask*, and *grant*, and *help*, and *go down stairs*, you know; the other words are French' (1796). She was of the Johnson circle and her distrust of Gallicisms was probably an echo. But although linguistic xenophobia is endemic, French verbal invasions continue, and after a few grumbles the trespassers are anglicised and forgiven. We may therefore expect that what has happened to *demanding* and *according* and *descending* will sooner or later happen to vogue-

---

[1] *Letters*, ed. William Aldis Wright (1889), 342, 289.

words like *intriguing* and *amusing* and *gesture*, as it has already
happened to such jargon as *garage, camouflage,* and *chassis,* although
we still retain the French pronunciation.[1]

The invasion of Gallic words originally came from the upper
fashionable and intellectual strata. In the first class we have such
well-established fashion-jargon as *chic, vogue, mode,* and *ensemble,*
and, in the second, the tedious iteration of *amusing* and *intriguing*
for interesting or attractive. The first group has a natural origin in
the French dominance of fashion, the second is more temperamental, beginning as an intellectual pose, and ending as a meaningless habit. Yet, here the usage is not as recent as may be supposed.
Horace Walpole came very near to *amusing* in its contemporary
anglicisation as far back as 1773, when, in a playful letter to the
Countess of Ossory, he refers to one of his periodical attacks of gout:
'Here I am going into my twentieth week, and in pain from head to
foot, though not more than is *amusing*—at least I bear it with so
much tranquillity, that I cannot conceive why they make such a rout
about Job's patience.' He is deliberately anglicising for the *italics* are
his own. And, in 1878, William Cory, referring to a premature
announcement of his decision to marry, says 'the gossips in N.
Devon must wait, but will not be much "intrigued" till April.
Again the word is deliberately used for it wears his own inverted
commas.

In our time, Gallicisms feared in the past have been successfully
absorbed into the language, but as fear of some kind is necessary to
verbal salvation Americanisms have become the pet phobia of
contemporary purists. This fear is not merely pedantic or fussy: the
invasion threatens to alter the very structure of the language, and
it is more serious because Americanised *radio* and *talkies* have a
world-wide influence. Whether the influence is good or bad remains
to be seen. At present it has not spread much further than to conversation or to back-chat or badinage, which seems to be taking the
place of conversation. The best American writers still write English,

---

[1] The French invariably naturalise English verbal invaders by giving
them a French pronunciation. Thus 'High-Life' (a multiple-shop firm) is
eeg-leef, 'beef-steak' becomes *biftek,* and so on. Gallicisms are quickly
anglicised by the average man—if left to himself: 'garage' becomes
garridge, and 'Ypres', Wypers. Phonetic spelling will one day catch up to
common usage. The process operates in reverse with 'Paris', always
pronounced phonetically, except in the vulgarism *Gay Paree* of the
Victorian and Edwardian music halls, which is in the same low class as
Monty for 'Monte Carlo'.

American being reserved for talk. For one George Ade or Ring Lardner there are a hundred Will Rogers, not all of them, alas, so entertaining. But, again, fear of Americanisms is not entirely contemporary. As long ago as 1845 Landor wished that Anne Marsh had not used in her novel *Mount Sorrel*, 'the vile Americanism of *realise* for comprehend or conceive'. But such fears are groundless and we are greatly indebted to American verbal inventiveness for a host of words and epithets which have added to the strength and variety of English without making it American.

ix

The introduction of a startling word into a descriptive or colloquial passage is rarely disinterested even when it serves a useful purpose. It is often an effort on the part of the author to do for his reader what he has to wait for time to do for himself: it is a short cut to recognition. If, for instance, Bernard Shaw had wished for fresh publicity, his use of the unpleasant word *bloody* in *Pygmalion* would have served his purpose. As it was, Miss Doolittle's 'Not *bloody* likely!' introduced his works favourably to innumerable people who had hitherto ignored or sneered at him. But words which explode or shine with an epigrammatic brilliance have other than personal or spectacular uses. 'The art of the pen is to arouse the inward vision', said George Meredith. 'That is why', he continued, 'the poets who spring imagination with a word or a phrase, paint lasting pictures.'[1] A chance word, happily placed, may arouse the imagination and communicate the author's meaning more effectively. Some writers are sensitive to this magic quality in words and take a delight in verbal display. Words to them are like precious stones, and, as we know, even the most exquisite gems must be properly set if they are to reveal their full beauty and significance. But writers should not make words perform tricks for which they were never intended, and a distinction should be made between the epigrammatic use of words, and the epigram which depends for effect upon a witty conclusion, as in Coleridge's 'Summer sets in with its usual *severity*', or Wilde's 'Nothing succeeds like *excess*'.

The deliberate search for the unique word[2] in the sense that it is

---

[1] *Diana of the Crossways*, 137.   [2] I use the epithet '*unique*' *word* as it expresses my meaning with greater precision than the more popular *mot juste* which seems to have strayed into common usage without sufficient justification. H. W. Fowler calls it 'a pet Literary Critics' word, which readers

something more than the right word is an attempt to give to language that is old and a little weary something of the glamour of its lost youth; and it must not be assumed that the unique word is always a show-word of the more mannered writers. Outstanding or exciting words may legitimately occur in any writing, mannered or plain. All words are unique at birth but they lose their original distinction by contact with other words. In many instances the original meaning would be forgotten if it were not preserved in dictionaries. But a forgotten word, once in common use, may renew its life by a fresh association in prose or poetry. The unique word at its best is not unique in itself but in its relation to other words. And it is nearly always a familiar word playing a new part which surprises and enlightens simultaneously.

Good specimens are often found running wild particularly in familiar epistles. 'Is there in nature aught so fair . . . as the *mild* Majesty of private life?' Elizabeth Iremonger asks Miss Heber;[1] Anne Douglas Sedgwick, describing the effect of Spring in Battersea Park speaks of the *pyrus salicifolia* as 'another *rapturous* tree',[2] and Samuel Richardson tells Lady Bradshaigh that 'at fifteen or sixteen, a girl starts into woman; and then she throws her *purveying* eyes about her . . .'.[3]

An outbreak of startling words may be a symptom of over-sophistication, or it may be the natural ingredient of playful conversation, likely to occur during any cultured period: a clever verbal exaggeration bordering on but not quite achieving wit. This art of placing ordinary words in surprising and agreeable contexts has had practitioner throughout the nineteenth century to the present day. It would be possible to collect a chain of specimens from, say, Jane Austen to Eric Linklater. Jane Austen's indulgence in the practice is occasional, rather shy or perhaps sly, and one of the best

would like to buy of them as one buys one's neighbour's bantam cock for the sake of hearing its voice no more'. He is unable to trace it in French dictionaries or in English, so contents himself with associating it 'vaguely with Flaubert'. *A Dictionary of Modern Usage* (1926), 364. [1] *Dear Miss Heber . . . An Eighteenth Century Correspondence.* Ed. Francis Bamford. Introduction by Georgia and Sacheverell Sitwell (1936). It is possible that this particular use of *mild* was a convention of the period for it occurs in a letter of Coleridge to Thomas Poole, 14th October, 1803, when describing his infant daughter, who smiles 'as if she were basking in a sunshine as *mild* as moonlight'. *Unpublished Letters of S. T. Coleridge*, ed. E. L. Griggs (1932), i, 293. [2] *Anne Douglas Sedgwick: A Portrait in Letters* chosen by Basil de Selincourt (1936), 101. [3] *Correspondence* (1804), vi, 60.

examples says that the 'stain of illegitimacy, *unbleached* by nobility or wealth, would have been a stain indeed' (*Emma,* 1816). Eric Linklater is more generous with himself and, in keeping with our habits, more adventurous, as when he speaks of a country 'blanched and dead . . . under a killing *democracy* of snow' (*Juan in America,* 1931). It would be possible also to construct a chain of examples from a particular function rather than from representative writers, and, appropriately, the most complete might come from the criticism or appraisement of wine. These references are often playful, but there is always, as might be expected, a serious intent, rescued from solemnity by whimsicality. Sydney Smith is obviously playful when he speaks of '*neat* wines', in a letter of 1829; but Anthony Trollope intends Mr. Dobbs Broughton to be more serious, in *The Last Chronicle of Barset* (1867), when he refers to a wine merchant's stock of '*tidy* Bordeaux'. An amusing contemporary instance is given by John Fothergill in *An Innkeeper's Diary* (1931). Two 'pundits' of Cambridge are dining at his inn and discussing the wine. 'It's rather *broad,*' says one. 'Yes,' the other replies, 'but, mind you, it's a *clever little* wine.' The tendency to preciosity when consulting the wine-list was made the subject of a humorous drawing in the *New Yorker,* 27th March, 1937, which had this caption: 'It is a *naïve* domestic Burgundy without any *breeding* but I think you'll be amused by its *presumption.*' The unique word, in its more obvious phases, that is when it becomes 'brilliant' or 'significant', is usually self-conscious. On the other hand, naivety may also produce a similar effect, as in *The Young Visiters* where Daisy Ashford, aged ten, refers to the appearance of the King wearing 'a small but *costly* crown'. Such expressions are generally and more appropriately used in conversation rather than in print. Roger Fry had a genius for surprising word-contexts of this kind. One of the most characteristic is recorded by Virginia Woolf in her biography of the artist. He was expounding the aims of the Omega workshops to an interviewer when they came to a chair with bright blue and yellow legs and brilliant bands of intense blue round a black seat. Fry described it as 'a *conversational* chair; a *witty* chair . . . much more *amusing* than an *ordinary* chair', adding that he could 'imagine Mr. Max Beerbohm sitting on it'.

x

The test of the unique word is that it comes to stay not because it is unique but because it is inevitable. When a word becomes a commonplace it has achieved its full purpose; it will henceforth be mobilised as a private in the army of words which make up the language. Mere cleverness can never achieve that end, and it is only bearable when recognisably playful, lightly witty, and free from strain or effect. Rupert Brooke seems to strive too much with his adjective in

> *When your* swift *hair is quiet in death:*

swift is not neatly welded, but if its use is satirical then, in the words of Professor Garrod, 'it would be silly to make too heavy a quarrel' with the 'silliness' of such an expression.[1] Oscar Wilde's more familiar *shrill* green is another and more acceptable example of this kind of show-word, for in spite of its deliberate cleverness it is not memorable for cleverness alone. It does express something, if, perhaps, in too shrill a manner. Anyone who uses it in a similar context without quotation marks runs the risk of being charged with plagiarism. On the other hand, Gray's '*madding* crowd' which must have been almost as shrill at its inception, is now a commonplace, and more remarkably, his '*genial* current of the soul'.

There are periods when the search for the unique word becomes a fashion, for literary fashions are not confined to subject, form and style. They affect all sections of literature, fashion in words often preceding fashion in style. Fashionable acceptance of a word or anything else can be but temporary for the essence of fashion is change, and once the novel application of a word becomes unfashionable its special significance is apt to pass out of use. A word which has passed through an experience of the kind will not go entirely out of use, but since fashions rarely repeat themselves without definite variations, it is not likely to recur in its old relationship: it may be born again but it will be born different. It is possible to trace the rise of contemporary 'vogue-words', such as *meretricious, amusing, sophistication, intrigue, awareness,* among the intelligentsia, from whom it descends to the haunts of the low-brow,[2] where atrophy presently supervenes and the once fashionable word receives decent burial in the pages of a dictionary.[3] But such epi-

---

[1] *The Profession of Poetry* (1929), 168. [2] See 'The Over-worked "Pattern",' by the author in *The Times Literary Supplement*, 11th August, 1945.
[3] Popular journalism uses slang, vogue-words, etc., as a condition of its existence. The vogue at present is for Americanisms and not always the best of them, as for instance: 'He has *gifted* a notable fifteenth century treatise to Melbourne Public Library.' 'The Londoner's Diary.' *Evening Standard,* 24th August 1938.

demics are less likely to occur in classical periods, although in so formal an epoch as the eighteenth century Boswell could charge Johnson with 'inflation of style' by the unnecessary use of 'common but apt and energetic words'.

xi

We must turn, however, to a romantic era for more conspicuous examples, such a period as that epitomised by Richard le Gallienne in 'White Soul', a typical essay of the Eighteen Nineties, where there is an invocation for verbal guidance in phrases which recall the conceits fashionable in Elizabethan and Jacobean England. His purpose will not be content with 'a quill dropped from an angel's wing', he must have 'whitest paper . . . ear sensitive, tremulous, heart pure and mind open, broad and clear as the blue air for the most delicate gossamer thoughts to wing through', and he must have 'snow-white words, lily-white words, words of ivory and pearl, words of silver and alabaster, words white as hawthorn and daisy, words white as morning milk, words "whiter than Venus' doves, and softer than the down beneath their wings"—virginal, saintlike, nunnery words.'[1] But it was Aubrey Beardsley, the typical illustrator of the decadence, who, in a digression from the graphic arts, used his pen for the arrangement of words in sentences with much the same audacity as he had shown in the arrangement of lines and dots in those drawings which had not ceased to thrill or shock the 'middle classes'. His adventure in prose was brief and fragmentary; it began as a serial in *The Savoy* (1896), with the title *Under the Hill: A Romantic Story*, but owing to acceleration of the malady from which he was so soon to die no more than two instalments appeared or were written. The prose, as mannered as his drawings, is spangled with words which behave with the studied 'brilliance' encouraged by *fin de siécle* taste. The fragment was composed of the introductory chapters of a story of Venus and Tannhäuser. The dandified hero approaches the heroine, as he quells the 'little *mutinies* of cravat and ruffle', while she amid the '*slender* voices' of her court, prepares to receive him arrayed in a pair of '*tender* gloves' which do nothing to obstruct the view of her '*malicious* breasts, full of the *irritation* of loveliness . . .'.

Such words and their contexts are something more than unique: they are conceits and explosives, rather than experiments in the

[1] *Prose Fancies* (1894), 198–9.

search for the right word. They are the affectations of genius, and one of the poses of a literary fashion which indulged in the game of *épater le bourgeois* and did not hesitate to set art before nature by the inversion of words and phrases as well as of ideas and conventions. There were thus *grey* roses and *green* carnations, and Oscar Wilde described a sonnet-sequence as being composed of *coloured-marbles*. Such period-words will always interest the student of literature, especially in its romantic aspects, for emphasis upon novelty is a symptom of romanticism. They are the romantic toys of a class and bear much the same relationship to the main stream of language as *caviare* to the *plat du jour*.

Insistence upon verbal surprise even in a period of preciosity, is not always precious. In the Eighteen Nineties Hubert Crackenthorpe, a classic among romantics, used the device with distinction and reticence. He needs no extraneous supports for his simple and direct effects, and there is perhaps a diffidence about his use of unexpected words as though he felt he was straying from the austere path of classical excellence at the bidding of his period. He does not seem to encourage his verbal offspring to show off or to stand out from the crowd. Yet one cannot be other than grateful for *fidgeting* spiders, the *finikin* arrangement of trees in Normandy, the *witty sparkle* of Florence, and the *niggardly* pavement of a street in Naples. He makes a more obvious concession to his period in 'dark evil-looking flies' with long *sneaking* legs, and a night full of *stifled* light, but generally his unique words are not gate-crashers, they are properly introduced into a well-mannered prose as when ships *herd* at Marseilles, or when a London slum in June *attempts a rural air*, or the *rumour* of life in Richmond Park is hushed at sundown.[1]

xii

Yet indulgence in literary conceits which was often no more than a vogue in the Eighteen Nineties, is a frequent diversion of many writers even during periods which make no attempt to specialise in conceits and which openly discourage preciosity. The conscious preciosity of the Eighteen Nineties continued far into the following decades in such writers, born out of their due time, as Baron Corvo, and Ronald Firbank. Corvo throws back to Rabelais, but without the master word-spinner's prodigality or audacity. He took a similar

---

[1] *Vignettes* (1896).

pleasure in inventing words of his own and digging up words so curious and so long forgotten that they were almost inventions. The results are too often the expression of his own whims and resentments rather than contributions to the treasury of good writing. Occasionally he permits himself to be normally expressive as when he refers to the rain streaming down in *frigid lances*, but usually he seems to be doing little more than relieve his feelings by throwing chunks of his private and contemptuous vocabulary at the society or civilisation which has no place for him. But whatever his motive he is frequently suggestive in the manner of Edward Lear and Lewis Carroll yet without their good humour or sense of fun. Even when he burbles he is vindictive. Thus we are introduced to a '*glaucomatic* don at Oxford', a '*facinorous* cringer', '*flocculent females*', 'fierce and *bariausie* Venetians, and an '*ever-bacterical* poodle'. For the rest, his inventions, derived largely from memories of Latin, Greek, French and Italian, mixed with the jargon of science and theology, are Gargantuan museum-pieces such as *lambrequins, fulgurations, clup-a-cluppy, didacity, minnocks, jubation, eximious, bunted, wabble, dedecorous, muliarity, gubernated, capotism, nidderings, physidoyls, pudihundery, turpilucricupidity, obsequiated, banausie, anile, imperscutable, membrature, Ipsesepunieus,* and *Heautontinorymenos*.[1]

Firbank, on the other hand, peacocked his prose with conceits in the manner of Wilde and Beardsley. You may open his books anywhere to find examples. He speaks of a 'restless blue-bottle, attracted by the wicked *leer* of a chandelier', of a girl walking 'up the drive with her face to the sun, her body shielded behind a spreading *bouquet of circumstance*', of workers 'nursing small *lugubrious* baskets'. You can hear echoes of the period even in non-decadent writers.

H. G. Wells, for instance, has never quite lost the habit of verbal strutting, and in his recent *Experiment in Autobiography* he refers to his father's shop at Bromley as being '*extensively* unscrubbed', to a sociological problem being '*immensely* unexplored', and to Joseph Conrad's 'dark *retreating* face'. His most persistent verbal mannerism is an addiction to vogue-words and he has a high-school girl's love of top-heavy words like *enormous, vast, immense* and *extensive*. Examples like the following from the

[1] The specimens are all taken from *The Desire and Pursuit of the Whole*, written in 1909 and first published with an Introduction by A. J. A. Symons, in 1934.

Autobiography may be found in many of his books. Reconstruction has been '*enormously* reinforced by the spreading of material success' and his life's 'general problem is *vastly* simple'. He is also fond of amusing himself and puzzling his readers by the use of a scientific word like *rugose* for wrinkled, in a reference to the gods in William Blake's designs. Even so unsophisticated a writer as Thomas Hardy seems to anticipate the conceit of the Eighteen Nineties with the '*high-shouldered* Tudor Arch'[1] of an English church tower, in *A Pair of Blue Eyes* (1873); the '*shrivelled voice* of the heath', the evening '*tan*' of the landscape, and the '*posture* of affairs', in *The Return of the Native* (1878); and the '*vehement* tread' of De Stancy in *A Laodicean* (1881).

xiii

There was a revival of the convention which became a fashion at the close of last century between the two main acts of the world-war. It reached its height (and perhaps its swan-song) in the work of Edith Sitwell. Her method is frankly experimental, science rather than art, since she adopts the attitude of a reformer extending the boundaries of language. Her aim is to express sensations by surprising contexts, the terminology of one sense being used to bring out hidden qualities of another: light and colour by sound symbols, water by form, and forms by speech. 'Where the language is insufficient to convey a meaning, a sensation, I use another, and by this means I attempt to pierce down to the essence of the thing seen, producing or heightening its significance by discovering in it attributes which at first sight seem alien. . . . The apparent strangeness comes . . . from the fact that all expression is welded into an image, not removed into a symbol that is inexact, or squandered into a metaphor.'[2] In contemporary writing this method is in the tradition of Oscar Wilde's *shrill* green through Rupert Brooke's *swift* hair and Ronald Firbank's *bouquet* of circumstance. But what probably began as a pose or a lark has been raised into a doctrine.

Some of her experiments play about tradition, as when *bird-voiced* fire *screams*, for we are familiar with roaring, chattering, and purring flames; and when we hear that

> *The busy* chatter *of the heat*
> Shrilled *like a parakeet,*

---

[1] He applied the same epithet to Amiens Cathedral, which he called a '*high-shouldered* edifice' in *A Laodicean* (1881). [2] Edith Sitwell, ' Some notes on My Poetry,' *Selected Poems* (1936), 23.

we feel that we are near to the archetypal Nineties. Her favourites are between hearing and another sense, and she certainly succeeds in startling us into a new and sharper attention. Her use of *creak* in connection with light created a sensation when it first appeared in 'Aubade':[1]

> *Jane, Jane,*
> *Tall as a crane,*
> *The morning light* creaks *down again.*

She is apparently so pleased with the effect that she does it again and again. Thus we are offered 'cold wind *creaking* in my blood', 'crazy *creaking* chalets,' 'crystal buds that *creak*,' *creaking* water, and rain that *creaks*. This sensitiveness to sound ranges far and wide, giving us such images as stars that *howl*, buds that *whimper*, fleece that *sighs*, flowers that *cluck*, trees that 'swell with *laughter*', *cackling* grass, *jangling* dew, *giggling* curls, and a *castanetted* sea. But other senses are brought into play, augmenting form and colour by such novel contexts as *glazed chintz* buttercups, *pig-snouted* darkness, *blunt* rain, *green* heat, *fair-haired* breezes, *hen-plumed* seas, 'an *allegro* negro cocktail-shaker' and 'wines as *plumed* as birds of paradise'. *Fur* as an adjective is almost as popular as *creak*. We have a *furry* wind, faces '*furred* with cold', and '*furred* buds of satyr springs long dead'. Intellectual and moral concepts are also prodded into new vitality, often humorously, as in 'milk's *weak* mind', '*sly* dumb air' or sinister as a sin which

> *Like a* weasel *is nailed to bleach on the rocks*
> *Where the eyeless mind* screeched *fawning* . . .

She has also words that *sting* like mosquitoes, a parlour that 'runs on *feathered* feet' to meet the homing sailor, and 'Black streets *tumbling* down a hill'.

I admit a certain unfairness in thus segregating words which, however loudly they announce themselves, are not separate show-pieces but integral parts of a poetic design which is intended to be as modern in outlook and idiom as the pictures of Picasso, Matisse, Derain, Modigliani, or the music of Stravinsky or Walton. If we grasp that fact, we are assured, 'the whole matter becomes easy'. The

---

[1] 'When Miss Sitwell spoke of light *creaking*, there was a deal of noise. Yet, in common speech, we acknowledge the correlation of colour and sound. We speak of bright colours as loud.' L. A. G. Strong, *Common Sense about Poetry* (1932), 158.

difficulty is due to our unfamiliarity with 'the habit of forming abstract patterns in words' in which 'nobody has gone so far as the modern poet has'. That may be true, and although novelty may give undue prominence to a word that is both unique and right, that prominence should be temporary. The danger is that habitual search for surprising words and verbal contexts, even in the name of modernity, devitalises expression by overloading it with idiosyncrasy; the result being that words and 'patterns' become more important than content or meaning.[1]

xiv

The fashion of gaining verbal effects by unfamiliar contexts and connotations which broke bounds in the Nineties has existed in some measure at all times, if only as occasional idiosyncrasy or playfulness. In the sixteenth century the conceit was an ingredient of even popular literature. It is conceivable that the groundlings at the Globe Theatre were as ready to applaud verbal dexterity as enthusiasts at Covent Garden to-day to applaud the tonal acrobatics of a popular soprano or tenor. The fashion is pushed to its logical conclusion by Lyly. But it is unfair to judge an author entirely on the extravagances imposed by fashion. Shakespeare knew how to sail with the wind, but he also loved a word for its own sake. He might easily have congratulated himself on '*dusty* death' and it was surely not out of respect for the 'futile decalogue of mode' that he made morning

Flatter *the mountain-tops with sovereign eye.*

He was giving a verb the chance of its life and readers a new and precious impression of the effect of the morning sun on mountain peaks.

The fashion became more self-conscious among the poets of the seventeenth century. In John Hagthorpe's *Divine Meditations and Elegies* (1622) there is a '*cordiall* Violet'; and William Lathum has an '*obsequious* Marigold' in his *Phyala Lachrimarum* (1634) a year earlier than George Wither's '*grateful* and *obsequious* Marigold' in his *Emblems* (1633).[2] Milton, especially in his earlier period, enjoyed a playful context or a new epithet. Many of his verbal adventures and experiments are as fresh as when they were first

[1] See Notes. [2] Daniel George, *Now and Then* (Autumn, 1942).

minted, although some of them have probably put on novelty by becoming obsolete. Comus is rich in fresh and happy contexts, such as *'pert* Fairies', *'dapper* Elves,' *'dimpled* Brook,' and

> *Follow me as I sing*
> *And touch the* warbled *string.*

But none of these has the inevitability of the key-word in one of the most familiar couplets in *L'Allegro*:

> *To hear the lark begin his flight*
> *And singing* startle *the dull night.*

The reader is legitimately startled into attention by the suggestive placing of a common word as when Shakespeare 'springs imagination' by making the rising sun *flatter* the mountain tops. Tennyson's hidden beauty in a *'lonely* word' is an example. The use of *lonely*, like Shakespeare's *flatter* and Milton's *startle*, also startles us into attention, but with a difference. There is a hint of preciosity due perhaps to Tennyson's reference in the poem to 'hidden beauty'. But although there is none of the eccentricity of Beardsley or Wilde, words in contexts of this kind can never pass into verbal currency, like his own *'slip* into my bosom and be lost in me'. This sounds like an improved version of Coleridge's use of *slid* in *The Ancient Mariner*:

> *She sent the gentle sleep from Heaven*
> *That* slid *into my soul.*

In the eighteenth century when *'moping* owl', in Gray's *Elegy* was new and surprising, the unique word was taboo. But Dr. Johnson did not object so much to Gray's use of new contexts in the *Elegy* as to certain innovations in the shorter poems. The then recent habit of 'giving to adjectives, derived from substantives, the termination of participles', is neither condemned nor approved, but although *'cultured* plain' and *'daisied* bank' arouse no objections, he is 'sorry to see, in the lines of a scholar like Gray, the *honied* Spring.' 'The moral is natural,' he adds, 'but too stale; the conclusion is pretty.' Horace Walpole's cat in the ode 'On a Favourite Cat, Drowned in a Tub of Gold Fishes', is called a *nymph*, 'with some violence both to language and sense.' *The Progress of Poesy* has many expressions and words to which the Doctor objects. Gray is 'too fond of words arbitrarily compounded, such as *many-twinkling*': we may say *many-spotted* but scarcely *many-spotting*, whilst *velvet-green* 'has something of cant'. The conclusion is that 'an epithet or metaphor drawn from Nature ennobles Art; an epithet or metaphor drawn from Art degrades Nature'—which nowadays we might call an over-simplification as well as being contrary to contemporary usage. What Dr. Johnson really objected to, without knowing it, was an early intimation of the romantic revolution which was ultimately to overthrow so many of his own principles and those of the century which he bestrode.

XV

The unique word is not necessarily a new word, such as *incarnadine* and *cloud-capp'd*, first used by Shakespeare in *Macbeth* and *The Tempest*, or a newly placed old word, like *'ditties'* in Keats's *'Ode on a Grecian Urn.'* A deliberate use of archaism often misses fire as in Keats's introduction of *brede* in the same poem, and Rossetti's attempt to revive the Elizabethan *relume*. On the other hand the passage of time often gives unique qualities to words, such as Milton's 'over thy *decent* shoulders drawn'[1] and Marvell's *'quaint* honour turned to dust',[2] Shakespeare's 'nor shall death *brag* thou wanderst in his shade'; or, to take a modern example, Coventry Patmore's *'gadding* butterfly'. W. B. Yeats rightly thought that the element of surprise in contemporary poetry was achieved by the use of a word with no poetic ancestry. Commenting on the use of *moderate* in Dorothy Wellesley's poem *Horses*:

> *The wild grey asses fleet,*
> *With stripe from head to tail, and* moderate *ears.*

'No poet of my generation', he says, 'would have written "moderate" exactly there; the close of a long period, the ear expecting some poetic word checked, delighted to be so checked, by the precision of good prose.'[3]

---

[1] Pope uses the word in the 'Elegy to the Memory of an Unfortunate Lady':

> *By foreign hands thy dying eyes were closed,*
> *By foreign hands thy* decent *limbs composed ...*

[2] The surprise of Ligeia in *Comus*,

> Sleeking *her alluring locks,*

may be another instance of this kind of ripening, as Philomel's song, in *Il Penseroso,*

> Smoothing *the rugged brow of night.*

[3] Intro. *Selections from Poems by Dorothy Wellesley* (1936).

The unique word at its best is an unexpected yet inevitable ordinary word, such as *rich* in Keats's *Ode to a Nightingale*:

> *Now more than ever seems it* rich *to die*
> *To cease upon the midnight with no pain;*

or *sleep* in William Blake's *Jerusalem* :

> *I will not cease from mental fight,*
> *Nor shall my sword* sleep *in my hand,*
> *Till we have built Jerusalem*
> *In England's green and pleasant land;*

or *unhappy* in Wordsworth's *Solitary Reaper*, or *flash, inward* and *bliss* in 'I wandered lonely as a cloud':

> *Will no one tell me what she sings?*
> *Perhaps the plaintive numbers flow*
> *For old,* unhappy, *far-off things,*
> *And battles long ago;*
>
> *They* flash *upon that* inward *eye*
> *Which is the* bliss *of solitude;*

or, again, Wordsworth's use of *haunted* and *uneasy* in *The Prelude* (ix, 159) :

> *. . . his sword was* haunted *by his touch*
> *Continually, like an* uneasy *place*
> *In his own body.*

Dorothy Wellesley's 'unique' use of the ordinary word *moderate* has much the same quality as *rich* or *uneasy* as used by Keats and Wordsworth over a hundred years ago.

xvi

These citations illustrate not only the right word in the right place, but the word which is not only right, but whose rectitude has special significance, combining propriety, inevitability, and novelty —an effective blend of all three. The unique word is convincing as well as surprising, inevitable and epigrammatic. It explains as well as amuses by throwing a new ray upon idea or thing. Joseph Conrad understood its real business when he said it was 'like a flash of limelight on the facade of a cathedral or a flash of lightning on a

landscape when the whole scene and all the details leap up before
the eye in a moment and are irresistibly impressed on the memory
by their sudden vividness'.[1] Competent use of unique words adds to
the power of the writer and to the zest of the reader by infusing
language with surprise. It does so because it is a revolt against the
muddiness of stagnant language clotted with clichés, platitudes and
smug commonplaces; it is a protest against tired words, tame and
cowardly words, polite, genteel, attenuated words, and words that
have worn thin or waxed fat, dull, empty, shallow words:
words in short that have become psittacisms.

xvii

But it is not necessary to use words loosely in order to confuse
observation or expression. The normal accretion of memories, the
inevitable conventionalisation of meanings, are always ready to
distort and falsify not only what we think but what we see. Aldous
Huxley has put it neatly. 'A Vocabulary', he says, 'is a system of
Platonic ideas, to which we feel . . . that reality ought to correspond.
Thanks to language, all our relations with the outside world are
tinged with a sort of ethical quality: before ever we start our observations, we think we know what it is the duty of reality to be like.
For example, it is obviously the duty of all oranges to be orange; and
if, in fact, they aren't orange, but, like the fruits of Trinidad,
bright green, then we shall refuse even to taste these abnormal and
immoral caricatures of oranges. Every language contains, by
implication, a set of categorical imperatives.'[2] Words and phrases
are often the graves of ideas where thoughts and ideas are em-
balmed long after they are dead. Most people are word-bound.
Phrases, as Mark Rutherford said, are 'more directly responsible than thought for our religion, our politics, our philosophy,
our love, our hatred, our hopes and fears'.[3] We are conditioned
by words and phrases throughout life and we often find that our

[1] *Letters from Conrad to Edward Garnett: 1895–1924* (1928), 4. Even so
shrewd a critic as T. W. H. Crosland misapplied the term in *Who Goes
Racing* (1907), one of his once popular satires: 'If one wanted to write up
over the Stock Exchange the *mot juste*, one could write only a single word,
namely Fraud.' This word may be deserved or undeserved, but it has
none of the qualities of surprise, special significance or novelty which
might have earned for it the dubious epithet *mot juste*. [2] *Beyond the
Mexique Bay* (1935), Albatross Ed. 18. [3] *Miriam's Schooling* (1890), 68.

verbal loyalties survive long after the symbolic words and phrases have lost their original meaning. For that reason alone, apart from the pleasure of examining subtleties of style and tracking them down to their whimsical origins, a regard for words is an essential part of the equipment of the fit reader.

CHAPTER VIII

THE EGO AND HIS BOOKS

'There is no real antithesis between personal and impersonal art: the opposition is a false one.'—J. MIDDLETON MURRY, *The Problem of Style* (1922), 41.

'No good thing is produced with "perfect detachment" or without passion. None of my work is detached or pretends to be.'—ARNOLD BENNETT, 2, v, 1927, *Arnold Bennett*. DOROTHY CHESTON BENNETT (1935), 300.

'We have really nothing to write about but ourselves.'—A.E. (GEORGE RUSSELL). Qt. JOHN EGLINTON, *A Memoir of A.E.* (1937), 235.

---

i

It is popularly believed that because the function of writing is to promote and exhibit what the author intends, reading is nothing but tuning oneself into a book in a spirit of reverential subjection.[1] Much reading does, indeed, proceed upon that assumption, but such an attitude of subjection invests the author with a power to which he is not entitled and the reader with a submissiveness which he cannot always guarantee, even if he would.[2] Each has his rights, yet the

[1] 'Everything is tedious when one does not read with feelings of the author.' Wordsworth, 1802. *Early Letters*, Ed. Selincourt (1935), 306. 'Do not dictate to your author; try to become him. Be his fellow worker and accomplice.' Virginia Woolf, *The Common Reader* (1932), 259. [2] Fielding rightly looked upon himself as a pioneer of fiction, 'the founder of a new province of writing,' and for that reason he says, in the Preface to Book II of *Tom Jones*, he is at 'liberty' to make 'what laws he pleases therein' and

author, welcome as he may be, survives by sufferance, for the reader possesses the sovereign privilege of choice with an instinctive, if not always a conscious preference for his own integrity. These faculties are generally in abeyance, but their presence, hidden or revealed, indicates the existence of obligations on both sides which may be presumed to strike the essential balance between desire to be read and bias for the readable. In the continuous if not always conscious effort to strike this balance, a reader may find it easy to appreciate what a writer is saying, but not, which is equally important, why he says it.

ii

The deliberate exploration of the inner life, and the interpretation of its phenomena, are one of the outstanding characteristics of modern literature. A new way of explaining the mysteries of the soul of man by reference to primitive memories inherited from the remote past of the species has opened up hitherto unmapped territories of human behaviour. Under this influence observation has become radio-active, seeking to look through as well as at phenomena by constantly challenging accepted appearance and revaluing traditional values. The venerable suspicion that things are not what they seem has been given a new meaning by psychologists, and readers are learning how to seek the intrinsic and the significant not in what is expressed but in what has caused the expression.

The exploitation of the Unconscious has added a new phase to our conception of the inner life, and, confirming the suspicion that all literature is subjective, it has introduced a new element into interpretative criticism. That element is not concerned so much with technique as art, as with technique as behaviour. The attitude of the first is that of a connoisseur, and of the second that of an anthropologist. The one is curious about forms, the other about what is behind the forms. At all times the two methods have existed side by side, sometimes even in closer association, and this will continue but with a wider outlook and more exacting demands upon meaning. Renan, for instance, is content to call philosophy another kind of poetry. He was thinking in forms. Jung is even more precise. 'Philosophical criticism,' he says, 'has helped me to see that every psychology, my own included—has the character of a subjective confession.'

to expect his readers 'to believe in and to obey them'. Yet he does not regard his readers as his slaves. 'I am indeed,' he says, 'set over them for their own good only, and was created for their use, and not they for mine,'

Modern criticism is so much in agreement that it is engaged in exploring and charting the mysterious realm called the Unconscious, with the result that much of literary creation is looked upon as the art of making and interpreting discoveries from the same vast resources.[1] In this conception a man of letters becomes one of the sensitive points at which the Unconscious becomes conscious. A book is no longer an objective treatise, history or story, but a revelation of an author's adventures in the hitherto unexplored and unapprehended depths of himself:

'Tis Revelation what thou thinkst Discourse.[2]

The writer not only gives himself in his book—he gives himself away. 'Thus,' says Empson, 'one finds it hard in reading some passages in Keats, to realise that they were long enjoyed empirically, without the reassuring aid now given us by sexual symbolism.'[3] Readers are compelled to readjust themselves to these new conditions, to take Wyndham Lewis literally when he advises us to

Spy out what is half there—*the page-under-the-page.*

iii

Many of those who feel the truth of the growing opinion that literature is largely autobiography would find themselves in difficulties if they were asked for precise details in support of that opinion. Yet it is a true explanation of the inner meaning of a large number of imaginative, critical, and historical works. This does not mean that each work of the kind is a deliberate but disguised record of the main details of an author's life, but rather that it has been inspired by an innate and uncontrollable desire on the part of a writer to project himself into words and sentences with no other object but his own satisfaction. Projection of this kind can and does take place in all the chief literary forms, in poems, essays, novels, biographies, and histories. Moods and feelings, dreams and reveries, take charge of writers so that they become autobiographical without effort whether they like it or not, and for the same reasons readers are equally bemused by the image of themselves which they see re-

---

[1] 'Poetry . . . is most easily written in slight digression. Because it is, like dreaming, a natural device of the Unconscious to smooth over a disturbance; the formation of a pearl by the oyster round the irritating grit.' F. L. Lucas, *Journal Under the Terror* (1939), 130.   [2] Dryden, *Religio Laici*, 70–71.
[3] *Seven.Types of Ambiguity*. William Empson (1930), 308.

flected in all kinds of books.[1] H. G. Wells is doubtless thinking of himself and his own irrepressible subjectivity when he asserts that the normal human being has a 'passion for autobiography'.[2] But he might have gone further and pointed out that the average human being is more of an autobiographical than a reasoning animal.

The egoistic basis of most literature complicates the already complex association of writer and reader, because the writer is not only determined to be himself, but, at the same time, to placate the reader by appearing to be disinterested. There is nothing discreditable in the desire to please, but many writers dislike the necessity of having to do so, believing that it is a reflection upon their own integrity, and in order to safeguard their *amour-propre,* such writers declare that they write to please themselves. It is not necessary, however, to take their statements too literally. Writing is not a simple act, and the more sincere it is the more complex it becomes. Neither is it a game nor a pastime to be taken up or neglected at will. Writing is the effect of an impulsion which relieves an inward tension, and although the results may please, the process, or parturition as it might well be called, can be other than pleasurable. Within limits an author may write to please himself, but even then, not solely to please himself. He may persuade himself that he has no one but himself to consider, but unless he is a megalomaniac he hopes not only to attract readers but to please them as well. 'Every sort of artist demands human response,' says H. G. Wells, 'and few men can continue to write merely for a publisher's cheque and silence, however reassuring that cheque may be. A mad millionaire who commissioned masterpieces to burn would find it impossible to buy them.'[3] In a famous couplet Hilaire Belloc put the attitude of the normal author:

> *When I am dead, I hope it may be said:*
> *His sins were scarlet, but his books were read.*

It may be assumed that readers are so far partners in the production of books that without them writers would cease to function.[4]

---

[1] 'In *Paradise Lost* the sublimest parts are the revelations of Milton's own mind, producing itself and evolving its own greatness; and this is so truly so, that when that which is merely entertaining for its objective beauty is introduced, it at first seems a discord.' S. T. Coleridge, 'Notes on Milton', 1818, in *Lectures on Shakespeare*. Bohn Ed. (1914), 525. See Notes. [2] *You Can't be too Careful* (1941), 110.   [3] Preface to *The Country of the Blind and Other Stories*.   [4] 'Without a public poetry can hardly continue.' F. R. Leavis, *New Bearings in English Poetry* (1932), 211.

THE EGO AND HIS BOOKS

Many books have been written in hope of reward, but the sources of authorship are deeper than the love of gain or the necessity of earning a living. There is a force which impels genius to express itself regardless of emolument or applause, or, in the last and doubtless neuropathic resort, of audience or spectators. Even the desire to please is not disinterested. A writer may be pleased to please as a means of justifying the self-exposure of which most writers are conscious.[1] The primary aim of all authorship that is not frivolous or mercenary is to reveal the author to himself.[2]

Writing, as Disraeli expressed it, is also a safety-valve of the passions,[3] or, as George Gissing believed, a respite from the burden of life. 'Write I must, it is the only refuge.'[4] It was in this spirit of self-preservation that Goethe transformed 'any fair Circe who was in danger of transforming him from his true self' by turning her 'into an image' and 'embalming her in a book'.[5] Yet authorship, even when it is what we now call escapist, a safety-valve or an anodyne, is not enough, it is controlled finally by readership. The reader completes the writer, and the writer uses the reader for his own ends: as an extension of himself. The reader is the writer's stage, and as in the theatre the presence or absence of an audience affects the action, so the numerical strength and quality of readers have a profound influence on a writer's work. Writing is acting before real or imaginary readers.

Many writers are doubtless impelled by the same motive which induces a bore to tell and retell the story of his life to anyone who will listen to him. The origin of the desire to dramatise oneself is obscure, but it is probably a compensatory manoeuvre, an attempt to recover experiences from the past or to release by expression inhibited thoughts, or incidents which have hitherto been lived only in reveries and dreams. Prolongation of the sensation of living is

---

[1] Meredith winced at the prods of his critics although aware of the consequences of publication: 'When I thrust myself into the pillory of publishing, the smack in the face and the pat on the shoulder are things in the day's order.' Letter to Rev. Augustus Jessop, 1871. Qt. S. M. Ellis, *George Meredith* (1919), 267.   [2] 'My earnest desire is to reveal myself first of all and probably last of all to myself, to give birth to the man I have been concealing within me.' Georges Duhamel, *Salavin*, Trans. Gladys Billings (1936).   [3] *Disraeli.* André Maurois. Penguin Edition (1937), 138.   [4] *Letters of George Gissing to his Family* (1926), 211. Warburton told Doddridge that he would not write at all 'but as a relief to the morbid lowness of spirits, and to drive away uneasy thoughts'. Qt. *Conversations with Northcote.* Hazlitt. Ch. IV.   [5] F. L. Lucas *Journal Under the Terror* (1939), 236.

never far away from literary impulse. Literature is thus one more protest against mortality. 'Was death invented that there might be poetry?' If so, it is, after all, not so senseless an arrangement.'[1]

iv

A writer does at least two things every time he takes up his pen. He writes not only what he wants to write, but what caused him to want to write it. The one is conscious and the other subconscious, and the subconscious bears the same relation to the conscious as the submerged portion of an iceberg to that which is visible. This inchoate realm is always trying to reveal itself; revelation is always self-revelation, and it is always taking place. The writer could not stop it if he would. 'He who knows how to read me', says Paul Valéry, 'will read an autobiography in the form. The matter is of small importance.' It is not necessary to go all the way with Valéry. Matter does matter even though we admit that form and its ingred-, ients, vocabulary, quotation,[2] allusion, metaphor, and even punctuation, are revelations of self making objective as well as subjective writings equally autobiographical. This applies to good as well as bad, to creative as well as critical literature,[3] to all books, in fact, not deliberately constructed as tools such as directories, gazetteers, and text books. It is only such biblia a-biblia that are written solely for the convenience of the reader.

It may be the intention of a writer to objectivise his mental states, but he never accomplishes his aim because he can no more detach himself from his unconscious memories and instincts than he can step over his own shadow.[4] History is life seen through a temperament; like fiction, it is a projection of the historian into events, whether real or imaginary.[5] To Pater 'history was only an

[1] William Cory, *Letters and Journals* (1897), 348. [2] Edmund Wilson says that Matthew Arnold 'possesses an uncanny gift for introducing quotations 'with a personal significance and accent'. *Triple Thinkers* (1938), 26. [3] Joseph Conrad thanked Edward Garnett for an article 'not as an appreciation of myself, but as a disclosure of you'. *Letters of Joseph Conrad to Edward Garnett* (1928), 140. [4] 'One might, at the risk of impertinence call it (Ezra Pound's *Hugh Selwyn Mauberley*) quintessential autobiography, taking care, however, to add that it has the impersonality of great poetry: its technical perfection means a complete detachment and control.' F. R. Leavis, *New Bearings in English Poetry* (1932), 139. [5] John Wilson Croker in the *Quarterly Review* (March 1849) declared that Macaulay's *History of England* 'must be regarded chiefly as an historical romance', and that it would 'never be quoted as an authority on any question or point of the history of England'.

extension of his own ego, and he saw himself whithersoever he
turned his eyes'.[1] His *Imaginary Portraits* are unconscious portraits
of himself in various psychological poses, much as Renan's Jesus is
'a sort of Renan'.[2] A similar identification, as I have shown, holds
good in criticism, the critic revealing himself while criticising the
work of someone else; and there is abundant evidence in support of
Oscar Wilde's dictum that 'the highest and lowest form of criticism
is a mode of autobiography',[3] although he himself was only defending his own subjective method. In support of this theory it is not
necessary to seek further than Coleridge, the most profound of
English critics, who consistently extracted himself from everything
he interpreted, and drew the best of all self-portraits in his explanations of the character of Hamlet, in whom he sees himself as in a
mirror: 'I have a smack of Hamlet in myself, if I may say so.'[4]

Writers are only interested in their own point of view: they see
only what they want to see, and, although rarely inclined to admit it,
what they want to see is themselves. A large, perhaps the major,
part of all writing is pointing at things or persons or ideas which
interest because they reflect the writer. When Gorki talked with
Tolstoy, he noticed that the great upholder of selflessness listened
with indifference and even incredulity to any reference to things he
could not put to his own use: 'like a collector of valuable curios, he
only collects things which are in keeping with the rest of his
collection.'[5] This characteristic is humorously illustrated by the
anecdote of Whistler and Oscar Wilde who being observed in what
appeared to be an endless discussion were asked what they found to
provoke so much talk. 'When Whistler and I are together', Wilde
replied, 'we talk about each other.' 'On the contrary,' said Whistler,
'when Oscar and I are together we talk about me!' Writers inevitably look upon things and events, as well as ideas and images,
emotions, memories and experiences, as the raw materials of their
art. Even a realist is only realising himself. Synge is a good instance,
for he was a self-conscious artist who deliberately adopted the West
of Ireland, which happened to be his native country, as his theme
on the advice of Yeats, who discovered him in Paris as deliberately
adopting French realism and the Latin Quarter as his raw material
and territory. His drama is romantic but although his studies of

---

[1] Paul Elmer More, *The Drift of Romanticism* (1913), 99.   [2] Edmund
Wilson, *To the Finland Station* (1942), 42.   [3] *Dorian Gray* (1891) Preface.
[4] 'Note Book' Appendix, *Lecture and Notes on Shakespeare*, Bohn Ed.
[5] *Fragments from a Diary*, Maxim Gorki (1924), 161

Wicklow and the Aran Islands aim at realism, 'Ireland is to Synge what the colours on a palette are to a painter, a something wherewith to depict one's own soul. He does not perhaps so much use himself to interpret Ireland as he uses Ireland to interpret himself.'[1] It was the same with the books he read, and in early life he read much. 'Other writers existed for him only as part of his own being—only in so far as they reinforced his personal tendencies or made clearer the vision wherein he was absorbed.'[2] It is the same with other writers big and little.[3]

It would be rash even to suppose that such an obvious tool as a dictionary might escape subjectivity: but the old Adam, or the eternal Narcissus, creeps in even here. Dr. Johnson's *Dictionary* reveals many more of those prejudices which Boswell delighted to recall and is scarcely less personal than the *Lives of the Poets*, the most subjective critical work of first rank in the language. The *Dictionary* has for long been superseded. Today it is consulted only by the scholar interested in historical philology, or by the general reader for entertainment or for knowledge of its compiler rather than for the precise meaning of words. Johnson's subjectivity is not confined to his definitions, it governs his selections and particularly his omissions. His aim was not to be personal, but, honest as he was, he could not be impersonal. Vast scholarship went to the task and wide special reading, but, as Sir Walter Raleigh has pointed out, 'the knowledge of the English language which he had thus acquired was not always serviceable for a different purpose. In some respects it was even a hindrance. Johnson's *Dictionary* was intended primarily to furnish a standard of polite usage, suitable for the classical ideals of a new age. He was therefore obliged to forgo the use of the lesser Elizabethans, whose authority no one acknowledged, and whose freedom and extravagance were enemies to his purpose.'[4]

v

The private disappointments of a writer are apt to determine his philosophy, just as poverty or the fear of poverty makes Socialists. In

---

[1] Maurice Bourgeois, *John Millington Synge and the Irish Theatre* (1913) 91. [2] *Ib.* 52. [3] George Moore, as might have been expected, also used Ireland to interpret himself. When he returned for a period to Ireland, he told himself that his interest was the so-called Celtic revival: 'but he went to Ireland intuitively, and *The Untilled Field* was the first fruit of that renewal.' Charles Morgan, *Epitaph on George Moore* (1935), 23. [4] *Six Essays on Johnson* (1910), 82.

fact all criticisms of life, all philosophies, whether secular or religious, all ideologies whether formal or informal, are endeavours to explain a personal attitude towards life,[1] to turn, in the words of Remy de Gourmont, 'personal impressions into universal laws'.[2] Resentment often plays a bigger part than inspiration even when philosophy or social criticism takes a fictional form. Sherwood Anderson noted this characteristic in the novels of Sinclair Lewis: 'As we read, we feel that . . . in some secret inner part of himself, he has been, at some time in his life, deeply hurt by his contact with life and wants to get even. He seems to want to pay life back, get even with it by showing people up . . .'[3] Philosophies are often little more than apologies, resentments, or in the current jargon, 'wish fulfilments.' In recent years the subjective basis of philosophy has been widely recognised. We are always paying our ideals the compliment of creating them in our own image. Ortega y Gasset is convinced that the philosophical concept, usually looked upon as the last resort of the objective, is a means of implementing the philosopher's own life rather than a means of persuading others. 'The concept', he says, 'is one of man's household utensils, which he needs and uses in order to make clear his own position in the midst of the infinite and very problematical reality which is his life. Life is a struggle to maintain itself among men. Concepts are the strategic plan we form in answer to the attack.'[4]

Mark Twain was a writer who confused criticism of life with the expression of his own spiritual discomforts. He had sacrificed his integrity as an artist to worldly success and the artist he repressed never forgave him. Even when he had become the leading man of letters of his time and a world-famous personality he could not escape the feeling that all was not well, and he proceeded to discover a scapegoat. As there was no particular person to blame, he blamed humanity: 'The victim of an arrested development, the victim of a social order which had given him no general sense of the facts of life and no sense whatever of its possibilities, he poured vitriol promiscuously over the whole human scene.' But that, as Van Wyck Brooks observes, belongs to pathology, not satire.[5] The so-called

---

[1] 'The truth is, I now see, Coleridge's talk and speculation was the emblem of himself.' Thomas Carlyle, *Life of Stirling* (1851), 78. [2] Qt. J. Middleton Murry, *Problem of Style* (1922), 40. [3] 'Man and his Imagination,' *The Intent of the Artist*. Ed. Augusto Centeno (1941), 42. [4] *The Revolt of the Masses* (1932), 143. [5] Van Wyck Brooks, *The Ordeal of Mark Twain* (1922), 244.

philosophical element in his humour is an unconscious apology for himself apropos of human frailty and inconsistency. He expresses his grievances against conventional restraints and domestic control by proxy of Tom Sawyer and Huckleberry Finn, and the ironic sayings of Pudd'nhead Wilson are the unconscious expressions of Mark Twain's betrayals of his own intuitions.

This unrest increased until 'the whole man became a spiritual valetudinarian',[1] and he devoted much time and thought during his later years to a grand exposure of the failure of mankind. It was to have been so frank and ruthless that, characteristically, he decided to withhold publication during his own life, but was eventually tempted to issue part of it anonymously under the title *What is Man?* Whatever was thought of this book when it was first published, and whatever he himself thought of it, there can be no doubt now that he was consoling and defending himself. 'It is really his own mind he is describing . . . Mark Twain reveals himself in old age as a prey to all manner of tumbling, chaotic obsessions. . . . A swarming mass of dissociated fragments of personality, an utterly disintegrated spirit, a spirit that has lost, that has never possessed, the principle of its growth.'[2]

The desire to make converts is a form of egoism.[3] One of the most familiar forms of this kind of projection is the never distant temptation to mix opinions on morals, religion, or politics with all sorts of unlikely themes Few authors are immune from this seemingly irresistible impulse. You find it in themes which are ostensibly objective, and even, as in the case of E. Nesbit, in tales written to entertain children—a characteristic she shared with Hans Andersen. Her biographer recalls how she was always 'inclined to introduce into her stories references to matters which engrossed her —Socialism in particular—but she had done so with an adroitness which disarmed criticism. By degrees the habit grew upon her until any perceptive reader might easily have formed a pretty clear idea of numerous likes and dislikes of hers in no way relevant to her subject matter'. The impulse developed until it became almost a mannerism, so that 'one would need to be fairly obtuse . . . not to

[1] *Ib.* 25.   [2] *Ib.* 285–6.   [3] 'Philosophers dearly love to call their utterances "truths", since in that guise they become binding upon us all. But each philosopher invents his own truths. Which means that he asks his pupils to deceive themselves in the way he shows, but that he reserves for himself the option of deceiving himself in his own way.' Leo Shestof, *All Things are Possible.* Trans. S.S. Koteliansky (1920), 71.

gather from the study of two or three of her later books . . . that she was a Socialist, a Baconian, and a resister of the Women's Suffrage Movement. *The Magic City* itself, though intended for children, contains a cut at the women who were then fighting so vigorously for equal franchise'.[1]

vi

Writers who construct imaginary utopias are helping themselves in advance of the feast. Sir Thomas More, though an active participant in the affairs of the world, always fostered an otherworld for his own private consumption. He was an ascetic who admired the propertyless condition of the Franciscan monks, and when he came to build his *Utopia*, prince and bishop were dressed in the Franciscan mode. Bacon on the other hand preferred outward show, his passion for ostentation was abundantly expressed in both his life and his works. He was a convinced citizen of the world and would have lived in it even more fully if that had been possible. This attitude is reflected in *The New Atlantis*, especially in his interest in luxurious clothing. It is no idle fancy, for instance, when he describes a professor who wears gloves set with precious stones attended by young men arrayed with equal splendour.

All writers have reveries of one kind or another, and the more persistent of them are the reflection of some unfulfilled desire. The longing for self-expression is always the result of self-suppression of one kind or another, but not always sexual. Frustrations and introspection are also related. Invalids and others who are isolated from normal experience or function are invariably introspective. If you can't act you brood.[2] Self-pity is auto-intoxication. Whatever may ultimately be discovered about such things, for our knowledge is still elementary, there can be no doubt about the effect of the frustrations of pain, either physical or emotional, upon literature.

Goethe had illusions of grandeur and to console himself for his middle-class origin he succeeded in persuading himself that he was not the child of his lawyer-father but of a love-affair between his mother and a prince. When Shelley described poets as 'the un-

[1] Doris Langley Moore, *E. Nesbit* (1933), 258.   [2] 'When one has little life in one, or a feeble sense of life, one is the more clearly inclined to observe interior phenomena. That is what made me a psychologist so early.' Maine de Biran *Journal Intime* (Paris, 1927), ii, 162. Qt. P. Mansell Jones *French Introspectives* (1937), 49.

acknowledged legislators of the world', he was consoling himself for the failure of his own youthful political ambitions, much as Coleridge was thinking of himself when he said that 'no man was ever a great poet, without being at the same time a profound philosopher',[1] and William Morris, who labelled himself 'the idle singer of an empty day', believed that he was 'born out of his due time', and fashioned, in *News from Nowhere,* the sort of conditions under which he as a poet and craftsman would like to have lived.

vii

Utopism is often associated with sexual aberration or abnormality, and the desire to save mankind is a symptom of a warped or frustrated life. *Paradise Lost* and some of his prose essays would have been different from what they are if Milton had been happily married. Anatole France attributes the *Contrat Social* to Rousseau's frustrate life. The philosopher was 'ugly, feeble, and deformed', and he felt impotent beside his more charming and physically attractive brother. 'There', said Anatole France, 'you have the origin of the *Contrat Social.* It is because Jean Jacques was a cold fish that he set the whole earth on fire.' For the same reason, Anatole France reminds us, most revolutions in the East have been caused by eunuchs, and Napoleon, 'like the greater number of despots . . . was a perturbed spirit and set the world by the ears because he was incapable of enjoying his own bed.'[2] There can be little doubt also that the defective sex of Carlyle and Ruskin is reflected in their work, doubtless to the advantage of our common intelligence. Tolstoy's anxiety about the morals of civilisation was the reflection of his own unbalanced sex-life. Throughout his life he was sex-shy and as a young man he neither felt 'strong love' nor believed in it.[3] And that 'artist in conspiracy and intrigue' Michael Bakunin, now known to have been impotent for the whole or the greater part of his life, devoted the whole of his time and energy to violent agitations for a utopian dream which his fellow men as violently rejected. 'His tumultuous passions, denied a sexual outlet, boiled over into every personal and political relationship of his life, and created that

[1] *Biographia Literaria* (1817), xv, 2.   [2] *Anatole France Himself,* J. J. Brousson, Trans. J. Pollock (1925), 211. This could be said, probably, with even more truth of Hitler, whose book, *Mein Kampf,* is the testament of a self-pitier.   [3] Paul Biryukov, *Tolstoy's Love Letters.* Trans. Koteliansky and Virginia Woolf.

intense, bizarre, destructive personality which fascinated even where it repelled, and which left its mark on half nineteenth century Europe'.[1]

viii

The subjective character of poetry is generally admitted, and few now-a-days would question Coleridge's dictum that 'all sensibility is a self-finding', which must have seemed extravagant a hundred years ago.[2] All poets are like W. H. Davies who, in Walter de la Mare's phrase, 'dyes his objects with himself,'[3] for most poetry is the repercussion of a personal experience. Something similar occurs in the appreciation of poetry, which would seem to be a transference of sensibility from poet to reader. Admissions of this subjectivity are not difficult to find. One by Coleridge, who pointed out that in *Paradise Lost*, and 'indeed in every one of his poems—it is Milton himself whom you see; his Satan, his Adam, his Raphael, almost his Eve—are all John Milton'. And Coleridge, egotistic poet and critic himself, frankly admits that it was 'a sense of this intense egotism' that gave him 'the greatest pleasure in reading Milton's works'. 'The egotism of such a man is a revelation of the spirit.'[4] Another is from Aubrey de Vere who as frankly recognises the biographical basis of poetry. 'To me', he writes, 'there is often a deep though latent biographical interest in poetry, and I have often regretted that poems were not arranged in the historical order of their composition, while myself endeavouring to make out that order as I might, and thus see the image of a life looking forward through the mist, and revealing itself the more because it did not profess to do so.'[5]

Further, it has been observed by Stephen Spender that even the most objective of writers are entirely personal 'in the sense that they are wholly acceptable only to a person whose isolation of experience is identified with his own'.[6] This idea is supported by Tillyard in several examples from poetry and particularly from *The Rape of the Lock* and *The Prelude*. Pope's poem, he says, 'offers the curious spectacle of one of the rarest and most quiveringly alive sensibilities possessed by any poet, elegantly and successfully masquerading

---

[1] E. H. Carr, *Michael Bakunin* (1937), 258–24.   [2] *On the Constitution of Church and State* (1830). Ed. H. N. Coleridge (1939), 193.   [3] *Pleasures and Speculations* (1940), 63.   [4] *Table Talk*, 18th August, 1833, (1874), 278–9.   [5] *Memoir of Aubrey de Vere*, Wilfred Ward (1904), 327.   [6] *The Destructive Element* (1935), 194.

under an objective poetical form.' In this poem, so graciously formal
and urbane, 'the sensibility is everything . . . the moral . . . weak
and shadowy . . .what matters is the fierce though tenuous appre-
hensions of the doings of the fashionable life.'[1] He comes to a similar
conclusion about the 'matter-of-factness' of *The Prelude* which was
Wordsworth's 'oblique expression' of the 'fundamental . . . trust
and reverence of his own experience'. It was only by being direct
that he could 'achieve his proper obliquity'.[2]

The conclusion I would draw is that both writers and readers are
egocentric, and that the writer who attempts to disguise his virtues
or his vices is even more open to be caught in the act than such a
professed subjectiviser as Anatole France, who boasts that he is
unable to hide his faults,[3] or George Moore, who confesses that he is
not afraid of making himself ridiculous.[4] But the reader has the
writer at a disadvantage for whereas a writer cannot always escape
from self-exposure, a reader may keep himself to himself. The act
of publication places a writer at a disadvantage, in this respect, for
he condescends when he publishes. He may have written disinter-
estedly and independently but once he decides to publish he suggests
a partnership and thereby subjects himself to the will and scrutiny
of another. Writers expect readers to be submissive; some authors,
as I show at the beginning of this chapter, going so far as to advocate
submission as a condition of reading, but they are never certain
whether they will get it. These conditions are fundamental and the
only way in which they can function successfully is for the writer to
write and the reader to read in his own way, that is, to please
himself, for 'what has man of his own to give his fellow man, but
his own thoughts and feelings, and his observations so far as they
are modified by his own thoughts and feelings'.[5]

[1] *Poetry: Direct and Oblique* (1934), 21. [2] *Ib.* 96–7. [3] Pref. *Life and
Letters*, 11. [4] *Vale* (1914), 51. [5] S. T. Coleridge, *Lectures and Notes on
Shakespeare*. Bohn Ed. (1914), 227.

CHAPTER IX

THE CULT OF AMBIGUITY

'What is not vague is difficult, what is not difficult is nothing.'—PAUL VALÉRY, *Leonardo da Vinci*. Trans. THOS. MCGREEVY (1929), 16.

'A few of us would like to pipe up, in a modest way, against this indiscriminate cult of clearness. We suspect that we are sometimes over-dosed with lucidity in leading articles and sermons, in novels and verse.'—C. E. MONTAGUE, *A Writer's Notes on His Trade* (1930), 72.

'Obscurity lies not in the poet, but in ourselves. We are clear and logical, at the cost of being superficial or inexact.'—HERBERT READ, 'Obscurity in Poetry,' *In Defence of Shelley* (1936), 150.

---

i

A considerable amount of contemporary criticism is engaged in discussing innate or designed obscurities. It is not an easy task, for even clarity cannot be taken at its face value, and franknesses and abandonments are often found to be reticences or pruderies in reverse. But the phenomenon of obscurity is neither new nor wholly undesirable.[1] Obscurity in one of its forms is a characteristic of most writings and not, as some believe, merely a pose, or the result of incompetent technique or confused thinking. It may not be true that 'everything which counts is veiled';[2] but it is certainly not true to say that everything which is veiled counts, any more than it is wise to cast suspicion on what is unveiled and clear.

[1] See Empson, *Seven Types of Ambiguity* (1935), 284, *et seq.* [2] Paul Valéry, Qt. G. Turquet-Milnes. *Paul Valéry* (1937), 100.

164

There are many reasons, other than incompetence or expediency, why a writer cannot always express his exact meaning, even when he is free to do so. It often happens that the writer of genius has the greatest struggle to achieve clarity. Subtlety, novelty and self-concern are always getting in the way. Many modern writers are aware of these complications, and if some make a virtue of them, others strive to overcome them.

A. E. Housman admitted that he found it difficult both 'to know the truth about anything' and 'to tell the truth when one knows it'; and he found the search for words which would not 'obscure or pervert it' an 'exhausting effort'.[1] But clarity of expression is a matter of degree, and it is equally important to be able to see through the glib as well as the opaque; there is also a sharp difference between involuntary and intentional obscurity. Emerson told Carlyle that 'Every writer is a skater who must go partly where he would, and partly where the skates carry him. . . . The variations to be allowed for in the surveyor's compass are nothing like so large as those that must be allowed for in every book.'[2] The number of different ways of saying anything is a constant surprise to readers as well as to writers, to creators as well as to critics, and even inevitability of expression is relative. But whatever differences of opinion exist, and some there will always be, contemporary criticism would now agree with Robert Browning when he says:

> *Art may tell a truth*
> *Obliquely, do the thing shall breed the thought,*
> *Nor wrong the thought, missing the mediate word.*[3]

ii

Some writers are driven into obscurity to escape from the expediency of being interesting or amusing. They see standards being lowered to attract readers, and quality reduced by subtlety. Those who adopt such an attitude are on the side of the angels because the writer who is determined to be entertaining at all costs, that is, to

[1] Qt. Laurence Housman, *A.E.H.* (1937), 185. Perhaps there is no more remarkable instance of marked expression than in the poetry of A. E. Housman which has achieved immense popularity without any apparent understanding of its meaning. There are some curious reflections upon this phenomenon in James Agate's *Ego* 3 (1938), 26–7. [2] *Correspondence of Carlyle and Emerson* (1883), ii, 264. [3] *The Ring and the Book* (1868–9), xii, 859–61.

put entertainment before intrinsic value, is a mountebank, if not a charlatan, for to write down to your reader is to water your intellectual stock. Vulgarisation is objectionable not because it is vulgar but because it involves the writer in misrepresentation. Glib and facile styles are suspected because they are not seldom masks of shallowness or cupidity.[1]

On the other hand there are writers who, from shyness of their kin, or the public, or fear of critics,[2] deliberately say less than they mean, just as there are those who delight in bewildering their readers, and sometimes in flattering them by mystification. Gilbert satirised this kind of writer in *Patience*:

> *If this young man expresses himself*
> *In terms too deep for me,*
> *Then what a remarkably deep young man*
> *This deep young man must be.*[3]

But such jibes, however consoling to the Philistine, are rarely helpful to the serious observer of life and letters, and deliberate obscurity of the kind is less frequent than some commentators suppose.

Charges of obscurity are often brought by readers as well as writers against members of the younger generation who are knocking at the literary door with an unfamiliar rap. But these objectors are rarely unanimous and there are sharp differences of opinion upon the validity and status of those forms of obscurity which have received the sanction of custom. Coventry Patmore, who had no objection to the esoteric when it was an instrument of religion, especially his own religion, was inclined to the opinion that all secular esotericism was no better than 'charlatanism that would have no meaning or

---

[1] Of Max Müller: 'Considering he is so clear, it is astonishing how deep he goes. Perhaps I ought to put it the other way. At his depth it is remarkable that he should be so clear.' T. E. Brown, 24th February, 1896. *Letters*, Irwin (1900), ii, 160.　[2] 'I am in danger of degrading the truth and force of my work to meet the judgment of ignorant, careless, and often incompetent critics.' Coventry Patmore, Qt. Derek Patmore *Portrait of My Family* (1935), 152.　[3] This sort of snobbery is not confined to the intellectual fringe; like most peculiarities of the kind, it is probably a response to some inner need. Tom Moore has an anecdote which supports the idea. At a Yeomanry dinner at Chippenham, in 1819, he proposed the health of Lord Lansdowne 'in a speech which about three persons out of fifty understood a syllable of: but such men like to be talked to unintelligibly; they take it as a tribute to their understandings'. Memoirs (1853), ii, 294.

imperfect meaning pass with the world for mysterious significance'.[1]
Macaulay, who was proud of the clarity of his own style, blamed
readers for priggishly approving of obscurity. 'How little the all-
important art of making meaning pellucid is studied now!' he
exclaims in his diary, on January 12th, 1850. 'Hardly any popular
writer, except myself, thinks of it. Many seem to aim at being
obscure. Indeed they may be right in one sense; for many readers
give credit for profundity to whatever is obscure, and call all that is
perspicuous, shallow.' The curious thing is that Macaulay was
thinking of Emerson's style! 'But, Coraggio! and think of A.D.
2850!' he concludes, 'where will your Emersons be then? But
Herodotus will still be read with delight. We must do our best to be
read too.'[2]

iii

The fit reader rightly objects to stupid or careless obscurities, and
even the average reader prefers what he believes to be simple and
direct writing: no beating about the bush—no frills—and above all
no highbrow stuff! This dislike of mental effort inevitably leads to the
acceptance of a degenerate jargon which ultimately destroys all
taste for precise expression or even for simple and direct writing.
The strength and clarity of such masters of English prose as Bunyan
and Cobbett, or Bernard Shaw and Hilaire Belloc postulate a certain
ardency in their readers. These writers do not cater for the intellectually lazy or the mentally deficient. Even popular fiction survives its period of popularity if it is well and truly written.

Anthony Trollope admired and practised clarity in prose and he
had a robust suspicion of all ambiguities. He objected to Bacon's
'Latin riddles, in which the meaning is intentionally hidden by the
uncouthness of the phraseology.' In such pedantry he saw only
an attempt to disguise shallow thought, for 'the depths of philosophy
often owe their marvels to the conceits of philosophers'.[3] Objections
to such ambiguities are legitimate. A clear style is as necessary as a
legible calligraphy and neither, as we know, need interfere with
idiosyncrasy. Poetry as well as prose should be sensitive, logical and
clear; but immediate convenience does not prevent readers from
being served with a jargon of simplicity which may be more ambiguous than well-conducted prose in its more deceptive phases.

[1] *Courage in Politics and Other Essays* (1921), 74. [2] Qt. Trevelyan, *Life
of Macaulay* (1909), ii, 234. [3] Qt. Sadleir, *Trollope* (1927), 354.

The general attitude has been stated and approved by Somerset Maugham. He has no patience with writers 'who claim from the reader an effort to understand their meaning'. He realises that some writers are, for technical reasons, more difficult than others. Such difficulties are normal and can be overcome by education. There are, in his opinion, two reprehensible kinds of obscurity, one due to negligence the other to wilfulness. Most readers would agree that even if negligence may be explained it cannot be defended. But the wholesale condemnation of obscurities, wilful or otherwise, may lead the critic into serious artistic losses and if persisted in might ultimately land him in the intellectual gutter. The obverse of this medal is fear of clarity which in the Eighteen Nineties continued to express itself in the manner of Bunthorne, in *Patience*, and the pose has had a renaissance in recent years, the objection being focused upon 'simplification' instead of 'the obvious'.

It should not be forgotten that art and wilfulness are allies, indeed, one would be impossible without the other. You achieve nothing by condemning a writer to obscurity for ambiguity. It is the business of the critic who is not morbidly subjective to understand and expound the ambiguous as well as the obvious. The contrary attitude has produced innumerable incongruities. It has forced even so distinguished a writer as Somerset Maugham to see nothing but 'meaningless verbiage that no one thinks of reading' in 'those French writers who were seduced by the example of Guillaume Apollinaire', and little more than pretentiously dressed platitudes in the works of Stéphane Mallarmé.[1]

iv

Deliberate obscurity is not the fad of eccentric or incompetent authors or of the mere poseur, but a recurrent characteristic of literature. It is a natural phenomenon and, like all such phenomena, exposed to artificial exploitation. Among natural obscurities are the inherent and accidental incidents which dog the footsteps of language and literary expression,[2] including ignorance, leading to woolly and inexact thinking, and incompetence, leading to confused writing. A style may be temporarily obscure because it is profound,

[1] *The Summing Up* (1938), 31–34.   [2] 'Most of the really difficult passages in Shakespeare are obscure not from the rarity of the words employed, but from the confused and rapid syntax.' Sir Walter Raleigh. *Six Essays on Johnson* (1910), 82.

or closely packed, or merely because it is new or strange.[1] The habit
or necessity of using a technical jargon can make writing obscure
to all but the initiated. Slang is closely related to jargon and may be
as obscure as a foreign tongue until it spreads from its original class
or circle to be ultimately welded into the language. Artificial
obscurities are equally varied but when not esoteric they are to be
attributed to temperament or experimentation, and, therefore,
have some claim to be classed among natural phenomena. Temperamental obscurities though artificial in effect are natural in origin, and
only become artificial when the originator inspires imitators who
make a fashion of what may be no more than temporarily unavoidable and unpremeditated difficulties of style.

Herbert Read affirms a 'positive value in obscurity . . . in opposition to those who expect poetry to be as plain as a pikestaff'.[2] 'All
poetry', according to Dr. Tillyard, is 'oblique; there is no direct
poetry'.[3] That may or may not be true, but there is no doubt that
many and perhaps all poets are occasionally ambiguous or obscure
for purposes which are inexplicable to them or which seem good to
them. Coleridge warned the reader of Milton to be 'always on his
duty', because 'he is surrounded with sense; it rises in every line;
every word is to the purpose. There are no lazy intervals; all has been
considered, and demands and merits observation. If this be called
obscurity,' he says, 'let it be remembered that it is such an obscurity
as is a compliment to the reader; not that viscious obscurity, which
proceeds from a muddled head.'[4] In our time poetry has been composed ostensibly for the entertainment of the poet himself and a few
of his friends. The cult of the obscure, sometimes called 'private
poetry', among contemporary writers and readers seems to have
immunised itself against Gilbertian satire by frankly evoking and
enjoying some meaning other than that apparently intended by the
author. It is usually achieved by concentration upon expression and
manner rather than upon meaning. The pose, for it may be no more,
is sometimes paraded as a virtue. T. S. Eliot, in his preface to the

[1] J. W. Croker complained that Byron was obscure, in *Childe Harold*,
'because he dealt in metaphysics, and in the workings of a dark soul.' *Croker
Papers* (1884), i, 97. [2] 'Obscurity in Poetry', *In Defence of Shelley* (1936),
150. He distinguishes obscurity from ambiguity. 'Obscurity should be distinguished from ambiguity. . . . Ambiguity is essentially *grammatical*;
obscurity is imaginative . . . it arrives *before* the logical, and therefore
grammatical, stage of expression.' *Ib.* 151. [3] *Poetry: Direct and Oblique*.
E. M. W. Tillyard (1934), 5. [4] *Lectures and Notes on Shakespeare and
other English Poets*. Bohn. Lib. (1914), 529.

Selected Poems of Ezra Pound (1928), illustrated the method out of his own experience: 'As for the meaning of the *Cantos*, that never worries me, and I do not believe that I care. I know that Pound has a scheme and a kind of philosophy behind it; it is quite enough for me that he thinks he knows what he is doing; I am glad that the philosophy is there, but I am not interested in it.'

There have doubtless been poets' poets from the earliest sophistic-ated times, and it is further probable that a good many poets have looked to poets for early understanding if not appreciation, as a preparatory step towards wider acceptance. Bulwer Lytton, who was no advocate of esotericism, admired Coventry Patmore's earliest works, and seemed to tolerate their obscurity of expression. 'You seem to me', he wrote, 'to lean more towards that class of Poets who are Poets to Poets not Poets to the Multitude.'[1] There can be no reason why poets should not write for one another rather than for the general public, but if they do they have no cause for complaint if the public neglects them. Whatever Coventry Patmore was in his early work, he tended to become a poets' poet in his later phases, but it was a long time before his brother bards paid him the compliment of genuine understanding. Curiously enough he scored a popular hit first. It is doubtful, however, if the Victorian public saw in *The Angel in the House* more of what its author intended than the mere surface story with its obvious and familiar sentiments. It is only in recent years that the privacy of that poem has been unveiled.

Obscurity amounting to esotericism is inevitable in the work of those poets who seek to refine and subtilise thought and feeling. It is evident in the experimental work of Gerard Manley Hopkins, Richard Watson Dixon, and Coventry Patmore, each of whom approved of occasional esotericism for himself, whilst resenting it in the others. Gerard Manley Hopkins was not 'over-desirous' that the meaning of his poem, the *Wreck of the Deutschland*, should be always 'quite clear'. To understand the poem, he told Robert Bridges, it was necessary to get 'weathered to the style and its features', and even then, as in the case of T. S. Eliot and Ezra Pound, complete under-standing was not necessary, on the contrary, 'sometimes one enjoys and admires the very lines one cannot understand.'[2] There are difficulties throughout the poems of Hopkins, frequently involun-tary but oftener the result of his own experiments in prosody, which lead to what Robert Bridges calls 'oddity and obscurity', and since,

[1] *Portrait of My Family.* Derek Patmore (1935), 53. [2] *Letters of Gerard Manley Hopkins to Robert Bridges* (1935), 50.

he points out, 'the first may provoke laughter', at a poet who is always serious, the latter 'must prevent him from being understood (and this poet has always something to say).'[1] Yet Hopkins was no believer in lack of clarity for its own sake, and he criticised Bridges himself for obscurity, and thought 'continued obscurity one of the faults of Patmore's *Unknown Eros*.[2] A few years later obscurity was the burden of a series of epistolary commentations on Patmore's poems, made direct to the poet. Patmore expressed gratitude for these criticisms, but he made no attempt to answer them; and, significantly, although he adopted suggestions for verbal alterations, he left the obscurities as they were.[3]

Coventry Patmore, reconciling himself to esotericism in theology, quotes St. Bernard on the subject with approval, but although he reserves his own right to obscurity in poetry, he resents it in others, especially when, as in Hopkins, it is due to experimentation in metre and construction: 'System and learned theory are manifest in all these experiments; but they seem to me to be *too* manifest. To me they often darken the thought and feeling which all arts and artifices of language should only illustrate; and I often find it as hard to follow you as I have found it to follow the darkest parts of Browning —who, however, has not an equal excuse of philosophic system.'[4]

His struggle with Dixon's *Mano* is fortunately documented so that we are able to understand his attitude towards obscurity in the poetry of others. He was introduced to *Mano* by Hopkins in August 1883 and procured a copy towards the end of September. On October 10 he expressed his first doubts: 'I am reading *Mano*, but with some disappointment. It is full of vigour and manly and even great styles; but I think that a reader, alert, as I am, to watch for indications of the inner motive of the poem, ought to be enabled to discover it more clearly than I am yet able to do.' Though puzzled he is inclined to appreciate, and on October 31 he would like to talk it over with Hopkins: 'My failure to see in it all that I was led to expect is very likely my own fault. It is full of weighty merits and must not be lightly criticised.' Some nine months later (July 26, 1884) he is still puzzled, and is obviously moved by favourable opinions about *Mano* from favourable sources, but he has 'little hope of being able to see in it all that some who are quite as good judges as I am seem to

[1] *Poems of Gerard Manley Hopkins*. Edited with notes by Robert Bridges (1930), 98. The specific causes of these obscurities are carefully analysed in the Notes. [2] *Ib.* 82. [3] *Further Letters of Gerard Manley Hopkins* (1938), 147–245. [4] *Ib.* 205.

see in it'. A month later he makes up his mind in reply to an expository letter from Hopkins which unfortunately is lost. He admires the poem for 'its depth of thought, tenderness of feeling, and gravity of manner, and its many memorable lines and passages'. But he suspects a hidden *motif* which he fails to catch. 'If, as I suppose', he concludes, 'there is much more meant than meets the ear, and the *primary* interest is symbolic, then it seems to me that the veil under which the real significance is hidden is much too opaque. "Fit though few" readers may be a good prayer for a Poet; but the Author of *Mano* will find very few indeed who are fit for his mystery—supposing there be a mystery.' The well-known obscurity of *Mano* is not denied even by its admirers and what comes out of this record of struggle to understand is an obscurantist's objection to obscurantism in a brother poet. Patmore is quite content to banish *Jonah* from his own canon, not so much 'on account of its extreme obscurity as on account of its hopelessly unpleasant tone', in fact, he fears 'it is scarcely obscure enough'. The explanation is that obscurity with him is tactical whereas with Dixon it is innate and mystical. With Patmore obscurity is a disguise, with Dixon it is a condition.

Meaning, as we know, varies with time and person, but in a good many instances what is obscure to one age, or reader, is intelligible to another.[1] But whether all writers will ultimately be made clear to all readers is by no means certain, nor is it desirable. The democratisation of meaning is limited by the ability of the reader to understand: 'writing down' confuses meaning.

Even the fit reader is faced by obscurities which curb his pace and sometimes prove insurmountable. Patmore's experience with *Mano* is but one instance, and easily explained because of the peculiar character of the poem. But the prevalence of obscurity is proved by the struggles of commentators with the texts of poets like Shakespeare, Milton, Dryden and Pope, all of whom seemed clear enough to their own contemporaries. Dr. Johnson, who believed that 'few lines' of Shakespeare 'were difficult to his audience', found it necessary to examine at least five kinds of obscurity in the plays, four of which were due to accident or time. They are: (1) Careless-

---

[1] 'A good deal of recent poetry seems to be addressed to a posterity which will understand it better than we do ourselves; and of A. E. too it may be said . . . there shall come a time in which . . . his poetry may assume an importance greater than is allowed it now as a mere contribution to imaginative literature.' John Eglinton, *A Memoir of A.E.* (1937), 175–6.

ness in printing, due in the main, to the hurry of surreptitious publication. (2) Shifting fashions in language. (3) Lack of standards and experimental licence permitted in Elizabethan English. (4) Use of allusions and quotations familiar at the time, and, finally: (5) 'The fullness of idea, which might sometimes load his words with more sentiment than they could conveniently carry, and that rapidity of imagination which might hurry him to a second thought before he had fully explained the first.'

Unlike ordinary obscurity esotericism does not prevent the appreciation of poetry or prose without any desire to penetrate their hidden meanings.[1] *Hamlet* and *Measure for Measure* may veil dark secrets in their author's life, but that has not checked their acceptance by generations of readers who have no thought for such mysteries. And so for three centuries the *Sonnets* of Shakespeare have been widely enjoyed by readers who have taken them at their face value, but they have found no generally accepted interpretation of their meaning among the many critics and commentators who have peeped behind the words. The reader has, in fact, read into them his own meaning, and, indeed, one of the delights of reading is the opportunity of exploring the deeps and deeper deeps of both prose and poetry by processes which are not necessarily intellectual. That no doubt is why so fit and fastidious a reader as Edward FitzGerald confessed to a liking for 'reading things' he didn't 'wholly understand; just as the old women love sermons'. He compares the taste to our admiration for Nature, and instances the charm he finds 'in the half meanings and glimpses of meaning that come through Blake's wilder visions', although he is aware that those 'difficulties arose from a very different source from Shakespeare's'.[2] Misunderstanding based upon ignorance or innocence would seem to be equally satisfying. Samuel Butler knew a man who was converted to Christianity by reading Burton's *Anatomy of Melancholy* which he mistook for Butler's *Analogy*,[3] and Bernard Shaw tells of a slightly deaf old lady who sat at the feet of Charles Bradlaugh, at the Hall of Science, under the impression that the eloquent Atheist was a Methodist. The discovery of hidden meanings may add to the

---

[1] Commentations are interesting as revelations of the commentator. J. W. Croker thought Warburton's metaphysical enthusiasm led him to give Pope 'a meaning which Pope never meant', so that the commentator was harder to understand than the poet. *The Croker Papers* (1884), ii, 144.
[2] 19th November, 1833. *Letters*. Ed. William Aldis Wright (1889), 23.
[3] *The Note Books of Samuel Butler* (1912), 311.

appreciation of poetry as autobiography or psychology, but neither
stands in the way of the appreciation of poetry as poetry, and we have
it on the authority of Coleridge that 'Poetry gives most pleasure
when only generally and not perfectly understood'.[1]

V

Complaints about obscurity are often no more than objections to
change. The poet Gray, who now appears to be so lucid, was
charged with obscurity in his own day. Mason tells us that Gray was
advised by his friends to 'subjoin a few explanatory notes' to *The
Progress of Poesy* and *The Bard* but 'had too much respect for the
understanding of his readers to take that liberty'.[2] Meredith and
Browning are typical examples from the recent past. Even so
intelligent and experienced a reader as Edward Dowden had such a
struggle with *Diana of the Crossways* that he wondered whether
Meredith was worth the trouble, for 'breaking stones on the road'
was 'light labour in comparison' with the effort to understand him.[3]
Frederick Tennyson confessed that, with the exception of *The Blot
on the Scutcheon*, 'through which you may possibly grope your way
without the aid of an Ariadne', the rest of Browning appeared to
him like 'Chinese puzzles, trackless labyrinths, unapproachable
nebulosities'.[4] It is difficult for readers of this generation to imagine
why a general charge of obscurity was ever brought against
Meredith, but obscurity in Browning cannot be denied for he
was often obscure to himself,[5] and is still difficult for many normal
readers.

Yet most of the styles which seemed wilfully perverse to their
first readers present no difficulties for us. Few today, for instance,
would find obscurity in George Eliot's works, yet Anthony Trollope
complained that he had to read passages in *Daniel Deronda* 'three

---

[1] *Anima Poetae* (1895), 5.   [2] *Life and Letters of Thomas Gray* (1774).
When Richard, Lord Edgcombe, heard Gray read *The Progress of Poesy* to
a company which included Horace Walpole, George Selwyn and 'Giely'
Williams, he turned, after Gray had read the second stanza. to Williams,
and said: 'What is this? It seems to be English but by God I don't understand a single word of it.' *Diaries of Silveston Douglas, Lord Glenbervie.*
Ed. Bickley (1928), i, 135.   [3] *Fragments from Old Letters* (1916) 175-6.
[4] *Alfred, Lord Tennyson. By his Son Hallam, Lord Tennyson* (1897), i, 382.
[5] 'Sometimes he gave the impression that he himself did not know the meaning of what he had written.' F. R. G. Duckworth, *Browning: Background
and Conflict* (1931), 135.

times' before he was able to understand what the writer intended;[1] and, yet more surprising, Gerard Manley Hopkins could not 'make out the meaning' of *The Voyage* in Tennyson's 1864 volume.[2]

On the other hand it is not surprising that Whitman puzzled his early readers. The style alone was enough to do that, and in addition there was the novelty of his theme, and above all, his own contradictory statements about many of his most challenging poems. At times it seems that he had the same liking for causing bewilderment as Samuel Butler. But that was only apparent. Whitman's undoubted courage as poet and thinker broke down at certain points, and just as he was not above log-rolling his own book, so he did not scruple to disguise his intention if he thought that frank admission or explanation might cause trouble. He seemed to lose heart most over *Calamus*. The fit reader of today has no hesitation in attributing a homosexual motive to that section of *Leaves of Grass* but Whitman prevaricated whenever he was questioned on the subject. It was not the usual excuse of being 'large enough' to be contradictory with which he dodged difficulties created by his more familiar affirmations, but a persistent and what seemed a deliberate desire to bewilder or mislead. The outstanding instance refers to the inquiries of John Addington Symonds, the most distinguished and friendly of his early English critics. Symonds legitimately craved enlightenment and for years badgered Whitman for explanations without success. He wanted to know frankly whether the poems in *Calamus* were homosexual or not. Whitman agreed that Symonds was right in asking the questions, but, he added, 'I am just as right if I do not answer them,' and, he went on to say, that 'I often say to myself about *Calamus*—perhaps it means more or less what I thought myself—means different: perhaps I don't know what it all means—perhaps never did know. My first instinct about all that Symonds writes is violently reactionary—is strong and brutal for no, no, no. Then the thought intervenes that I may be do not know all my own meanings . . .' But although he quibbles about his meaning, he concludes that he will have to write Symonds 'definitely about *Calamus*—give him my word for it what I meant or mean to mean.'[3] It is quite possible that Whitman did not know what he meant but his ambiguous explanation suggests some other reason.

[1] *Autobiography*. Ed. Sadleir (1923), 225. [2] *Further Letters of Gerard Manley Hopkins* (1938), 75. [3] Qt. Horace Traubel, *With Walt Whitman in Camden* (1908), 76–7.

One of the more obvious reasons for the admitted difficulties of Henry James is the leisurely deliberation of his technique. Reading a Henry James novel is like looking at a slow-motion picture through the wrong end of a telescope. To what extent this obscurity was cultivated is not always certain. That he wanted to be understood, at least in some of his moods, is indicated by one who had many opportunities of observing him at close range during his ripest years. According to this authority, he despaired of intelligent comprehension when he was 'acclaimed as the author of *Daisy Miller* by persons blandly unconscious of *The Wings of Dove* or *The Golden Bowl*'.[1] Every serious writer hopes for intelligent comprehension, yet Henry James, despite attempts to disguise it, deliberately purged his mind and observation of obviousness, with the result that he is still a puzzle to some of his most appreciative readers. Some passages in his works suggest that the only intelligent comprehension could come from himself, and there are grounds for supposing that he was aware of it.[2] Samuel Butler, on the other hand, took a Puck-like pleasure in bewildering his readers. *The Fair Haven*, though serious enough, was written in such a way as to make it perilously like a piece of leg-pulling. Butler wrote as he did 'with a view to stupid people not seeing through it at all, and very clever people being in a good deal of doubt'.[3]

vi

Some of the poets and novelists of our own time are making still more daring excursions into the borderlands of expression. Whether language was given to men so that they could hide their thoughts, or whether G. K. Chesterton was right when he charged the modern mind with thinking that lucidity was more bewildering than mystification, there can be no doubt that today there is a cult of obscurity. Books are being written which have to be explained by other books.[4] It is necessary to decode the early work of Gertrude

[1] Theodora Bosanquet, *Henry James at Work* (1924), 13. [2] 'With *The Turn of the Screw*, he has carried his ambiguous procedure to a point where it seems almost as if he did not want the reader to get through to the hidden meaning.' Edmund Wilson, *Triple Thinkers* (1938), 138. [3] *Letters between Samuel Butler and Miss E. M. A. Savage*, (1935), 38. [4] The reader of modern poetry must be 'prepared to adopt an unaccustomed attitude in order to perceive unfamiliar forms. He must be willing to learn the language with which the poet creates awareness of a changed world.' Babette Deutsch, *This Modern Poetry* (1936), Foreword.

Stein and the later work of James Joyce before you can unravel their meaning, and if the earlier poetry of T. S. Eliot did not need decoding, to understand it was like struggling with an unfamiliar jargon. A considerable expository literature has grown up around *The Waste Land* of T. S. Eliot and Joyce's *Ulysses*; while it is necessary to learn a new vocabulary of his own manufacturing and almost to develop new stages of consciousness in order to comprehend Joyce's later novel *Finnegans Wake*.[1] Gertrude Stein's early work baffles most readers who find it impossible to discover any coherence in her fantastic style. 'She has outdistanced the Symbolists in using words for pure purposes of suggestion, she has gone so far that she no longer even suggests. We are the ripples expanding in her consciousness, but we are no longer supplied with any clew as to what object has sunk there.'[2]

The conscious stretching of the texture of language is not new. Valéry looked upon it as inevitable: 'In all language sooner or later a *mandarin's language* appears, sometimes far removed from the customary language; but generally this literary language is derived from the other, from which it draws words, figures of speech, and phrases best fitted to express the effect which the literary artist aims at.'[3] He instanced Mallarmé who made up 'a language entirely his own by a refined choice of words and by using exceptional turns of speech which he invented or adapted, always refusing the immediate solution suggested to him on every side'. His aim was to defend himself, 'in the details and elementary functioning of mental life, against automatism.' It was not a pose as many critics have too readily believed, but a mark of honesty in a poet who was resolved at all costs to maintain the integrity of his art by keeping faith with his intuitions. 'In order to remain faithful to the inner language of form, the poet must invent words and create images, he must mishandle and stretch the meaning of words.' Further, it is a mistake to demand an explanation of this honest objectivity: 'The poem must be received directly, without ques-

---

[1] 'Rather than sacrifice one atom of his (Joyce's) truth to detail, he is arcane and incomprehensible; and it is impossible not to feel he enjoys his own mysteriousness. It gives some kind of fillip to his self-engrossment.' J. Middleton Murry, *Discoveries* (1924), 139. [2] Joyce 'did not, after all, quite want us to understand his story *Ulysses*, as if he had, not quite conscious of what he was doing, ended by throwing up between us and it a fortification of solemn burlesque prose—as if he were shy and solicitous about it, and wanted to protect it from us.' Wilson, *Axel's Castle* (1932), 243–4. [3] Qt. *In Defence of Shelley and other Essays*, Herbert Read (1936), 159.

tioning, and loved or hated, until finally the strange words are accepted without questioning, but always with fresh recognition.'[1]

Nor is the defence of obscurity new. Joubert recognised that 'in style the introduction of pleasing ambiguities is a great art'. Nietszche said 'all that is profound loves the mask'. Baudelaire believed in an '*obscurité indispensable*' for poetry: and his taste as we know had the support of the Symbolists, some of whom turned obscurity into a fine art. Mallarmé and Valéry carried the idea a step further. They not only wrote with obscure intent but made it difficult also for would-be readers to obtain their books. Valéry's poems 'are always out of print and his other writings are always being published in editions so expensive and limited as practically never to circulate at all.'[2]

vii

The modernists, however, are not out to tease their readers with obscurities. The best of them have the 'high seriousness' of the Victorians.[3] Ambiguity is imposed on them by the novelty of circumstances as well as by depth of vision. They believe that life is real, life is earnest, and that things are not what they seem. Not for them the familiar path, they must, in Thoreau's phrase, 'make tracks into the unknown'. Wyndham Lewis is frank about it. He warns his readers not to expect a work of the classic canon, and advises him to

> *Take binoculars to these nests of camouflage—*
> *Spy out what is half there—the page—under-the-page.*
> *Never demand the integral—never completion—*
> *Always what is fragmentary—the promise, the presage—*
> *Eavesdrop upon the soliloquy—stop calling the spade spade—*
> *Neglecting causes always in favour of their effects—*
> *Reading between the lines—surprising things half-made—*
> *Preferring shapes spurned by our intellects.*
> *Plump for the thing, however odd, that's ready to do duty for*
> *   another,*
> *Sooner than one kowtowing to causation and the living-image of*
> *   its mother.*

[1] Herbert Read, *Ib.* 162–3.   [2] Edmund Wilson, *Axel's Castle* (1932), 89.
[3] 'T. S. Eliot's verse is a mixture of genuine obliquity and disguised statement. Possibly he deliberately disguises statement in order to give some appearance of a continuous obliquity to his verse, just as the writer of the old formal epic or tragedy deliberately heightened the trivial to get a formal consistency.' E. M. W. Tillyard, *Poetry: Direct and Oblique* (1934), 131.

I sabotage the sentence! With me is the naked word
I spike the verb—all parts of speech are pushed over on their
  backs.
I am master of all that is half-uttered and imperfectly heard.
Return with me where I am crying out with the gorilla and the
  bird.[1]

This sounds like a parody of something in Walt Whitman, but those who know the work of modern poets will recognise that it is not a parody but a further example of contemporary striving for expression. It is a mind at high tension, sweated of tolerance for the past and forcing old forms into strange new shapes and patterns.

There is a stage in the history of all art when technique becomes dissatisfied with its conditions and strives to become something else. Wordsworth's poetry, for instance, was latterly in danger of becoming philosophy or theology, and Rossetti's pictures tried to turn pigment into poetry. Walter Pater's belief that art aspired to the condition of music was probably an oblique defence of the inevitable musical trend of a prose style which he composed by welding together sentences and epithets each one of which had been written on a separate sheet of paper and tested for its rhythmical values like a bar of music before being given its place in the final composition.[2]

viii

In a period of acute self-consciousness, such as the present, the arts are so unsettled that they seem to be indulging in a continuous class-war—aspiring to any condition rather than that to which they were born. In *The Waste Land*, according to Stephen Spender, 'we have reached a stage when poetry refuses to become poetry,'[3] just as in James Joyce and Gertrude Stein English is in revolt against being English. One of the causes is certainly an accentuated self-consciousness with its inevitable neuroses and psychoses. Resentment of the common heritage of art, or speech, or habits is invariably morbid, and may become abnormal, or even subnormal. Some psychologists believe that undue engagement with a 'private language' is a symptom of insanity.[4]

[1] *One-Way Song* (1933), 29–30. [2] It is significant that W. B. Yeats begins his *Oxford Book of Modern Verse* (1936) by printing as *vers libre* Pater's purple patch on *La Gioconda* from the essay on Leonardo da Vinci. [3] *The Destructive Element* (1935), 149. [4] See Alfred Adler, *The Science of Life* (1930), 64.

179

Ambiguities may be natural steps towards the clear expression of new ideas or unresolved feelings. They are a sign of striving, and even if in trying to say more writers are forced to say less, the experiment may lead to a fuller meaning of experience. Others are mere fashions,[1] and often fashionable only with a class or a small group of intellectuals. And although it would be a mistake to associate romanticism too closely with the choice of words or a method of expression rather than with a mental state which constitutes an attitude towards life, obscurity in so far as it is prompted by a liking for mystery is as romantic as the constant desire for surprise or novelty; in fact, the desire for mystery is an attempt to hold the sensation of novelty by withholding the actual experience.

In a realistic period the romantic writer is inevitably although not deliberately repressed, so takes to disguise, that is, makes a mystery of himself by dressing up his style in obscurities and ambiguities, in much the same way as the romantic poseur rejects what is plain and accessible for what is quaint and distant. When the realistic pose is ascendant he tries to run with the hare and hunt with the hounds and as fashion or convention forbid him to use the properties of romanticism—purple patches, fine phrases, rhetoric—he embroiders the lean and athletic prose and poetry of the time with mystifications which are no more than an admission of his own perplexity, when they are not that inevitable symptom of romanticism, a yearning for originality complex. The pursuit of originality is the business of the mountebank rather than the man of letters, but originality is not despicable when, like beauty, it arises naturally out of a sincere attitude and an assured technique. Even then it is a characteristic of manner rather than of matter: manner plus inspiration. Even a Shakespeare can do no more than give a new turn to an old idea or emotion, originality being a variation of the life-stream which is often so delicate, or indeed so minute, as to defy investigation, or to escape detection by all but the most observant of readers. Attempts to contract out from the life-stream of letters ends in freakishness.

ix

Interactions of the romantic and classical appear in all periods. Predominance is a matter of degree, and the characteristics of

[1] 'The obscurity fashionable today . . . is largely a form of poetic diction, though not the poetic diction Wordsworth fought so hard to get rid of.' Forrest Reid, *Private Road* (1940), 210.

180

each have a tendency to overlap.[1] But there is no doubt that marked love of novelty in art and life is a romantic characteristic. In the eighteenth century novelty as the implementation of enthusiasm[2] was taboo, and it is still suspect with classically minded readers and writers. When it was not an eccentricity, the result of incontinent enthusiasm, it was believed to be a trick or advertisement.[3] Coventry Patmore, one of the most original poets of the last half of the nineteenth century, would have repudiated any charge of novelty-seeking in his own work. It was, in his opinion, 'the greatest triumph of the poet to clothe the comparatively tranquil current of healthy and universally experienced affections in that continual slight novelty of language which the greatest master of criticism has pronounced to be the essence of poetic diction.'[4] Patmore is indirectly upholding his own method, but it is none the less true that it is the least violent and the least eccentric elements in prose as well as poetry which endure longest in the appreciation of readers. The innate need for variety can and should be satisfied by the observance of a 'continual slight novelty'. On the other hand, the pursuit of novelty for its own sake stimulates rather than satisfies appetite for variety, in the end leading to the insecurity, in life as well as in art, which is a characteristic of the present age.

[1] See F. L. Lucas, *The Decline and Fall of the Romantic Ideal* (1936).
[2] Enthusiasm had not shaken off its seventeenth century association with religious delusions and excesses. To many cultured adults 'enthusiast' was synonymous with 'fanatique'. 'Sir, he is an enthusiast by rule': when Dr. Johnson thus 'characterised an ingenious writer of his acquaintance', he was expressing disapproval of that writer's works. *Boswell's Johnson.* Hill (1887), iv, 33. [3] 'I have enquired of two learned gentlemen, their opinion of the works of Mr. John Hutchinson; men of piety and extensive knowledge and charity, yet who know each other. They both agree in discountenancing that gentleman's *whimsies* (one of them called them) and those of his followers. Men generally (they say) incapable (but by propagating novelties) of making any figure in the literary world.' Samuel Richardson, 13th December, 1756. *Correspondence*, Barbauld (1804), v, 161. [4] *Courage in Politics and Other Essays* (1921), 60.

CHAPTER X

WRITING IN DISGUISE

'I had realised to myself a series of portraits, and had been able so to put them on the canvas that my readers should see that which I meant them to see. There is no gift which an author can have more useful to him than this.'— ANTHONY TROLLOPE, *An Autobiography* (1883), Ch. v, i.

'Poets mean what they say . . . even when they do not say what they mean; from our failure to recognise that proceed nearly all the faults of our criticism.'—H. W. GARROD, *Poetry and the Criticism of Life* (1931), 38–9.

'Of its nature, camouflage is a reality which is not what it seems. Its appearance, instead of declaring, conceals its substance. Hence the majority of people are deceived. The deception can only be avoided by one who knows beforehand, and in general, that there is such a thing as camouflage.'—ORTEGA Y GASSET, *The Revolt of the Masses* (1932), 149.

'Style, personality—deliberately adopted and therefore a mask—is the only escape from the hot-faced bargainers and the money-changers.'— W. B. YEATS, *Dramatis Personae* (1936), 79.

---

i

A writer may put into his work less of what he has experienced than of what he has repressed. André Gide is an example. 'He has allowed to blossom in his work the secret instincts, the occult desires and subversive ideas driven down into the

182

unconscious by conventional ethics.'[1] But he was not wholly unconscious of what he was doing, for in the Preface to *La Tentative Amoureuse*, he admits that our books are 'aspirations towards other lives, for ever forbidden'. Groddeck discovered that both Ibsen and Wagner buried all sorts of secrets in their works, 'so that in every fresh reading one discovers new treasure.'[2] But he says Wagner was innocent and Ibsen conscious of what he was doing. Buried secrets are the cause of much of the ambiguity and confusion in modern letters. The least reticent of writers are often telling half-truths when they are under the impression that frankness could go no further. On the other hand those writers who pride themselves on their secretiveness tell us more than they imagine. The discretions of a George Moore, for instance, are even more indiscreet than his indiscretions. Few, if any, writers have done more than hint at what they have discovered in the 'dim forests of the soul',[3] and when they do more than hint they take the precaution of projecting themselves into a fictitious or symbolical character.[4]

And just as there is an automatic element in writing so there is an automatic element in reading. If for instance it was necessary for Tennyson to drug himself into ecstasy by repeating his own name to himself, like a Hindu saying his Mantras, before he could tap the subconscious sources of poetry, so, it may be assumed, is some such process necessary to bring the reader into tune with himself. It is only by intensive reading, and often re-reading, that we may hope to taste the full flavour of certain books; and then they add a quality to our lives which will endure as long as we do.

ii

There is no certainty that what a writer has to say will be comprehended as he intended, or as he wished, for a book may have as many facets as readers or readings, and appreciation or condemnation may be the result of misjudgment or misunderstanding. The reader's reasons for the appreciation of books often surprise the author. Flaubert felt that success might be a missfire, for 'even when a book succeeds the success you win is never the success you were after'. He thought it was the farcical side of *Madame Bovary* that made it a

---

[1] Léon Pierre-Quint, *André Gide* Trans. Dorothy M. Richardson (1935), 162. [2] *Exploring the Unconscious.* [3] Lord Alfred Douglas, *Sonnets* (1909), 16. [4] See *ante*, pp. 80-1.

success.[1] Thomas Hardy was indignant at a notice of *Tess* in the *Quarterly Review*, and remarked ironically, 'How strange that one may write a book without knowing what one puts into it—or rather what the reader reads into it.'[2] George Gissing was surprised at the serious acceptance of *The New Grub Street*: 'Writing it, I believed it trash, for it was wrung, page by page, from a sluggish and tormented brain . . .' it seemed, however, to contain something which appealed to 'a great variety of readers'.[3] Bernard Shaw devotes so much space to telling his readers what he means because he knows that 'the lesson intended by an author is hardly ever the lesson the world chooses to learn from his book'.[4]

Contemporary observers have noted that the admirers of D. H. Lawrence 'fail to notice what he intends for them',[5] and 'how marvellously' the readers' attitude towards a book by George Moore changed that of the author. When Moore wrote *A Mummer's Wife* he had a definite idea of what he was doing; but when the novel was published he was surprised to find it praised for qualitites which he did not know it possessed. 'No critic', he says, 'seemed cognisant of the merits and demerits which I saw and which in turn delighted and tortured me. As the public verdict continued to affirm itself, I will say, to realise itself, the book I knew of was changed, metamorphosed, disappeared, and another bearing no more than a distant family resemblance to my *Mummer's Wife* was gradually forced upon me. I have since forgotten the old, and accepted and am content with the *Mummer's Wife* of critics and friends.'[6]

There is no reason to suppose that this instance is unique, nor need there be undue surprise, for changes in an author's aims take place during the writing of a book as much as during the reading of it. 'One does not write the books one wants to write,' it is recorded in the *Journals* of Edmond and Jules de Goncourt, for 'there is a fatality in the first hazard that dictates the idea of the book. And there is an unknown force, a superior will, a sort of compulsion to write, which commands the word and guides the pen; so much so that at times the book which comes forth from your hands seems not to have been born of yourself at all; it amazes you like a thing that was in you unknown to yourself.' Both brothers felt this about

[1] *The Goncourt Journals.* Trans. Galantière (1937), 81. [2] *Later Years of Thomas Hardy*, Florence Emily Hardy (1930), 7. [3] *Letters* (1926), 318. [4] *Man and Superman* (1903). Epist. Ded. x. [5] F. R. Leavis, *For Continuity* (1933), 125. [6] Qt. Hone, *Life of George Moore* (1936), 119.

their novel *Sister Philomène*.[1] There are several reasons for what the Goncourts call 'the persistent fatality of books', one of the most obvious being unconsciously controlled by contemporary ideas. 'We,' they say, 'whose racial and family sympathies incline us to favour the Pope, who have no feeling against any man who is a priest, we find ourselves writing, urged on by some irresistible force in the air, a book harmful to the Church. Why? But who knows the why of what he writes.'[2]

iii

Philosophers and poets sometimes project themselves into an idea or a thesis with results surprising to themselves. They may even follow a whim and find it true. Samuel Butler was fond of starting hares and persuading himself they were lions—and he may yet prove to have been right! *Life and Habit* began as such a hare, and as it turned into something more powerful it scared him. 'The theory frightens me,' he told Miss Savage, 'it is so far-reaching and subversive—it oppresses me, and I take panics that there cannot really be any solid truth in it . . .'[3] On the other hand he was aware that there was invariably something behind his 'written words' which the reader could not grasp. He believed it was due to 'the sense of wrong which was omnipresent' with him for several reasons: the collapse of an old friendship, the opposition of the Darwins to his theory of evolution, parental tyranny in early life, and an 'ever-present' anxiety about money.[4]

Robert Bridges recognised the existence of involuntary misrepresentations of emotions and in his study of Digby Mackworth Dolben he gives an account of the dilemma of the young poet whose Pegasus had bolted with him. 'The poetry which Dolben wrote to describe these emotions cannot escape the reproach of courting misrepresentation. It is indefensible: but it should be remembered that he would not himself have defended it. He would over-indulge the poetic sentiment of the moment, and afterwards condemn the extravagance. He would often laugh at himself (his sister wrote to me of him) "as if he saw that his poetry had got out of hand". And the fault is really a failing in his artistry. Just as a philosopher, when he has chosen his premises, will argue out his system to conclusions altogether at variance with his convictions,

[1] *The Goncourt Journals.* Trans. Galantière (1937), 98.   [2] *Ib.* 258.
[3] *Letters between Samuel Butler and Miss E. M. A. Savage* (1935), 156.
[4] Qt. Edmund Wilson, *Triple Thinkers* (1938), 219.

so an artist in developing his conceptions may perplex his intention, and be led into extravagant and unpremeditated positions.'

Even so matter-of-fact a writer as Anthony Trollope was faced with subleties of a similar kind, and in one of the asides which occasionally held up the easy flow of his narratives, he confides to the reader that all is not going as he intended. The novelist, it seems, often fails to depict all he has imagined. 'When he flies to pen and ink to perpetuate the portrait' he has conceived, 'his words forsake, elude, disappoint, and play the deuce with him', until in the end, the man he ultimately describes 'has no more resemblance to the man conceived than the signboard at the corner of the street has to the Duke of Cambridge.'[1] To some extent this is a condition of all imaginative writing, and especially of the creation of characters in fiction. The better they are the more they are likely to develop wills of their own. The heroine of *Diana of the Crossways* surprised Meredith in this way. 'She has no puppet-pliancy', he told Mrs. Leslie Stephen 'the truth being, that she is a mother of Experience, and gives that dreadful baby suck to brains. I have therefore a feeble hold of her; none of the novelist's winding-up arts avail; it is she who leads me.'[2]

iv

Another symptom of this anxiety takes the form of apology for real or imagined lapses from moral rectitude, and it is often used with ill-disguised cunning by pornographers as an excuse for deliberate defiance of the moral code. The author, generally a novelist, is not in these circumstances endeavouring to check the capers of his subconscious self so much as to overcome tradition or custom. It is symptomatic of the guilt of the novelist who realises that he has transgressed the unwritten law of the English novel which insists upon a purpose other than pure fiction or narration. The English novel at its best is always didactic. It began so with Richardson and Fielding, the example was followed by Dickens and Thackeray, continued by Meredith and Hardy, and it remains so with Wells and D. H. Lawrence and Aldous Huxley.

Novelists apologise when they feel that their love of fiction for its own sake has run away with them. One of the most curious of these apologies occurs without warning near the middle of *Mr. Midshipman Easy* after an orgy of stirring action.

Captain Marryat was obviously enjoying himself, but evidently

---

[1] *Barchester Towers* (1859), Bohn Ed. 187–8. [2] *Letters* (1912), ii. 560–1.

feeling that his readers might also succumb to the delights of pure fiction, it was necessary to remind them that he had a higher purpose, not only as the author of *Mr. Midshipman Easy* but as a novelist. He devotes four full pages to a defence of himself as a propagandist of reforms in the Royal Navy and the Merchant Service, and he excuses the entertainment of his yarns on the ground that it was necessary to gild the philosophic pill! 'We do not write these novels to amuse,' he proclaims, 'we have always had it in view to instruct, and it must not be supposed that we have no other end in view than to make the reader laugh.' He goes so far as to claim that to lash crime and folly and to uplift virtue and morality is 'the true art of novel writing'. The entertainment of his readers is camouflage. 'If we were to write an elaborate work, telling truths, and plain truths, confining ourselves to point out errors and to demand reform, it would not be read', therefore he 'selected this light and trifling species of writing, as it is by many denominated', as a channel for conveying 'advice in palatable shape'. Though he creates a character and weaves it into a story 'it becomes as much a beacon as it is a vehicle of amusement'.[1] There is no doubt of Marryat's zeal for reform, but that so accomplished a storyteller was primarily a reformer may be doubted. But he obviously felt that his gifts as a novelist were getting out of control and tried to allay his anxiety by placating the many who still looked upon novels as a 'light and trifling species of writing'. He may be presumed to have had no moral objection to the light and trivial tastes of fiction in which, willy-nilly, he became a master, but at the same time he was proud of the reforms he brought about, and had no intention of letting his readers overlook his desire to improve the bad conditions seafaring men had still to endure.

v

Sometimes the uncontrollable element leaps impishly into prominence despite the efforts of a writer to take full command of his own genius. It is not uncommon for the politest of writers to lapse unaccountably into vulgarity as though in the grip of an atavistic power imagined non-existent or well-mastered. A Keats may lapse into cockneyisms as easily as a Shelley into tub-thumping; much of Wordsworth's poetry was destroyed by the 'meddling intellect' which he both feared and defied, and Coleridge the poet and philoso-

---

[1] *Mr. Midshipman Easy* (1836), Ch. IV.

pher was cut down in the prime of life by the Chadband within, whom he could never control. Dual personality is common especially among artists of all kinds. Edward Gordon Craig gives an example from the theatre in his study of the character of Ellen Terry— who is composed of E.T. and Nelly . . . two persons in one body— 'Nelly who never had a doubt, E.T. who was essentially cautious on most occasions: Nelly, wild as nature itself, E.T., attentive to civilisation: Nelly, who didn't care a rap whether she had a penny or not, and E.T., careful as anything: Nelly, all impulse and every impulse right as rain, E.T. thinking twice about things, or even then never quite sure about anything.'[1]

In more recent years George Moore provides us with a very explicit example of this irregularity of creative genius; and it is useful as well as explicit because he himself was aware of the perverse imp which was always ready to take hold of his pen the moment he was off his guard. George Moore was continuously re-writing, or suppressing those of his works which he thought so ill-conceived as to be beyond redemption in style or polish. Some of these works, such as *Evelyn Innes* and *Sister Teresa*, he looked upon as the result of an outbreak of immaturity and would not reprint, but there were others, *Mike Fletcher*, *Vain Fortune*, *Parnell and his Island*; plays like *Martin Luther*, *The Strike at Arlingford*, and *The Bending of the Bough*; and two volumes of verse: *Pagan Poems* and *Flowers of Passion* which he would have liked to suppress entirely. That being impossible, he suggested that if they were ever reprinted they 'should be issued as the work of a disciple—Amico Moorini'.[2] But Amico Moorini, as Charles Morgan points out, was not George Moore's disciple or friend: 'He was his enemy who, though beaten down a thousand times, always rose up from under his foot.'[3]

The life of every artist is the tale of his struggle for expression against circumstances, environment, economics, temperament and his own complexes. All, or nearly all, of these things want him to do something else and must be subdued, side-tracked or sublimated. A glance at the dates of the volumes which Moore would not admit into the canon of his works indicates that he was at war with his perverse double for the greater part of his writing life, and only subdued him during his final years. He created defence works such as *Hail and Farewell*, *The Brook Kerith* and *Heloïse and Abélard*,

[1] *Ellen Terry and her Secret Self* [n.d.], 142.　[2] *The Lake* (1921), Pref.
[3] *Epitaph on George Moore* (1935), 13.

which the force of forces represented by Amico Moorini could not penetrate. The deliberate tread of his style, its slow motion, its wariness, its cautious and subdued rhythms, were tactical and left no opening for glib or vulgar infiltrations. George Moore's style could not have become so great an accession to English literature unless he had fought and won this victory over the lowbrow impudencies of his subliminal self. If he had taken the line of least resistance he might have been no more than a pornographer with an outlook upon life not much finer than that of the toff or masher he nearly became, with a sensibility not much better than that of a dirty-minded scribbler of bawdy remarks on a privy wall. George Moore's style is what it is because George Moore willed it so and he willed it so to satisfy, not his moral but his aesthetical conscience. He says, in the preface of *The Lake* from which I have already quoted: 'a writer's aestheticism is his all; he cannot surrender it, for his art is dependent on it.' Few writers have taken so keen an interest in expounding their aims, but these seventeen words contain the gospel of letters for George Moore and in the superb style of his final disguise there is no surrender.

vi

Reading, it will be seen, is complicated by the subterfuges and diffidences which writers are impelled to adopt as countermeasures against these uncontrollable activities of their genius. And with the passage of time their protective measures have inevitably produced a technique which might almost be called a ritual implemented by symbols and conventions which become unchanging literary habits for many writers over long periods. The editorial 'We', and the mock-impersonal 'One', each so threadbare as to deceive nobody, even if that were the intention, may be taken as familiar examples. The editorial 'We' can be justified on the ground that editing is often a corporate craft. Few editors nowadays speak for themselves alone. The use of 'one says' sometimes indicates a broader outlook than 'one's own', but it may equally soften the exposure of 'one's self'. It may be as Sir Walter Raleigh has said that 'You' and 'Us' are 'a vain attempt to escape from the insignificance of 'I'.'[1] But it should not be forgotten that 'You' and 'Us' are also vain attempts to disguise an overweening consciousness of the significance of

[1] *On Writing and Writers*. Ed. George Gordon (1926), 25–26.

'I'.[1] It is true, as Raleigh also observed, that 'Ordinary writing is full of these protective disguises, some of them ridiculous enough'.[2] But the problem is not, as he thought, connected with loose writing and therefore curable by closer attention; it is complex and fundamental and common to all writing in varying degrees of subtlety. He is aware of that for he notes elsewhere the difficulty of attaining self-expression: 'How eagerly or stubbornly does "man" hide himself behind creeds, mathematical problems, and abstractions!'[3]

vii

Most writers are involuntary exhibitionists, writing being for them, as it was for Milton, a 'fugitive and cloistered virtue',[4] they are impelled by an intellectual shyness, a protective caution, to express themselves indirectly, and by implication,[5] masked and veiled. Art releases emotional pressure by self-expression at passion-heat, which invariably tends towards self-revelation however much disguised. Ruskin put it this way: 'You may read the characters of men, and of nations, in their art . . . for the character becomes passionate in the art, and intensifies itself in all its noblest and meanest delights . . . a man may hide himself from you, or misrepresent himself to you, every other way; but he cannot in his work: there, be sure, you have him to the utmost. All that he likes, all that he sees—all that he can do—his imagination, his affections, his perseverance, his impatience, his clumsiness, cleverness, everything is there.'[6] A book communicates such self-revelations more readily than a picture or a statue and is always so much more than its appearance, that the reader who is content to take words at their face-value misses, or may miss, what the writer meant but was too diffident, or perhaps too confident, to announce.[7] Unlike many subjective writers, D. H. Lawrence, who knew from experience what he was talking about, frankly faces the problem: 'The curious thing about art-speech is that it prevaricates so terribly,

[1] It is surprising in these egotistical times to find a contemporary apologising for using the first person: '(to revert to the first person of modesty) I do not think . . .' Leavis, *New Bearings in English Poetry* (1932), 150. [2] *On Writing and Writers*. Ed. George Gordon (1926), 25–26. [3] *Ib.* [4] Milton, *Tractate on Education.* [5] 'There is a modesty of mind as deep implanted in the soul of man as is the . . . modesty of the body.' R. B. Cunninghame Graham, *Thirteen Stories* (1900), Pref. ix. [6] *The Queen of the Air*, 1869 (1905), 139–40. [7] *Studies in Classic American Literature* (1924), 8.

I mean it tells such lies. I suppose because we always all the time tell ourselves lies. And out of a pattern of lies art weaves the truth. Like Dostoieffsky posing as a sort of Jesus, but most truthfully revealing himself all the while as a little horror.' Some of the greatest writers rarely venture further than a hint. Such subterfuges are rarely frank attempts to hide something. They are often unconscious preferences for understatement which actually reveals more than exaggeration, much as excessive or abnormal clothing may be less modest than nakedness. It is sometimes assumed that an author need be no more explicit than his work. Against that, however, is the popular demand for the expository. The general expectation of a book is that it should explain something, and a writer is supposed to aim at explanation, or to tell the reader something easily comprehended. The chief concern of many writers, and among them many of the best, is to dodge this responsibility. A writer may desire to reveal something to himself rather than to his reader, or he may wish to say something which he has hitherto suppressed without giving himself away. The result is reticence, the most familiar of all literary disguises, or alternatively the whittling down of a passage until it loses distinction in a blur of mediocrity or commonplace.[1]

There would seem to be two impulsions at work: one towards self-exposure and the other away from it.[2] Even self-knowledge is often resented too much because it is apt to conflict with the unspoken conception of self as a moral or a social entity, and, for that reason, involuntary self-confessions or self-exposures whether spoken or written are defensive explanations: self-justifications in the language of psychology, or, in common speech and literary usage, apologies.

Further, since writers are incapable of avoiding confessions, they endeavour to avoid the consequences by throwing a direct light only on the convention they have formed of themselves. This conflict caused Joseph Conrad much concern. His hypersensitive aesthetic conscience which urged him towards frankness was always being checked by the personal considerations of a discreet and even timid

[1] 'Mediocrity is the happiest mask which the superior mind can wear, because it does not lead the great majority—that is, the mediocre—to think that there is any disguise. Yet the superior mind assumes the mask for their sake—so as not to irritate them, nay, often from a feeling of pity and kindness.' Friedrich Nietzsche, *Human-all-too-Human*. Trans. Paul V. Cohn (1911), ii, 175. [2] Thoreau felt that he was 'cheapening' himself by trying to become a successful lecturer, 'that is', he says, 'to interest my audience.' *Journal: Autumn*, 390.

191

temperament. The peculiarity, often amounting to a lapse into mediocrity, is surprising in a writer of genius so individual and courageous in other respects. And it is all the more surprising since he was aware of the anomaly if not always of its full implications. Direct and oblique references to it occur throughout his works, and he is quite frank about it in the 'Familiar Preface' to *A Personal Record* (1916). In these reminiscences he promises his readers truth 'of a modest sort', and sincerity, but not at any cost. He is aware of the dangers of delivering 'oneself into the hands of one's enemies' and of embroiling oneself with one's friends, and is inclined to take the necessary precautions. These are the dangers 'incurred by an author of fiction who sets out to talk about himself without disguise'. The dangers are not imaginary since a novelist lives in and for his work. Then comes self-revelation inevitable with Conrad, in the form of an explanation which amounts to an apology. Fiction being autobiographical is liable to displays of sentiment on the part of the author which he thinks repugnant. Not that he would 'unduly praise the virtue of restraint', often 'merely temperamental', and the result of pride rather than coldness. The risk to be avoided is missing the mark: 'Should the open display of emotion fail to move, it must perish unavoidably in disgust and contempt.' Hence a regard for 'decency, even at the cost of success, is but the regard for one's own dignity which is inseparably united with the dignity of one's work'.

It is not only the poverty of the inner environment which a writer may seek to hide, but the riches. There are disguises for depth as well as for shallowness; for plenitude as well as for paucity. Some writers are obscure because they have little to hide, others because they have much. Henry James is one of the latter and his works are a varied and complex disguise for a rich and timid inner life.[1] He 'was of those to whom the future is always ominous, who dread the treachery of apparent calm even more than active ill weather.'[2] He found in writing his only peace for there he could both express himself and hide from himself. His 'ruminating fancy' sought in the novel an anchorage from the shifting scene, from the impermanence of actual life. If ever a man built an ivory tower for himself it was Henry James. His intricate style was but the first line of defence. Readers were treated as though they were trespassers, and there is

---

[1] 'That there was something incomplete and unexplained about James's emotional life seems to appear unmistakably from his novels.' Edmund Wilson, *Triple Thinkers* (1938), 148. [2] Percy Lubbock, Intro. *Letters of Henry James* (1920), i, 15–17.

an inner line of subterfuge and prevarication which make it still more difficult for even the more determined of them to penetrate into the interior of his mind. Should an advance be pressed he would not hesitate to deny knowledge of his own meanings or intentions, by disclaiming 'responsibility for what deliberately had been suggested',[1] or by offering explanations which were more confusing than the original statement.

viii

W. H. Hudson, a writer far removed from Henry James both in character of mind and artistry, was equally fastidious. His biographer tells us that Hudson could not understand how Richard Jefferies could have 'given himself away' so fully in *The Story of My Heart*. 'Hudson ever wished to keep his own counsel and his own secret.' His books are always subjective even when not frankly autobiographical, yet his 'only piece of common vanity' was that 'he was difficult to understand', and 'he was not going to let people comprehend him'. He had admitted so much in a letter; and although he changed as he grew older, 'to the end he obscured and hid his motives, his gratitude, his affections, so that some would look upon him as an impersonal creature . . . his instincts led him into such secretiveness as leads a bird to build her nest where none shall find it . . . his reticence was so immense that he made false trails to avoid being known.' He appreciated such subterfuges in wild life. 'The actions of birds who pretend injury to mislead those who might take their eggs or hurt their young had a great . . . a special delight and attraction for him.'[2] This characteristic is expressed in the objective pose of much of his best work. He exposes himself most clearly in fictions like *The Purple Land* and *Green Mansions*. In those tales he holds the mirror up to himself. But when he is holding the mirror up to nature as a field-naturalist he is equally reflecting himself. Nothing is recorded for its own sake: toad or humming-bird, deer or adder, rook or robin—the pumas of Patagonia, the

[1] Forrest Reid, *Private Road* (1940), 70. The reference here is to a 'protest of ignorance' in connection with *The Turn of the Screw*, 'when internal evidence of the story points to a quite definite knowledge.' The attitude was not peculiar, for Reid was informed by André Raffalovich that he once teased James by pressing for an explanation of what 'the Olympian young man in *In the Cage* had done wrong.' The novelist 'swore he did not know, he would rather not know'. [2] Morley Roberts, *W. H. Hudson: A Portrait* (1924), 274–5.

coast of Cornwall, or the glades of Richmond Park, are all peculiar to himself because that self was unique in its reverent and sensitive contacts with nature.

ix

Writers give themselves away most frequently and most obviously in their prejudices. The more knowing of them take care to disguise this very human, indeed very natural characteristic, for our prejudices may be the last attempt of instinct to control mind. Carelessness occurs when a prejudice is temporary or new-born. The poet and critic T. W. H. Crosland, is an easy catch for my first example. In his book on the *English Sonnet*, he gives a running commentary on the principal masters of that verse-form, and omits to say anything about Lord Alfred Douglas. The omission invites enquiry because only a year or two before Lord Alfred had published a volume of *Sonnets* to which Crosland had contributed an enthusiastic epilogue placing Douglas in the front rank of the masters of the sonnet. If he had changed his mind he should have said so, but there is no evidence that he had. The explanation is a temporary flux of prejudice due to circumstances which are well authenticated. Crosland had quarrelled with his friend, and he was taking his revenge by the familiar trick of suppression.[1]

Landor is an interesting case. He is neither novelist nor playwright but a little of each, and, like Bernard Shaw and H. G. Wells, though not so constructively, he is interested in public affairs. He is also a poet and most of his poetry is frankly subjective. No anthologist covering the lyrics of last century could ignore his finely chiselled verses, but his fame rests, properly enough, upon the broad and solid base of his work as a hybrid novelist-playwright. But in both verse and prose he is, again very properly, accepted as the glass of fashion and the mould of classical form, and his *Imaginary Conversations* are popularly supposed to do no more and no less than interpret the ideas of his historical puppets. Landor himself fostered this illusion. In the preface to the *Imaginary Conversations* (1822) the reader is requested to attribute none of the opinions to the author of the work, 'as proceeding from his conviction or persuasion, but to consider that they have risen and fallen in different periods and emergencies.' But in the dedicatory epistle which precedes the preface he reveals the quality of his unprejudiced

[1] See *The Life and Genius of T. W. H. Crosland*, W. Sorley Brown (1928), 381.

attitude in a naive admission that he has included among his *dramatis personae* 'a few little men, such as emperors and ministers of modern cut, to shew better the just proportions of the great; as a painter would place a beggar under a triumphal arch or a camel against a pyramid'.

This kink in the classical armour of Landor did not escape the quick eye of George Saintsbury who was as subjective a critic and, on occasion, as good a blusterer; and although Landor and he are not to be compared as artists, a little of Saintsbury's commonsense might have saved the master of classical prose from many dialectical absurdities. 'Greek or Roman, mediaeval or modern, political or amatory, literary or miscellaneous, the *Conversations* simply convey in stately English the soon well known and not exceedingly fresh or wide-ranging opinions of the author on mundane things, with occasional and not particularly happy excursions into things divine. ... If the subject is literature, woe to anyone who speaks ill of Southey or well of Gifford. Woe again to anyone who speaks ill of Milton; but let nobody speak good of him except in the particular way which is satisfactory to Walter Savage Landor. We must always speak well of Dr. Parr, for he was a friend of ours. . . . But we must not speak ill of Dr. Johnson, though he was a Tory and a churchman; for he was a man of the Midlands, and so a very honest fellow. Down with the wretch Pitt (against whom we took a grudge when we knew nothing about politics), with the ribald Canning (who was an Oxford man and a scholar like ourselves, but very successful when we were not quite that), and with the villain George the Third (who was a king and whose countenance did not please us). We do not like lords, but if we happen to know any particular lord and he is polite to us, or has pretty daughters with euphonious names, or is related or connected in some way with our own family, and has not quarrelled with us, let us speak of him and his with a sweet and rotund mouth. If anybody dares to interfere with our comfort whether at Llanthony or Fiesole, in Paternoster Row or elsewhere, let us attend to the sacred duty of literary justice by gibbeting the fellow in as Dantean a manner as we can manage.'[1]

x

Even humour must be treated with caution for it is not always as disinterested as it would seem. Its very disingenuousness makes it

[1] 'Landor', *Collected Essays of George Saintsbury* (1923), ii, 121–2.

invaluable as a mark. Mark Twain who made the English-speaking world laugh for over half a century had no intention of becoming a jester and 'it was a constant surprise to him at first that people laughed at his stories and gave him gold and silver for telling them!'[1] He was not only surprised: he was disheartened, because the humour that made him famous began as the self-defence of a frustrated artist who had made the mistake of becoming a pioneer in California during the gold rush. He disguised his chagrin with laughter and for the rest of his life he was treated as a professional funny fellow. The reason is clearer now than it could have been at the time. The humour with which Mark Twain appeased his own restraints and irritations appealed to the community of gold-seekers because most of its members were 'roughing it' and subject to similar annoyances in varying degrees according to sensibility. And what was a relief to the mining camps of the West was equally useful to the commercial communities of the East. 'The whole nation', says Van Wyck Brooks, 'was practically organised—by a sort of common consent—on the plan of a vast business establishment, under a majority rule unalterably opposed to all the inequalities of differentiation and to a moral and aesthetic development in the individual that would have retarded or compromised the success of a business regime. We can see, therefore, that if Mark Twain's humour was universally popular, it was because it contributed to the efficiency of this business regime, because it helped to maintain the psychic equilibrium of the Western pioneer.'[2] As the years passed Mark Twain became more and more dependent on the business regime and less and less of an artist and although his humour continued to give first aid to business men, for him it remained a mask. Life for Mark Twain was apparently no joke but he went on joking about it so that the world should not know his real thoughts and feelings.

There is something of the clown who laughs while his heart is breaking or the villain who smiles and smiles and remains a villain behind most humour.[3] Cowper found that 'being merry by force' dispersed melancholy, and, 'strange as it may seem,' he said, 'the most ludicrous lines I ever wrote have been written in the saddest mood, and, but for the saddest mood, perhaps had never been written at all.'[4] A laugh may be provoked to relieve tension, as in

---

[1] Van Wyck Brooks, *The Ordeal of Mark Twain* (1922), 101. [2] *Ib.* 211.
[3] 'Not only a man's laughter is significant, but the *history* of his laughter.' Edward Dowden, *Fragments from Old Letters* (1914), 90. [4] *Letters*, Ed. Frazer (1922), i, 218–9.

the harsh humour in some of Guy de Maupassant's stories, but laughter is also used to sidetrack intelligence. Such disguises are not always involuntary. Some are deliberate and transparent, as others are transparent without being deliberate, and some, and they are the most difficult to trace, are sly attempts to throw the reader off the track of the original inspiration. Such an author veils his thoughts in symbols as though they would lose value by exposure. What for him is rare and good must be veiled, not least the temple of himself.

xi

Reticences and diffidences must not be taken at their face value, for, as should now be clear, they are not always what they seem. They may be prompted by modesty, self-respect, fear, or vanity, and in each form if logically carried out they may engender all the acidity of resentment which follows disappointment or injured pride. Candid vanity is comprehensible and harmless; but there is a more prevalent form of vanity which often puts the reader off his guard because it is carefully veiled. Gustave Flaubert calls it *la vanité intérieure* and he is convinced that it is at the 'bottom of everything' and particularly of what 'one calls conscience'.[1] The English habit of self-depreciation is a symptom of a vanity which French writers understand so well. Self-dispraise is sometimes tactical but may be a form of self-indulgence:

> *There is a luxury in self-dispraise;*
> *And inward self-disparagement affords*
> *To meditative spleen a grateful feast.*[2]

In an age of advertisement and loose exposure of the emotions, the reader must be on the alert also for the pose of understatement and the stage-whisper of the self-advertiser who creates a legend of himself by too openly keeping out of the news.

A writer is generally making the best or the worst of himself. One, like Dickens, hides himself behind a fascia of indomitable cheeriness, another, like Dostoievsky, masks himself in spiritual gloom; a third, George Meredith, who used his grandfather as the model for the 'Great Mel' in *Evan Harrington*, never confessed that he himself was the grandson of a tailor. After remarking that in reading Hazlitt you 'feel the man . . . not the mean, querulous,

---

[1] *Pensées* (Paris, 1915), 1.   [2] Wordsworth, *The Excursion*, Bk. iv.

disagreeable' fellow he was, Somerset Maugham confesses that 'the man within us is as true in reality as the man, pitiful and halting, of our outward seeming'.[1] Disraeli 'used to improvise quotations, attributing to recognised authors ideas which he had not the nerve to express as his own'.[2] This trick is not so necessary in poetry where reality is traditionally discounted on the ground of fancy:

> *Ever let the fancy roam,*
> *Pleasure never is at home;*

or excused on the ground of poetic licence, although poetical forgeries, such as those of Chatterton and Macpherson, are possibly attempts at camouflage on the part of poets who have suspected the ordinary conventions of poetic production. Poetry makes acceptable realities which might not be tolerated in prose. Only the musician dare be franker than the poet. In its more complex forms music is a natural disguise, since it is rarely transmutable into exact intellectual terms. Some good judges believe that if Wagner had translated certain parts of the music of *Tristram and Isolda* into words the opera would have been suppressed for obscenity.

xii

Some authors deliberately tax the reader's intelligence, demanding almost as much subtlety in the reading as in the writing. They look upon avowals as bad form.[3] To be explicit is to belittle the reader's intelligence. Writers of this kind seem in the end to be content if but few succeed in tracking them down to their furtive meaning, for, like the reader, they seek not so much to give as to receive. It is sufficient reward that here and there someone may raise the veil and bring to the temple a tribute of perception or a sensitive response, even if such readers are detectives endeavouring to trace to its ultimate essence precisely what the writer meant: to work their way through what he thinks he meant to what he actually means.

In all books, those 'less subtle and fine, but more simple, sensuous and passionate',[4] as well as those which are crabbed, or merely shallow, there is a triple meaning: what the writer said, what he thought he said, and what he meant to say. Writers involuntarily

---

[1] *The Summing Up* (1938), 47. [2] André Maurois, *Disraeli* (Penguin Ed. 1937), 33. [3] 'To speak with perhaps ill-bred candour, I like as well to fancy you are *not* preaching to Unitarians a Gospel after their heart.' Carlyle to Emerson, *Correspondence of Carlyle and Emerson*, i, 38. [4] Milton, *Areopagitica*.

play hide-and-seek with their readers, and it is only possible to catch what is meant by hunting between the lines and within even the words. In this game the reader sometimes takes the initiative by hiding from the author, running away as he reads, or reading to satisfy some obscure private craving; thus if writers expose and disguise themselves in what they write, readers seek and deny themselves in what they read.

xiii

The disguise called 'obliquity' has been examined by E. M. W. Tillyard. Obliquities are associated less with whim than with the deeper human needs. Though not the sole province of poetry they are frequent in most great poems. One of the most suggestive instances given by him is that of the involuntary emergence of what he calls the 'great commonplaces' which 'have been gradually captured and consolidated through history'. Those commonplaces are the 'concern of the whole human race, and 'it is possible that they were first expressed in poetry'. Taking *The Iliad* for an example he shows that in addition to the story and the human conflicts, 'the poignant exhibition of the passions,' is a 'great commonplace . . . beyond the usual "heroic" mentality of Homer's day'. That commonplace is 'the idea that in the utmost extremities the things that unite men are stronger than those which divide them'.[1] It is, he says, one of the functions of poetry to keep these commonplaces alive, and obliquity is fundamentally necessary for their preservation and presentation, for, 'As the great commonplace can be so remote in its origins and so complicated in its history, no direct statement of it is likely to carry weight. We instinctively distrust the man who has the boldness to express one, and we require the most convincing proofs of depth of mind and width of experience before we can overcome our distrust: in fact we require the speaker to talk about most things before saying what he has to say. We may even prefer the ultimate obliquity of his omitting what he has to say altogether and implying it through an elaborate pattern of seeming irrelevancies.' But the obliquity may not always disguise an objective idea. The commonplace for instance, in Blake's song, the 'Echoing Green' 'that there is virtue in desire gratified' which 'had been moribund since the seventeenth century', however

[1] *Poetry: Direct and Oblique* (1934), 26–28.

199

much he had objectivised it had 'its value as being uniquely his own'.[1]

All the obliquities examined by Tillyard: Rhythm, Symbolism, Allusion, Plot, Character, Mythology, Rhetoric, and Geography, are unavoidable in writing and must be mastered if reading is to be full and profitable, for they are often the key to the intention and therefore to the meaning of an author. That meaning is coloured by the response of the reader to these stimuli, and conditions his bookmanship. Where the obliquities are literary in character, as most of them are, or propagandist, as often happens, the responses depend upon the innocence or the experience of the reader as a reader.

xiv

A complete understanding of *Paradise Lost*, for instance, demands a classical education, or, at least, wide and memorable reading in the classics, before its literary qualities can be fully savoured or fully understood. But even then the poem has a theological content which may mean less to us than it did to Milton, for, as John Bailey has pointed out, 'neither God the Father, nor the Son, nor Satan nor the angels have any kind of personality of their own: in the sense that Hamlet or Ajax or Faust or Hector or even Turnus have: they are merely vehicles through which Milton carries on an interminable argument about free will and cognate matters.'[2] Response to allusion fixes the intellectual class of a reader, for 'writers allude, not always with any notion of specific relevance, but in order to proclaim that they are fully aware of the tradition'. In the use of such allusions the author informs the reader that 'I am writing in the tradition, I am civilised, I know what I am about, I am in touch with a civilised audience whom I can count on to understand me'.[3] Allusion is always at its best in a classical and cultured age, but it exists at all times and swings from the mythological to the literary and from the literary to the actual according to the current standard of education, culture, and habits. If the allusions in the *Iliad* are to mythology what those in the *Odyssey* are to the *Iliad*, and those in *Paradise Lost* to the *Iliad*, the *Odyssey* and the *Bible*, a writer in a semi-cultured period, say Kipling, still clings to Homer and the Bible while introducing a whole range of allusions, historical, patriotic, geographical, mechanical and Masonic, which

---

[1] *Poetry: Direct and Oblique* (1934), 33–34. [2] *Letters and Diaries* (1935), 49. [3] Tillyard, *Op. cit.*, (1934), 186.

are almost as necessary to a complete understanding of his work as a knowledge of the Classics to an understanding of *Homer* and *Milton.*

XV

Style is another of the phenomena of literature which readers must treat with caution, for it often disguises as much as it reveals. It is, as Yeats knew from experience, as much a means of escape as a mode of writing. It is a subject also of endless bewilderment among critics, who have never agreed upon a precise definition of the word. In the common usage of criticism it is assumed to mean method, and is often confused with mannerism, and even idiom. With the emphasis which is one of the characteristics of his own style, Swinburne argues that 'there is no more important, no more radical and fundamental truth of criticism than this: that in poetry perhaps above all other arts, the method of treatment, the manner of touch, the tone of expression, is the first and last thing to be considered'.[1] Mannerism, choice of words and phrases, however, are only ingredients. Style is something more than presentation. Style is what it is as well as the cause of what it is; manner cannot be separated from matter. Style is a characteristic attitude towards matter which produces a recognisable manner or idiom: as Flaubert put it—'a way of seeing things.' Coventry Patmore emphasises this opinion when he calls it the 'rarest of all artistic merits' which 'consists, not in a singular way of saying but of seeing things'.[2]

Some of the more earnest writers fear style, believing that brilliance, cleverness, the startling phrase, anything that makes a word or group of words sparkle unduly, may be taken for attitudinising, or dressing up. There are considerable grounds for these fears, for style often enough is no more than a pose or a parade, and therefore a hindrance to reading because it invites you to look at the writer rather than at what he is doing. For that reason, no doubt, Renan devoted a whole year to the elimination of style from his *Life of Jesus*, and it could be argued also that Walter Pater, an apparently unrepentant stylist, doubted the authenticity of his method when he said that 'to the grave reader words too are grave; and the ornamental word, the figure, the accessory form or colour or reference, is rarely content to die to thought precisely at the right

[1] *Studies in Prose and Poetry* (1894), 137. [2] *Courage in Politics and Other Essays* (1921), 152.

moment, but will inevitably linger awhile, stirring a long "brain-wave" behind it of perhaps quite alien associations'.[1] The richly worked style, with its purple patches and unique words, which is always associated with Pater, may have been the unintended result of a frustrate struggle for the simplicity which we have been told is the last refuge of complexity.

Carlyle's style was devised as a weapon for attacking the industrial civilisation of his time. It ultimately took the form of an exaggeration of his forceful and aggressive talk, with first aid from the prose style of Jean Paul Richter. But mannerism developed slowly, his early writings being in the eignteenth century prose tradition which he handled with individuality and distinction. Yet he always enjoyed projecting his irate temperament into quarrelsome words and crabbed phrases, although he had been writing for about ten years before he achieved Carlylese. The new style began in *Sartor Resartus* (1831) and reached its height in his prose epic on the *French Revolution* (1837), which he looked upon as one of the 'savagest' books 'written for centuries', and upon its author as a '*wild man*'.[2] These and other similar comments made during the progress of composition reveal a studied consciousness of purpose and a feeling that he had achieved something unique in English letters. But at times even he seemed suspicious of the mannered pose of the style, believing that it might hold up his message. 'There are two parties to a good style,' he said, 'the contented Writer and the contented Reader,' and proposed to alter 'many a little thing' in his *French Revolution* 'with an eye to greater clearness'.[3] Towards the end of his life this repentant mood increased and, without materially altering his style, he concluded that the 'ultimate rule is to learn as far as possible to be intelligible and transparent, no notice taken of your "style", but solely of what you express by it'.[4]

Joseph Conrad who strove so deliberately to camouflage himself in a subjective objectivity, had an almost morbid contempt for fine phrases, due perhaps to a conscientious desire for simplicity and precision in a language which he only mastered after reaching manhood. His highest praise for Guy de Maupassant is that he 'stoops to no littleness in his art—least of all to the miserable vanity

[1] 'Style', *Appreciations* (1889), 15. [2] *New Letters of Thomas Carlyle* (1904), i, 55. Italics are his. [3] *Ib.* i, 33. An American critic explains Carlylese as the 'phenomenon of unconscious disguise, of fear lest the figure in the carpet become too clear'. Ludwig Lewisohn, *Expression in America*, 258. [4] *Reminiscences*, Ed. J. A. Froude (1881),ii, 41.

of a catching phrase'.[1] But there is something smug about Conrad's attitude, for he was posing in his own way and for his own purpose. He also wanted to bend the reader to his will. He shunned cleverness, but none the less, cultivated a style, even if he succeeded in persuading himself that it was as unobvious as the style of Swift—which it certainly was not.

xvi

It is evident from the foregoing examples that style is suspect. But it is also evident that all styles, questionable though some of them may be, are not equally undesirable. What Conrad feared was verbal attitudinising, dandyism, cleverness, and he thus aspired to, but never achieved, the brilliant reporting of Guy de Maupassant. There is much to be said for the aspiration, especially if, as T. E. Hulme observed, 'all styles are only means of subduing the reader.' If it is the business of a reader not to be subdued, as I believe it is, then all aggressive styles are bad, except for the reader who is a literary connoisseur or a psychologist. The best style is unobvious, and as free from attitudinising as from ornament, everything sacrificed to clarity, the reader being left free to form his own opinion of what is offered to him, as in the work of Jonathan Swift, which is in the front rank of all writings. An aggressive style is like high-powered salesmanship, and it generates suspicions similar to those known in business circles as 'sales-resistance', because it seeks to persuade you against your will. Writers who strut and shout are offensive for other reasons. Emphasis is impudence. Thinking aloud is bad manners. To be dominated by a book, even a good book, is like being bossed by a servant, or a canvasser—or a propagandist.

But all style is neither deliberate nor ostentatious. There is a style which is innate, expressed in form rather than in manner; peculiar to a man, bone of his bone, flesh of his flesh, and even if the character of his artistry is mannered, it is not lightly to be ignored, provided that manner and theme have meaning and balance. Edward Dowden had some such idea in mind when he said 'manner is matter of a fine kind, and to have enriched the world with a new style is to have opened a new set of human organs to new sources of feeling.'[2]

[1] *Notes on Life and Letters* (1921), 41.   [2] *Fragments from Old Letters* (1914), 85.

xvii

An author reveals himself in all his works and methods: perhaps least of all in deliberate portraits of himself. When you start writing about yourself, that is, when you admit to yourself and others that you are writing about yourself (but you are always writing about yourself) you are in imminent danger of writing about someone else, someone you think you were, or someone you think you are. Thus all such personal and intimate records are likely to be misleading, and the franker they are the further they tend to stray from reality. The inevitable desire to exaggerate or to subtilise ultimately turns all autobiographers into liars. Some disguise themselves by overstatement, others by understatement. An author may feel that he has exposed too much of himself, and he will adopt such disguises as obscurities, subtleties, opaque symbols, or even metaphors. Again he may resort to an apparently slavish or meticulous insistence upon facts and documentary evidence, or to the pose of a rollicking carelessness or a humorous obliquity.

Literature is largely autobiographical because confession or exhibitionism of some sort is inevitable. The desire to write is well-named *cacoethes scribendi*, for writing is not only scratching on paper, it is scratching the consciousness which itches for relief. When we write we have a disposition to scratch, and just as most people prefer to scratch in private so we seek to disguise our literary scratchings by writing in symbols or cyphers. If Samuel Pepys had made his confessions in a novel, instead of in a diary written in cypher, he would have used the camouflage of ambiguity—or braggart frankness. Many autobiographies are disguises even when they seem to be most flagrantly exhibitionistic. The autobiographer is taking part in a masquerade, dressing up, exhibiting himself not as himself, but as he fancies himself or as he would have you fancy him. Every autobiography is a *roman à clef* about the author.

An autobiography can be enjoyed if it is enjoyable, that is if it is well written, witty, profound, instructive, but it can only be judged as a self-portrait by comparison with the author's less personal performances and the portraits of him drawn by others. The present fashion for autobiographies does not indicate an outbreak of morbid exhibitionism, but a perfectly normal desire to dress up. Disguises are being adopted not abandoned. It is not more than once or twice in an era that an autobiographer desires or achieves nudism.

xviii

One of the reasons why autobiographers usually adopt the disguise of fiction is the common prejudice against talking about oneself. The prejudice persists in spite of the fact that the best talkers rarely do anything else, for most people enjoy talking about themselves once they have got over the initial shyness, and the majority who resist the temptation, from caution or cowardice, adopt a superior attitude towards the others. Most of us are probably frustrated egotists in this respect, and, incidentally, that may explain some of the popularity of autobiographies and memoirs. Almost any kind of self-confession can find readers, although there are few masterpieces in this class of literature.[1] All but the most inspired autobiographies are dull, because the style of an author is crabbed by knowledge of the prejudice against talking about oneself. They recall the atmosphere of a West End club where conversation is stifled by the legend of the club bore. Where the clubman becomes dull, the autobiographer tries to be bright. But brightness or smartness is no longer a substitute for self-revelation. An autobiography should be artless rather than artful, and the test of its validity is consistency with a central unchanging self, or point of view. Insistence upon objectivisation is often no more than morbid diffidence. The objective in art is protective like manners.

xix

The would-be autobiographer is further obstructed by the innate difficulties of self-exposition. It is not easy to talk truthfully about yourself, however sincere you may be. The scientist, with all his reticences and provisoes, may allow himself more latitude in expression because he knows he will not be charged with seeing only himself. The man of letters is not so confident. He may see further than the man of science but he is never wholly free of the consciousness that what he sees are phases of himself. Self-deception thus invariably dogs the steps of self-expression. Dramatisation involves exaggeration, and the more sensitive and introspective the writer the more he is inclined to enlarge upon his experiences, both internal and external.

[1] 'I wish we had diaries of the lives of half the unknown men that have lived.' Edward Fitzgerald, 19th November, 1833, *Letters*, Ed. Wright (1889), 22.

205

The habit is confirmed directly in Tolstoy's confessional works and indirectly in his novels. He is fond of giving a highly-coloured version of the sins of his youth and young manhood, and in his later years of commenting on them with an even more highly-coloured sense of sin. Recollecting those moral lapses he feels the 'torments of hell'. The 'whole abomination' of his past life 'poisons' his 'existence'. These confessions do not deceive careful observers of Tolstoy's life and art, notably among them his biographer, Paul Biryukov, who knew him intimately. Tolstoy, he says, 'wanted to convict himself, to punish himself for his past sins, and to do penance in public.' He recognises 'a touch of exaggeration' in these confessions. But 'in spite of exaggerations which we need not believe', Tolstoy was tormented throughout his life by the memory of youthful sins acting upon a 'moral consciousness' of so high a standard that it 'lit up his past life', revealing the 'stains in it . . . with peculiar vividness'.[1]

Exaggerated presentation is familiar to those who have experience of the confessional. Roman Catholic priests and officers of the Salvation Army know how to discount the statements of their penitents; the reader must also learn how to assess at their true value the confessions of authors. He must be able to separate pure gold from pinchbeck, to strip the exhibitionist of all lingering concessions to habit and custom, all remaining love of pose and instinct towards mimicry. But this stripping process is not negative. The parts you cut away in order to reveal what your author thought he was revealing are still a part of him, and necessary to a proper assessment once their relationship to the inner phenomena is understood. It should never be forgotten that most autobiographers are merely peeping at themselves: peeping at themselves round corners and through keyholes, and many of them are scared at what they see. Some out of politeness temper the wind to themselves and their readers by veiled references and other subterfuges. Thus that apostle and practitioner of frankness, Havelock Ellis, tried, in his autobiography, as he admits and as every other autobiographer must, to find a personal way of telling his own life, a way that is 'sincere without being crude, a way that tells all that is essential to tell and yet leave many things to be read, clearly enough by intelligent readers, between the lines'.[2]

[1] *Tolstoi's Love Letters with a Study on the Autobiographical Elements in Tolstoi's Works.* Trans. S. S. Koteliansky and Virginia Woolf (1923), 121.
[2] *My Life*, Havelock Ellis (1940), xiii.

xx

Nor are biographies as disinterested as their authors sometimes suppose. Every biography is inevitably an account of the biographer apropos of the subject. The biographer imagines he is an impartial seeker after truth and so he is, but in trying to portray the truth about another, he reveals the truth about himself. Johnson's *Lives of the Poets* is an obvious example of a great writer being unconsciously yet flagrantly subjective in an age which desired first and last to objectivise its ideas and observations. There have been many examples since, and some writers are not only conscious of what they have done, but frankly admit it. G. K. Chesterton's study of *Browning* is an instance. 'I will not say that I wrote a book on Browning', he confessed in his *Autobiography*, 'but I wrote a book on love, liberty, poetry, my own views on God and Religion (highly undeveloped), and various theories of my own about optimism and pessimism and the hope of the world; a book in which the name of Browning was introduced from time to time, I might almost say with considerable art, or at any rate with some decent appearance of regularity. There were very few biographical facts in the book, and those were nearly all wrong. But there is something buried somewhere in the book; though I think it is rather my boyhood than Browning's biography.' In spite of paradox; which is one of Chesterton's chief disguises this passage may be taken literally. We may believe that Chesterton's *Browning*, like *The Man who was Thursday* and *The Napoleon of Notting Hill*, is a chapter in the intellectual life of Chesterton (and we have his authority for so doing) because he was always conscious of a tendency for his biographies to become autobiographies. He believed that 'a real life of anybody is a very difficult thing to write' because, as he admits immediately afterwards, he himself found it difficult, and he was 'under no illusion' that he could make a good job of his own autobiography. His instinct was sound, for if Chesterton obscured his portraits of Browning and Blake, he also obscures his portrait of himself. The real G.K.C. is to be found in the biographies, essays and stories rather than in the autobiography.

207

CHAPTER XI

SELF-SEEKING IN FICTION

'Is there any other book read but *Rhoda*? And is not that admired because it shows everybody what they like best?—their own faces in the glass...'—MRS. PIOZZI, 11, xii, 1815, *Autobiography* (1861), ii, 136.

'The fictions, and thousand-and-one Arabian Nights, promulgated as fictions, what are they at bottom but this, things that are in thee, though only images of things?'—THOMAS CARLYLE (1836), *Miscellanies* (1888), vi, 82.

'Every writer, consciously or unconsciously, puts himself into his novels, and exhibits his own character even more distinctly than that of his heroes.'—LESLIE STEPHEN, *Hours in a Library*, 1874, i, 95.

'All the characters that we create are but copies of ourselves.'—W. SOMERSET MAUGHAM, Pref. *Cakes and Ale* (1940).

---

i

Novelists invariably and involuntarily write about others apropos of themselves. Some novelists are aware of it. They know that although the 'good novelist' has many models, 'he is himself his most versatile model and can serve for giant or dwarf; he samples all the portions of himself, puts on all the costumes, tries on all the wigs. Line by line he asks questions and answers them, loves and hates himself, attacks and defends himself.'[1] E. M. Forster says that a novel is based upon evidence plus an 'unknown quantity' which is the 'temperament of the novelist'

[1] Georges Duhamel, *In Defence of Letters*. Trans. Bozman (1938), 116.

and that 'unknown quantity always modifies the effect of the evidence, and sometimes transforms it entirely'.[1] A novelist of a younger generation narrows down this subjectivity to 'the average successful novelist' who is 'a more receptive and probably more exhibitionist specimen of the average man with the gift of the gab on paper'.[2] But once admit a temperament with power to transform the evidence and autobiographical action is inevitable.[3] This is more obvious in some novelists than in others, and it is particularly evident in the work of modern writers of fiction, many of whom do not disguise the subjective character of their work.

The pretence on the part of the novelist and the belief on the part of unskilled readers that a novel is no more than a story with only an impersonal relation to the writer has been disturbed by recent practice. A story can still be read for its own sake but a growing number of readers with no actual training in psychology has become aware of something behind the story. The attitude is not in itself new, but intensive criticism and analytical biography have created a new point of view from which it is seen that a writer's attitude towards life born of his own beliefs and experiences is as much a part of his work—often a more interesting part—as the bare incidents of plot or story. But whether admitted or not, a novel is composed of what an author has felt or experienced. He cannot make bricks without straw and the idea that the imagination can supply him with the raw materials of his fiction is an illusion. Imagination can do no more than help him to select and weld his impressions into novels or stories.[4] By doing so he is both expressing and satisfying a common need. He is feeding the hunger of human beings for information about each other. There would be no novels if social curiosity did not exist. Gossip is the archetype of the novel.

[1] *Aspects of the Novel* (1927), 65. [2] Richard Aldington, *Times Lit. Sup.*, 2nd July, 1938. [3] Edward Thomas pointed out that Lavengro 'has no value as a record of facts. It is a picture of a man revealing himself by his attitude towards his childhood and youth'. *Life and Letters of Edward Thomas*, John Moore, (1939), 316. [4] 'The short story of Tchekov was an innovation in literature. The immediate consciousness remains the criterion, and the method is based on a selection of those glimpses of the reality which in themselves possess a peculiar vividness, and by virtue of this vividness appear to have a peculiar significance. . . . To present such episodes with a minimum of rearrangement, as far as possible to eliminate the mechanism of invention, was Tchekov's aim. This is not to suggest that Tchekov in vented nothing; but his constant effort was to reduce the part of invention. He strove to link moments of perception, rather than to expand the perception by invention.' J. Middleton Murry, *Discoveries* (1924), 142–3.

It says what 'we say to ourselves in addition to what we say to one another.[1]

Whether the novelist is philosophically or sociologically or theologically minded he can do no more than record the reactions of human beings to the conditions he finds them in or imposes upon them. For many years moralists have suspected and denounced this kind of narrative and even novelists have sometimes doubted the authenticity of their own art.[2] Quite recently H. G. Wells, who looks upon literature as documentation,[3] has seen reason to doubt whether the novel would have any great importance in the intellectual life of a future which will presumably demand closer contact with reality and a more realistic assessment of personalities and affairs. Already 'we are moving towards a greater freedom of truthful comment upon individuals', and in that trend there would seem to be hope, for if the novel survives 'it will become more frankly caricature—comment upon personalities and social phases—than at present'. But even so he is in doubt and inclines to the belief that the novel will dwindle and die out and be replaced by more searching and outspoken biography or autobiography.[4] To some extent this is prediction after the event, for recent tendencies are in that direction. Novels have tended to become commentaries on social affairs, both personal and political; and biographies and autobiographies are often, as in Wells's own *Experiment in Autobiography*, as 'searching and outspoken' as law or good manners will permit. The novel, in fact, is becoming more biographical as biography encroaches upon the domain of fiction.

ii

Impartiality is never more than a mask, and often an ill-fitting mask causing discomfort to the wearer, as in the case of Flaubert.

[1] It is surprising to find Somerset Maugham upholding the opinion that 'neither an author's character nor his life has anything to do with the reader, who is concerned only with his works' (*Books and You*, 64) when we know, and he knows, that an author is explaining, hiding, or exhibiting himself in those works. [2] 'A modern novelist is half-ashamed of his art; he disclaims earnestly any serious purpose; his highest aim is to amuse his readers and his greatest boast that he amuses them by honourable or at least by harmless means. Leslie Stephen, 'Richardson's Novels,' *Hours in a Library* (1874), i, 84. [3] See *You Can't Be too Careful* (1941), 109. [4] *Experiment in Autobiography* (1934), ii, 502.

His aesthetic life, and it was the only life he knew, was a constant struggle to objectivise by means of realistic fiction an intractably romantic temperament. He is still popularly accepted as an objective writer (a tribute to his own emphasis, and the advocacy of his disciples), but objectivity with Flaubert was an ambition not an achievement, and at best a mark for an ingrowing sensibility which made living an anxiety and writing a torture. He has been called a martyr of letters, buried alive in literature, and like many martyrs in other walks of life he was a congenital self-torturer. His martyrdom was the result of a sense of inferiority which gave him no rest. More than most authors he doubted the authenticity of the work upon which he happened to be engaged. 'I am not sure at all of writing good things, nor that the book I am dreaming can be well done, which does not prevent me from undertaking it.' But he is impelled to go on by a deep impulse to relieve himself of a spiritual emotional stasis. 'I hope', he exclaims of this particular book, 'to spit into it the gall that is choking me, that is to say, to emit some truths, I hope by this means to *purge myself*, and to be henceforward more Olympian, a quality I lack entirely. Ah! how I should like to admire myself!'[1] His painful endeavours to express and repress himself simultaneously were probably masochistic; his complaints, advertisements. He was not content to work in a frenzy, but he liked to talk about his work, comparing it with an attack of herpes. 'I scratch myself while I cry,' he told George Sand, 'it is both a pleasure and a torture at the same time.' Yet he can never do what he wants to do (which, incidentally, was the impossible), because 'one does not choose one's subjects, they force themselves on one'.[2]

This confession was forced out of Flaubert by George Sand who had taunted him with groaning about the work he enjoyed and of devoting to it a passion for which she probably felt she could have found other uses: 'In spite of what you say about it, art could well be your sole passion, and your shutting yourself up, at which I mourn like the silly that I am, your state of pleasure.'[3] But whatever the cause of his passionate attachment to letters, the difficulties were imposed upon himself by the effort to disguise his opinions and mask his real attitude towards life. 'I do not think that the novelist ought to express his own opinion on the things of this world. He can communicate it, but I do not like him to say it . . . I limit myself, then, to declaring things as they appear to me, to expressing

[1] Gustave Flaubert to George Sand, *The George Sand—Gustave Flaubert Letters*. Trans. Aimee L. McKenzie (1922), 281.   [2] *Ib*. 116.   [3] *Ib*. 115.

what seems to be true. And the devil take the consequences . . .'[1]
Flaubert strove after an impersonal realism but the repressed
romantic was always hitting back. It gave him no peace. His realism
was a protest and a disguise. He is 'bursting with anger and
restrained indignation . . . and choking with convictions. But . . .
the artist should not manifest anything of his own feelings, and . . .
the artist should not appear any more in his own work than God in
nature. The man is nothing, the work is everything'.[2]

iii

It is not easy to say exactly when readers first began to understand
that fiction had an egoistic basis, but it is certain that familiarity
with the Russian novel accelerated the process. As late as the
Nineteen Twenties it was possible for Middleton Murry to assert in
an introduction to two of Dostoevsky's stories, that up to then the
public had found it 'difficult to conceive' that a novelist 'should be
anything but a teller of stories. . . . That he should be a philosopher
in the sense that his work should be the profound expression of his
attitude towards life; that this attitude should decide the manner in
which he presents his experiences; and finally that only by virtue of
the passion which the problem rather than the fact of life awakens
in his soul is he worthy to be called a great novelist—these are yet
far from being the commonplaces of criticism that they should be'.[3]
A fuller appreciation of Dostoevsky and other Russian novelists has
done much to bring about the change of attitude which has since
taken place. The processes of what ultimately became a more or less
open use of fiction for personal expression were gradual up to
Turgenev whose delicate artistry wore a carefully designed mask,
and Tolstoy who used the novel and the short story openly to express
his own inner conflicts and their torments, as well as to propagate
the prophylactic ideas which he endeavoured to practise.

With Dostoevsky the novel became a demonstration of personal
struggle between the inner consciousness of the author and the
outward circumstances of his life. 'He first explored the subconscious
hell which seethes in the depths of each man's soul, and whose
waters have since been charted with so much ingenuity by the
psycho-analysts.'[4] In the earliest English study of this novelist,

[1] *Ib.* 98–9. [2] *Ib.* 348. [3] Intro. Dostoevsky's *Pages from the Journal of an Author* [n.d.], vii. [4] Edward Hallett Carr, *Dostoevsky* (1931), 256.

212

Middleton Murry points out that 'Dostoevsky cannot be understood from his letters; to understand them demands first an understanding of his work. Without that, they are obscure; with it, almost superfluous. So it is with his life. There is not a single fact in it that cannot be deduced from his books; he lived in them and for them; they alone contain the anatomy of this tormented soul'.[1] The life of this tormented soul has naturally attracted the psycho-analytical critics, who have confirmed Murry's opinion. One of them goes so far as to say that 'What is especially valuable in him is the fact that it is impossible to draw a line between Dostoevsky the man, and Dostoevsky the artist, since all his art was an organic and necessary result of his actual inner experience, and not of the imagination of a littérateur.'[2] That remark is supported by the subsequent publication of documents relating to the life of Dostoevsky. But it could be applied equally to all novelists other than those who are mere hirelings operating as men-of-letters. The history of the novel is to some considerable extent the record of a struggle to put a man in the place of the littérateur, and in the latest phase of that conflict the leader has been Dostoevsky.

Most of the critics of Dostoevsky have acknowledged his indebtedness to himself for many if not most of the leading ideas and themes of his novels. It is not always easy to differentiate the subjective from the objective even in so subjective a novelist. André Gide, who needs no conversion to subjectivity either in Dostoevsky or himself, feels that it is 'imprudent' and 'even dishonest' to impute to an author the thoughts expressed by the characters in his novels; at the same time he recognises that the novel was Dostoevsky's medium of personal expression and that he had a trick even of using 'a colourless individual to formulate one of his cherished truths'. 'We seem to hear him speak from the lips of a secondary character in *The Eternal Husband* when the "malady of the age" is mentioned.' The book from which this extract is taken is a 'spiritual portrait' of Dostoevsky composed of materials taken from his novels.[3]

Edward Hallett Carr, who takes a more scientific view of literature, also sees danger in 'seeking autobiographical material in professed works of fiction'.[4] Yet in his cautious study of Dostoevsky he admits several instances of the novel being used to express the author's

---

[1] *Fyodor Dostoevsky: A Critical Study* (1916), Pref. viii–ix. [2] *Dostoevsky and his Creation: A Psycho-Critical Study*. Janko Lavrin (1920), 189. [3] André Gide, *Dostoevsky*, English Translation (1925), 197–8. [4] Edward Hallett Carr, *Dostoevsky* (1931), 121.

ideas or to resolve and soothe his personal dilemmas. He is aware of
the widespread use of the novel for the propagation of religious
and social theories, particularly in Russia: 'Practically every great
Russian novel of the classical period was more˙ or less a *roman à
thèse*. Even if we ignore novels like those of Herzen and Cherny-
shevsky, written on a specific propagandist thesis, the moral purpose
is almost as clearly marked in Turgenev or Tolstoy as in Dostoevsky.
. . . It would not have occurred to Dostoevsky to deny that his novels
were written with a purpose. One of the unrealised ambitions of his
later years was to write a Russian *Candide*; and if ever a story
deserved to be branded as a *roman à thèse*, it is Voltaire's masterpiece.'[1]

An early instance of this trend in Dostoevsky is the projection of
his own love of gambling into the hero of *The Gambler*, 'whose
utterances are autobiographical in almost every detail,'[2] and in *A
Raw Youth* there is a further attempt to excuse to himself the
disappointments of games of chance which he had sought to ration-
alise by the familiar use of a 'system'.[3] Again, the famous correspondence between Aglaya and Nastasya Philippovna in *The Idiot*
was based upon an imagined exchange of letters between
Dostoevsky's wife and his mistress.[4] The character of Marmeladov
in *Crime and Punishment*, particularly in its morbid self-pity is
drawn from the author's experience of that weakness, and 'the
sombre background of *Crime and Punishment* is but a dim reflection
of the black gloom of despair in which its tortured pages were
written.'[5] The theme of *The Possessed* is generally acknowledged to
be subjective and Prof. Carr adds that 'there is no reasonable doubt
that Shatov is a self-portrait, or it would be fairer to say a self-
idealisation of the author.'[6]

One of the principal themes of Dostoevsky's novels is that of the
'double' which every man carries within him. It is the idea put into
melodramatic form by Robert Louis Stevenson in *Dr. Jekyll and
Mr. Hyde,* and could be extended to cover most human activities,
as in the Hegel-cum-Marxian doctrine that every social system
contains the elements of its own destruction. Dostoevsky had a
'double' of whom he was morbidly conscious, and he used the novel
as a means of escape from its disturbing attentions. Carr agrees that
the 'double' is a part of the technical equipment of the writer, but
his citations of duality from Novalis, Alfred de Musset, Gautier and

---

[1] *Ib.* 188–9. [2] *Ib.* 162. [3] *Ib.* 162. [4] *Ib.* 160. [5] *Ib.* 145. [6] *Ib.* 224.

Baudelaire suggest that the association is not entirely technical. The subjectivity of poetry is now widely admitted, even that of poets less obviously subjective than Alfred de Musset and Charles Baudelaire, and there is no valid reason for exempting fiction from the same tendency, especially if it is realised, as it ought to be, that fiction at its best approximates to the condition of poetry in all but form—and sometimes even in that. Carr, however, admits that Dostoevsky may have adopted 'a literary conception of western origin . . . not only for literary purposes, but to introduce some semblance of order into his diagnosis of his own character'.[1] The assumption that he was sufficiently interested in the diagnosis of his own character and its relationship with his writing proves rather than disproves the presence of an autobiographical element in his novels. The conclusion is supported by the statement that the 'double' was 'a literary theme invoked first to diagnose a disease, and then to point a moral',[2] on the ground that interests cannot be segregated from their causes. The cause in this case was Dostoevsky's impulsion to identify his own unrest with the psychological experiences of the Russian people, and not solely to report and expound those experiences.

iv

It would be more difficult for a defender of the faith in objective fiction to deny the autobiographical character of Tolstoy's works, for, unlike Dostoevsky, he has made it easy for his readers to compare parallel passages in the novels, diaries and letters. In addition to that, most of his biographers and critics have commented upon the close association of art and ideas even in his least didactic works. Biryukov, his friend and biographer, goes so far as to say that if there were 'no facts to draw upon, we could, by arranging Tolstoy's works in chronological order, write his biography from them alone', for there is 'not a single work . . . in which traces of autobiography are not to be found'.[3] As in Dostoevsky you find in him a sense of duality and the desire to identify his ideals with the Russian people, with the difference that Tolstoy is conscious also of a universal identity. When he dreams and suffers it is not only for Russia but for mankind.

[1] *Ib.* 261. [2] *Ib.* 262. [3] 'Autobiographical Elements in L. N. Tolstoi's Works,' in *Tolstoi's Love Letters*. Paul Biryukov. Trans. S. S. Koteliansky and Virginia Woolf (1923), 73.

Tolstoy used dramatisation, projection, and all the other machinery of subjectivity, but it was only in his later phases that he became deliberately propagandist. The autobiographical element in his earlier novels is unconscious; and he comes so close to the upholders of art for art's sake as to repudiate any suggestion that he has drawn characters in *War and Peace* from living models. His attitude reveals the inevitability of subjectivity and the folly of trying to insulate it from what is called 'creative art'. And as Tolstoy admittedly, though 'unconsciously and unpremeditatedly', gave names to certain characters which closely resemble those of people he knew, so also we may assume, with Biryukov, that he created characters without being conscious of the mimetic processes which ruled his pen. Biryukov concludes that he 'created characters, and it seemed to him that he was creating something perfectly new that had never existed before, and yet portraits of living men came from his pen'.

It is not certain when he became consciously autobiographical, but if, as he himself might have claimed, there was no premeditated reflection of the two sides of his own character in the characters of Andrei Bolkonsky and Pierre Besukov (*War and Peace*, 1865-9), there can be little doubt that he knew what he was doing when he reproduced the spiritual crisis through which he was passing in the soul of Levin (*Anna Karenina*, 1875-7), and when he put 'his whole soul' into Nekhlyudov (*Resurrection*, 1899); and although, as we may readily believe, the characters in *The Kreutzer Sonata* (1890) are not drawn from life, the fear of sex which that deliberately didactic work reveals, is a Tolstoyan obsession, and would not have become the basis of the last and most widely debated of his advocacies if he had not believed that married life trespassed upon his activities as a prophet.[1] *The Kreutzer Sonata* is the result of a defect in Tolstoy and he found comfort in passing it on to humanity.

v

The difference between Dostoevsky and his successors is that Dostoevsky produced his novels under the impression that he was objectively revealing the Russian soul, which he identified with the soul of humanity struggling to free itself from the tyrannies of time and circumstances, whereas the modern subjective novelist is conscious that he is exploiting himself, often without even the

[1] See *The Life of Tolstoy: The Later Years*, Aylmer Maude (1910), 399.

excuse of an altruistic motive. It is doubtful, for instance, if Leonid Andreyev would have written anything unless he had been free, like H. G. Wells, to project his immediate experiences into his work. One of his favourite methods was to transmute the substance of a discussion (and he was always discussing) into a novel or story. His fictions are thus analogies of his intellectual and emotional encounters. When his collected works appeared in 1915 he told Maxim Gorki that 'beginning with *Bergamot*' all his work was to a large extent the history of their friendship.[1] But long before the birth of modern subjective fiction, writers were beginning to be aware of themselves as models or raw material for their novels.

And this characteristic was not confined to Russian fiction; Disraeli looked upon his novels as starting points for the next act in the life-long drama of Benjamin Disraeli. 'A novel was for him a means of analysis, the testing of an attitude, the rehearsal, as it were, of a political policy.'[2] It was not, as with some novelists, a substitute for life, but rather an aid to living, a tonic as well as what he called a 'safety-valve' for his passions. 'I wish to act what I write,' he said. On the other hand a novel may be compensatory, an attempt to live by the proxy of fiction what the author has failed to accomplish in real life. Anthony Trollope is convinced that Charlotte Brontë must 'have been in love with some Paul when she wrote *Villette*, and have been determined to prove to herself that she was capable of loving one whose exterior circumstances were mean and in every way unprepossessing'.[3]

The subjective character of the novel is less obvious to Anthony Trollope himself, although even he used fiction for the expression of his own preferences, and the release of his own personality. He never, for instance, abandoned the didactic attitude of his period even when he strove most to disguise it, and didacticism is always subjective. In his later life he took some pains to make his reader understand how frequently he had used characters for the expression of his own political or social convictions. 'They have been as real to me', he said, 'as free trade was to Mr. Cobden, or the dominion of a party to Mr. Disraeli; and as I have not been able to speak from the benches of the House of Commons, or to thunder from platforms, or to be efficacious as a lecturer, they have served me as safety-valves by which to deliver my soul.'[4]

[1] *Reminiscences of Leonid Andreyev* (1931), Maxim Gorki, 63. [2] André Maurois, *Disraeli* (Penguin Edition) (1937), 138. [3] *Autobiography*, Ed. Sadleir (1923), 250. [4] *Ib.* 165.

Every novelist either consciously or unconsciously projects himself into character and plot, and some go even further by turning a novel into a pictorial chart of the whole or part of their lives, often with results that are surprising and beneficial to themselves. Anne Douglas Sedgwick provides us with an example from her own experience. 'My books, I know, when they are at all good, are a phase of myself,' she said, 'and perhaps a deeper phase than I am able to express in my personal capacity.'[1] And she tells another correspondent that the writing of the novel, *Paths of Judgment*, had been of 'enormous value' to her 'apart from any intrinsic worth or originality . . . for it's being like an objectivising of all my thoughts, all my fears and faiths: holding them all at arm's length, making them visible, and really grasping them—or, at least, getting more hold of them than I've done before'.[2]

Charles Dickens was an unabashed subjectiviser; his histrionic personality dominates the stage in all his works. The greater part of *David Copperfield* is frankly autobiographical, and the love incidents, first with Dora and later with Agnes, represent the two phases of the author's passion, the real idealised because it was a failure, and the ideal sentimentalised because it was never consummated. In the Preface to this work, Dickens reveals himself to his readers more than in any other of his introductions. He confides to them that he was so overcome with emotion when he had finished *David Copperfield* that he 'was in danger of wearying the reader with personal confidences and private emotions'. When those words were written little was known of his domestic life, and it was assumed that they referred solely to the natural feelings of an author 'dismissing some portion of himself into the shadowy world,' and who was watching the 'creatures of his brain going from him for ever'. But we now know that they masked an unfulfilled dream of happiness. And when he said: 'Like many fond parents, I have in my heart of hearts a favourite child. And his name is David Copperfield,'[3] he was consoling himself with the memory of what might have been. But in spite of his need for personal expositions and his addiction to dramatic domination, there are hints throughout his works that he was also aware of the need of the reader for self-expression. A good example occurs in *Great Expectations* (chap. vii) when Joe Gargery and Pip discuss education:

[1] *Anne Douglas Sedgwick: A portrait in Letters* chosen by Basil de Selincourt (1926), 115.　[2] *Ib.* 72.　[3] *David Copperfield* ('Charles Dickens' edition), Pref.

'Give me', said Joe, 'a good book, or a good newspaper, and sit me down before a good fire, and I ask no better. Lord!' he continued, after rubbing his knees a little, 'when you *do* come to a J and a O, and says you, "here at last is a J – O, Joe," how interesting reading is'. Helping his readers to this sort of discovery was the essence of Dickens's great popularity.

vi

George Meredith, by his own admission, was 'cursed with a croak':[1] a novelist with a grievance, in fact, with two grievances. The first and most persistent, like that of so many writers, derived from the maladjustments of his early life; and the second from disappointment at the slow progress of his works towards widespread appreciation. He croaked about other things as well but these two were the chief and they provided him with themes and variations for several of his novels. Meredith was both snob and prig: he considered himself superior to his family and his books superior to most of the novels then before the public. He fretted himself on his pet grievances, and sought relief from the irritation they caused him by transmuting them into fiction. In *Evan Harrington*, which is a thinly disguised record of the chief repercussions of his own early life, 'Meredith was actuated by a petty and long-brooded personal animus against his relatives.'[2] The snobbery which made him ashamed of his descent from a tailor was characteristic of his period, and the struggles of deserving or cunning young men or women to climb from a lower into a higher class, which he was fond of depicting, was a stock theme of Victorian fiction.

The family relationship seemed to arouse in him all manner of hidden hatreds and irritations which found expression in a variety of ways throughout the novels, always for his own satisfaction, for these incompatibilities were unknown to all but his intimate friends and members of his family. Meredith's repression of his private affairs aggravated an unrest which found expression in *Evan Harrington*, *Harry Richmond* and *Beauchamp's Career*. But while he resented his descent from a shopkeeper he revealed a hidden admiration for his grandfather, Melchizedeck Meredith, the naval tailor of Portsmouth who rode to hounds and was received by the county families, and is immortalised as the 'Great Mel', in

[1] In a letter to Robert Louis Stevenson, 16th April, 1879. *Letters* (1912), i, 297. [2] S. M. Ellis, *George Meredith* (1919), 139.

Evan Harrington, and as 'Richmond-Roy', in *Harry Richmond*. It was not until the publication of *George Meredith, his Life and Friends in Relation to his Work* in 1919, by his kinsman, S. M. Ellis, that the subjective character of so much of Meredith's work became generally known.

At the same time his pride and sensitiveness must be obvious to all fit readers of his novels and poems and it does not require much reading between the lines and behind the words to discover a self-concern which finds expression, this time unconsciously, in *The Egoist*. Sir Willoughby Patterne is not George Meredith, but Sir Willoughby's attitude towards life is much the same as his. Temperamentally imperious, Meredith was sensitive to the external resistance such an attitude would create:

> *In tragic life, God wot,*
> *No villain need be! Passions spin the plot:*
> *We are betrayed by what is false within.*

These words from *Modern Love*, the sonnet-sequence on the crash of his first marriage, apply equally to all the disharmonies of his life. But his readers have no cause for complaint for if he had not been betrayed by what was within himself Meredith might have been no more than a nature poet of the second rank. As it is we have the novels, and the Meredithian theory of the Comic Spirit which can be applied profitably to himself, and we can indulge in one of those mental smiles approved by him when we contemplate this philosophic novelist hugging the family legend that the Great Mel came of unrecorded aristocratic stock. Claiming that he wrote for an 'acute but honourable minority', he never ceased to grumble because the majority neglected him. His struggle for integrity was equally comic, in the Meredithian sense. He capitalised his humble origin in fiction; revenged himself on the obtuse majority by adopting an increasingly crabbed and difficult style. The climax of his resentment was reached when he tried to denationalise himself by an act of wishful genealogy which, unsupported by any evidence, turned him into a Celt of Welsh origin, without reducing his appreciation of English character and the English scene, and indeed, most English things except the alleged English neglect of George Meredith. But in spite of the unpopularity of his writings Meredith managed to live the sort of literary life which many more successful writers might envy. He had numerous friends, was generally appreciated by his peers, and died at a ripe old age the recognised head of his profession and a member of the Order of Merit. Yet although he knew that 'a man who hopes to be popular must think from the mass' and not attempt to follow 'the vagaries of his own brain', he followed his own vagaries and never ceased to grumble at the small popular demand for his works. He never stooped to conquer, but he allowed resentment to crab his style, for instead of writing down to the public he deliberately and spitefully wrote above its head. The tortuosities of Meredith's style are often acts of defiance: he was asserting his independence by wilful originality.

vii

Henry James is a more obvious example of the subjective novelist, and he has left elaborate explanations of all his novels and how they came to be written, which provide direct confirmation of his egoism. In all these expositions of a method which is so peculiarly his own, the fundamental condition revealed is a conscious attempt to recover and fix particular memories, to cultivate what he calls 'the sense of the past'. I say conscious because he knew what he was doing: his novels are as autobiographical as his autobiographies. There are many points in both where he crystallises this passion for the past in a phrase or a sentence, and he was equipped by nature with a tireless and self-registering memory which constant practice made a perfect means of implementing the close-grained introspection of his novels. 'The more I squeeze the sponge of memory the more its stored secretions flow.'[1]

Experiences as ordinarily understood meant little to him. His life was almost without action even if we take into account the fact that he travelled from the New World to the Old and to various observation points in Europe and Great Britain, before he settled down at Rye in Sussex where he spent the last quarter of his life harvesting memories. 'The truth is', he tells us, 'much less in the wealth of my experience than in the tenacity of my impression, the fact that I have lost nothing of what I saw and that though I can't now quite divide the total into separate occasions the various items surprisingly swarm for me.'[2] He often expounds this condition of his genius and he puts it most clearly in the introduction to *The American*, where he says: 'I have ever, in general, found it difficult to write of places under too immediate an impression—the impres-

---

[1] *A Small Boy and Others* (1913), 66. [2] *Ib.* 108.

sion that prevents standing off and allows neither space nor time for perspective. The image has had for the most part to be dim if the reflexion was to be, as is proper for the reflexion, both sharp and quiet: one has a horror, I think, artistically, of agitated reflexions.'[1] Things and experiences must be merged into his personality before they become real. He can only describe (that is, for him, create) what he has brooded over in tranquillity.

He likes the past for its own sake, and not always his own past, nor is it merely a sentimental passion. He is sensitive to what Nietzsche called 'the pathos of distance' and seeks to reduce it by the reconstruction of scenes, events, and persons of the past by an effort of the will capable of infinite patience and laboriousness. Other times soothe as well as fascinate, but only when imaginative reconstruction helps him to enjoy the illusion of permanence. 'Rich and strange is the pleasure of finding our only way to be sure of it,' he says, apropos of an old aunt who typifies for him the American past. 'It was the Past that one touched in her. The American past of a preponderant unthinkable queerness; and great would seem the fortune of helping on the continuity.'[2] But it would be a mistake to suppose him capable of any very profound liking for the continuity of national characteristics whether American or British. His concern for the past was a method of conquering time.

The habit began when he was a boy: 'The only form of riot or revel ever known to me would be that of the visiting mind,' and he was 'quite fantastically aware' of a tendency to 'dawdle and gape'. The intensive cultivation of this sense of the past by subtle and minute recollection is essential to his spiritual welfare. His novels record the experiences of a soul in pursuit of the permanent. 'From the moment it is a question of projecting a picture,' he says, 'no particle that counts for memory or is appreciable to the spirit *can* be too tiny, and that experience, in the name of which one speaks, is all compact of them and shining with them.' In manhood as well as boyhood 'almost anywhere would do' to 'receive an impression or an accession, feel a relation or a vibration'. And he came to feel more and more 'that no education avails for the intelligence that doesn't stir in some subjective passion, and that on the other hand almost anything that does so act is educative, however small a figure the process might make in a scheme of training'.[3] He gives the process the useful name of 'retractive vision'.[4]

[1] *The Art of the Novel: Critical Prefaces* (1935), 27.   [2] *A Small Boy and Others* (1913), 133.   [3] *Ib.* 25–27.   [4] *Ib.* 44.

Such an acute sensitiveness to evanescence is morbid and probably the result of some incapacity in the normal function of living. More than one of his interpreters has noted the reflection of an increasing attitude of disappointment in his characters as he grew older. His 'later heroes are always regretting having lived and loved too meagrely', Edmund Wilson observes, and in such characters 'he seems to be dramatising the frustrations of his own life without being quite willing to confess it, without always fully admitting it to himself.' The incompleteness of his own life, his morbid sense of opportunities lost, of promises unfulfilled, are not only reflected in his works, they make those works subconscious prophylactics against his own dilemma.

viii

George Gissing, another example of the consciously subjective novelist, invented little and remembered less. Each of his novels is a reflection of himself and in some measure an attempt to purge himself of the miseries of poverty. He lived and wrote from hand to mouth. When accounting for the depressing atmosphere of his first novel, *Workers in the Dawn*, he said, in a letter to his brother, 'If you knew much of my daily life you would wonder that I write at all, to say nothing of writing cheerfully. But in that book, I have, so to speak, *written off* a whole period of my existence.'[1] In *The Private Papers of Henry Ryecroft*, written during the enjoyment of economic freedom towards the close of his life, he depicts himself as a refugee from the tyranny of Grub Street, but that is not the full story. Gissing's misfortunes began before he tried to double the roles of man-of-letters and literary hack. He was expelled from Owen's College (now Manchester University) for petty theft and a little later in a fit of pique or self-pity he married a prostitute. These lapses were enough to ruin any young life. But Gissing was not a wastrel; he had plenty of courage and his capacity for drudgery in the face of impossible conditions showed that he possessed character. If he had succeeded more quickly in earning a living by his pen he might have recovered sooner from the temperamental errors of his youth, and his novels would have reflected the scholarly calm of Henry Ryecroft surrounded by books in a country cottage instead of the gloom and resentment of a literary hack living precariously in an attic off Tottenham Court Road.

[1] *Letters of George Gissing to Members of his Family* (1926), 72.

ix

I refer here to André Gide, whose influence among French subjectivisers is second only to that of Proust, because of his direct confirmation of the theory expounded above, and also because he is so frankly aware of the psychological processes which help an author to find relief by projecting himself into a fictional character. While writing his autobiography, *Si le grain ne meurt*, he comes to the conclusion that 'intimacy penetration and psychological investigation can in certain respects be pushed further in the Novel even than in Confessions. One is sometimes disturbed in the latter by the "I": there are certain complexities one cannot try to unravel or to reveal without an appearance of complacency'.[1] He finds it easier 'to make a character speak' than to express himself in his own name, and the more easy the more a character differs from him. 'I have written nothing better', he says, 'than the monologues of Lafcadio and the journal of Alissa. In doing this kind of thing I forget who I am, if ever I knew. I become the other person.'[2]

x

There is no more direct contemporary example of this form of self-re-creation than that of George Moore who devoted a long life to self-exposure at first in the romantic and latterly in a more classical form. But in spite of demanding that 'we must stem the desolating tide of subjectivity', he never succeeded in dodging himself. His method was the promotion and exploitation of reverie, and he constantly revised and rewrote his books to weave into them new ideas and impressions of himself as well as to improve a style which was more than usually the man. That style was gradually and laboriously turned into a perfect medium for the expression of reverie. He thought himself into his books. He brooded over them until they flowed full of himself like rivers of dream. He could only remember persons and places after the experience of them had been soaked in his own personality. 'I am cursed with the worst memory for faces on any man of earth. Nevertheless I think I should know you if I were to meet you, but then I have *thought* about you. . . .

[1] *Journal des Faux-Monnayeurs*, 21st November, 1920. Qt. P. Mansell Jones, *French Introspectives* (1937), 112–3. [2] *Ib.* 15th November, 1923, 113.

Until I *see* my subject I cannot write.'[1] The second word emphasised
meant more for him than visualisation. Seeing was all the senses
distilled into a memory which sought to insinuate itself into the thing
or circumstance under contemplation. He once told a friend that
while writing certain passages of Sister Teresa 'he used to feel as
if he were himself a nun'.[2] In fact it has been said that he relied
upon memory and hearsay rather than upon direct observation. He
saw nature through the lens of art. 'Moore's landscapes', said
Wilson Steer, 'are based on pictures rather than nature.'[3] But
withal the George Moore of the confessional books is largely the
result of a dramatised pose. It is George Moore with variations and
the amatory variations are now generally believed to be fictions.
The painter, Jacques-Emile Blanche, who knew him well, 'had
reason to believe' that the love-adventures of Moore 'were all
mental'.[4]

xi

English novelists are seldom frank about the subjective character
of their works; they prefer to acknowledge it in an aside when they
feel impelled to refer to it, but more often the admission is disguised
in an obliquity. H. G. Wells is a notable exception. He has not
hesitated to interpret his life in the light of modern psychology to
make it clear that his art is fundamentally a projection of himself
into novels, stories and sociological essays.[5] At first the process of
compensatory dramatisation was unconscious but it gradually
developed into a deliberate method and for many years it has
continued to dominate his literary output. This subjective character
of his work has always been evident but until the publication of his
extraordinarily frank *Experiment in Autobiography* (1934) its
extent and determination could only have been detected by a reader
with some knowledge of psychology.

He seems to have resented his earlier novels because they were
not as deliberately subjective as they might have been, although
they were fairly obvious, if unconscious, attempts to resolve the
admitted social and emotional handicaps of his own impecunious
upbringing. Those novels 'had their function in their time but their
time has already gone by. . . . They were . . . protests against rigid
restraint and suppression' and 'helped to release a generation from

[1] George Moore to the Marquise Clara Lanza. *Life of George Moore*,
Hone (1936), 175. [2] *Ib.* 403. [3] *Ib.* 205. [4] Jacques-Emile Blanche, *Portraits of a Lifetime* (1937), 137. [5] See Notes.

restriction. . . . Aesthetically they have no great value. No one will ever read them for delight.'[1] He refused latterly to believe even that his early work bore a true approximation to the ideal novel. His 'so-called novels', as he calls them, 'were artless self-revelatory stuff, falling far away from a stately ideal by which they had to be judged.'[2]

As his fictions and essays became more sociological they became more subjective: commentaries upon social conditions apropos of himself. He calls *Mankind in the Making* (1903) the exhortation of a man who has not yet been able to establish, at any point, working contacts for the realisation of his ideas. 'Plainly,' he says, 'he is exhorting himself as well as others. Just to keep going.'[3] In his later books he is fully aware that he is adjusting himself and his ideas to external conditions as well as trying to adjust external conditions to himself. World-saving becomes Wells-saving. Complete awareness of the compensatory character of his work crystallises in the production of *The New Machiavelli*. The circumstances which urged this novel into being were immediate as well as remote. The immediate and precipitating cause was his failure to convert the Fabian Society to his own particular brand of Socialism.

On his own admission he was deeply disappointed at the result of his campaign and found it by no means easy to put an acceptable face on his retreat from the conflict. 'I had', he says, 'to swallow the dose that I had attempted to do something and failed completely. I had to realise that I had no organising ability and no gift for leading or directing people. To make up for that, I told myself I would write all the better.' There is no doubt in his own mind about the result: *The New Machiavelli*, 'with its pose of the deflated publicist in noble retirement, is obviously a compensatory production'.[4] But the Fabian defeat was only the immediate cause. There are remote causes which go back to early days when he was struggling against the conditions imposed upon him whilst employed in a draper's shop where he was an obvious misfit. He traces the history of the mood in the following passage:

'My revolt against the draper's shop was the first appearance of this mood. It was a flight—to a dream of happy learning and teaching in poverty. To a minor extent and with minor dislocation this fugitive mood no doubt recurred but it did not come back again in full force until my divorce. Then it is quite clear that it clothed itself

[1] *Experiment in Autobiography* (1934), 467.   [2] *Ib.* 494.   [3] *Ib.* 655.   [4] *Ib.* 736.

226

in the form of a dream of a life of cheerfully adventurous writing. The concealed element was that my work [as a schoolmaster] was boring me. That divorce was not simply the replacement of one wife by another; it was also the replacement of one way of living by another. It was a break away to a new type of work. I detect all the symptoms of the same flight impulse again about 1909, but then there was not the same complete material rupture with my established life. But *The New Machiavelli* (published in 1911) is quite plainly once more the release of the fugitive urgency, a release completed in imagination if not in fact. I realise now (and the queer thing is that I do realise only now) that the idea of going off somewhere—to Italy in the story—out of the tangle of Fabian disputes, tiresomely self-relevant politics and the routines of literary life, very nearly overwhelmed me in my own proper person, and the story of Remington and Margaret and Isabel is essentially a dramatised wish. I relieved my tension vicariously as Remington. He got out of my world on my behalf—and wrote in lofty tranquillity of politics in the abstract, *à la Machiavelli*, as I desired to do.'[1]

The tension to which he refers expressed itself in a desire to escape from the conditions of his own temperament and environment. The one doubtless reacted upon the other. He diagnoses his condition as claustrophobia, and it is revealed in all his books as an irritation under those conventional and circumstantial restraints which ordinary people bear with fortitude or indifference. Taken together those books form an iliad of adjustments which, beginning with his own complexities, gradually spread out until they embrace the affairs of the whole world. Wells seems to be seeking an ideal simplicity which shall ultimately adjust the conflicts of man and himself as well as those between man and man, and nation and nation. The desire for inward and outward seemliness is finally summed up in the idea of a World State implemented by an Open Conspiracy of men of ability and goodwill. The *Experiment in Autobiography* is a history of this attitude towards life which reaches its climax in *The New Machiavelli* (1911), *The Research Magnificent* (1914), and *William Clissold* (1926). The chief character in each of these works is an image of himself and a dramatisation of his own discontent. The autobiography makes all this clear, and doubly clear in its concluding paragraphs:

'I began this autobiography primarily to reassure myself during

[1] *Ib.* 738–9.

a phase of fatigue, restlessness and vexation, and it has achieved its purpose of reassurance. I wrote myself out of that mood of discontent and forgot myself and a mosquito swarm of bothers in writing about my sustaining ideas. My ruffled *persona* has been restored and the statement of the idea of the modern world-state has reduced my personal and passing irritations and distractions to their proper insignificance. So long as one lives as an individual, vanities, lassitudes, lapses and inconsistencies will hover about and creep back into the picture, but I find nevertheless that this faith and service of constructive world revolution does hold together my mind and will in a prevailing unity, that it makes life continually worth living, transcends and minimises all momentary and incidental frustrations and takes the sting out of the thought of death. The stream of life out of which we rise and to which we return has been restored to dominance in my consciousness, and though the part I play is, I believe, essential, it is significant only through the whole. The Open Conspirator can parallel—or, if you prefer to put it so, he can modernise—the self-identification of the religious mystic: he can say, "personally when I examine myself I am nothing"; and at the same time he can assert, "The Divinity and I are One"; or blending divinity with democratic kingship, "The World-State, cest Moi." '[1]

xii

Such detailed frankness would not have been possible a few years ago when few novelists were more than half aware of their autobiographical confessions and projections. Even so broody a writer as Joseph Conrad believed that he came to literature because he needed an occupation for his leisure rather than to satisfy any need of self-expression;[2] he continuously dramatises himself in the concept of an imaginative hero who is moved to the kind of action which Conrad desired but failed to achieve except in art. To justify that realisation of himself in fiction (for he is a moralist as well as an artist) he sought to prove that the artist was a man of action. Conrad's novels and tales rarely give the impression that they are fictions and nothing more. The overcareful storytelling is threaded with reflections of an ego which was always under self-observation. One figure stands out in all his seascapes and it is the figure of himself. 'The sailing of ships has been for Conrad what the writing

[1] *Ib.* 824–5.　[2] *Joseph Conrad his Mind and Method*, R. L. Megroz (1931), 29.

of books became, a means of externalising the activity of a mind which had a powerful tendency to introspection at the expense of the practical life.'[1]

He was aware of this dichotomy and, as I have shown elsewhere in this book,[2] struggled against it. He knew that 'every novelist must begin by creating for himself a world, great or little', in which he could 'honestly believe', and that 'this world cannot be made otherwise than in his own image' yet he was ready to resent any suggestion that he was not impartial and objective. Edward Garnett, Conrad's oldest friend, discoverer and adviser, risked this displeasure when he pointed out, in a review of *Under Western Eyes*, that the novelist revealed his hatred of the Russians in that work. Conrad showed resentment at once. 'If you seriously think that I have done that', he said, 'you don't know what the accent of hate is. Is it possible that you haven't seen that in this book I am concerned with nothing but ideas, to the exclusion of everything else, with no *arrière pensée* of any kind; or are you like the Italians (and most women) incapable of conceiving that anybody ever should speak with perfect detachment, without some subtle hidden purpose, for the sake of what is said, with no desire of gratifying some small personal spite or vanity.' It may have been Conrad's wish to write with perfect detachment, but he was not always successful in attaining his ideal and even then was not at his best. He was later to put on record, as a consolation for the 'hard slavery of the pen', the advantage 'a novelist has over the workers in other fields of thought . . . in his privilege of freedom—the freedom of expression and the freedom of confessing his own beliefs'.[3]

xiii

The habit of self-revelation in fiction is not confined to professional writers skilled in expressing themselves openly or furtively, still less to exhibitionists who are impelled to self-display by stronger motives. There are idealists, like the author of *John Inglesant*, who use fiction, often again unconsciously, to console themselves for conditions which they dislike yet from which they have benefited. The act is cathartic and relieves a repressed sense of guilt. Shorthouse was a Birmingham business man who lived comfortably at Edgbaston, which to him must have been something

[1] *Ib.* 84.   [2] *Ante*, pp. 191-2.   [3] *Notes on Life and Letters* (1921), 7-8.

of an oasis in the industrial desert called the Black Country. His was a typical example of that Victorian high-mindedness which looked upon beautiful thoughts, a quiet home life, and the pleasures of reading and the arts as legitimate refuges from the turmoil and devastations of an industrial system which had long since gone money-mad and turned whole areas of England into slag-heaps and slums. People of taste who profited by the system ran away from the devastated areas to the unspoilt countryside and some of them earned reputations as men-of-letters or patrons of the fine arts.

Shorthouse belonged to this class. He was a good man and gentle in all his dealings with man and beast, but he was self-satisfied and smug. His wife says that 'many of his descriptions of character are certainly true of himself', and she supports this opinion with extracts from *John Inglesant* (1880), and his lesser known novels, *Blanche, Lady Falaise*, and *The Countess Eve*, most of them favourable to her husband from the point of view of the comfortable classes of the period. Shorthouse projected himself upon the screen of fiction as a 'noble and distinguished' figure with 'an expression of perfect sweetness, combined with steadiness and gravity . . . who followed the good and the beautiful, and avoided instinctively the disgusting and difficult aspects both of life and thought'.[1] He had shut out the disagreeable part of the world from the charming platonic retreat he had made for himself and his friends, and his novels are an attempt to soothe an uneasy conscience.

xiv

Fiction is the most popular of all literary forms. It is so popular that facts of science and history, even the records of contemporary events, have to be romanticised before they are acceptable to the average man and woman. This is implied in the terminology of journalism. A news-item is a 'story', every incident out of the ordinary run of happenings is a 'romance'. We have romances of marriage, business, travel, fortune, discovery, murder, health, disease, and, in fact, everything that can be put into story form. The individuals who are thrown up in this continuous legend are always 'personalities'. Journalism may thus be raised to the rank of fiction, although the word 'dramatisation' is used to describe the process. But journalism differs from the fiction of the novel in that it is a general-

[1] J. Henry Shorthouse, *The Countess Eve*. Qt. in *Life and Letters of Shorthouse* (1905), i, 252–3.

isation, and however much it may depend upon personalities, its own attitude is impersonal. The relation of an editor to his readers is the same as that of shopkeeper and customer. He stocks what he thinks he can sell. News is merchandise, and it is selected and displayed, just as goods are bought and sold. The effect on the reader is much the same as that produced by the 'novel', 'fashionable', 'attractive' of the shops.

But fiction is not always mass-produced. When it is not merely merchandise, it is expression based upon an intimate response to life and its varied incidents as they are seen and experienced by a sensitive and imaginative person, that is, one who recognises the spiritual and physical facts of life and correlates them. The result, if competent, conveys his powers of comprehension and apprehension to his readers. Facts are stranger than fictions until they become fiction; but the reader of novels is in search of realities. The idlest novel-reader is continually pitting his own potentiality for experience against the real or imaginary experiences of the novel he is reading. He merges himself into the experiences of the novelist, feeling, according to capacity, what the novelist felt when creating his characters and incidents, and weaving them in a consecutive collateral narrative of his own.[1] It is not the story or the narrative, however, which has the deepest effect upon the reader, but the motives which impelled the author to expression. Edmund Wilson has outlined clearly what precisely are the conditions of creative fiction. 'The real elements of any work of fiction,' he says, 'are the elements of the author's personality: his imagination embodies in the images of characters, situations and scenes the fundamental conflicts of his nature of the cycle of phases through which it habitually passes. His personages are personifications of the author's various impulses and emotions: and the relations between them in his stories are really the relations between these.'[2]

XV

A recurring phenomenon of the interaction of author and reader is the readiness with which authors are charged with having libelled or defamed living people in the characters they have created. The danger is so great that writers of novels dealing with contemporary

[1] See Notes.   [2] *Axel's Castle* (1932), 176–7.

life protect themselves by stating that their characters are imaginary.
Nor are all such charges frivolous or predatory. It is 'natural' to discover oneself in novels and plays. That is one of their charms.
Georges Duhamel has said that 'if all the people who imagine they
have discovered part of their personality in *Salavin* were to proceed
against me I should spend the rest of my days in prison'.[1] The very
act of writing a novel is an inducement to such self-reflection. The
characters in a work of fiction are something more even than
reflection, they are both creations and creative. They exist in themselves as works of art and they exist as stimuli towards the rehabili-
tation of themselves in others. There is something more than wilful
paradox in Oscar Wilde's famous argument that we become what
the novelists have depicted.[2]

Literature generally and novels in particular encourage what
appears to be mimicry of thought and action. But the mimicry is an
illusion for in most instances such imitations are acts of recognition.
As we read, sleeping thoughts and repressed wishes are inevitably
disturbed because a writer of fiction maps out the unexplored
territories of ourselves. That is one of the explanations of the sensation common to all readers, that the writer of the book has expressed their own thoughts and feelings. Jane Welsh Carlyle had such
an experience when she read *Shirley* for the first time. She did not
think very highly of the book but felt that 'if' the then unknown
author 'have not kept company with me in this life, we must have
been much together in some previous state of existence. I perceive in
her book so many things I have said myself, printed without alteration of a word'.[3]

When Edward Dowden read *Daniel Deronda* for the first time he
so identified himself with the weaknesses of Daniel, 'which seem
. . . like a piece of my own experience,' that he watched the history
with 'a kind of personal anxiety'. And feeling, apparently, that he
had confessed too much, he supposed to his correspondent (the lady
who became his second wife) that 'hundreds of readers' must be
moved in the same way.[4] Charles Ricketts recalls a similar experience on first reading Nietzsche. 'I was half-frightened', he says, 'to
find in print so many things which I felt personally, and to hear
them from a mouth I loved so little.'[5]

---

[1] *In Defence of Letters.* Trans. Bozman (1938), 118. [2] See *ante*, pp. 74-5
[3] 17th November, 1849, *New Letters of Jane Welsh Carlyle* (1903), ii, 5.
[4] *Fragments from Old Letters* (1914) 156-7. [5] *Self Portrait of Charles Ricketts, R.A.*, Ed. T. Sturge Moore and Cecil Lewis (1939). 43.

xvi

When appreciating a novel the reader passes through the emotional experiences not only of the author, but those also of the characters depicted. The more excellent the novel the more profound the experience. The whole English-speaking world passed through the emotional experiences of Dickens during the middle decades of last century; and later, Dostoevsky was, for a time, to infect the intelligentsia of Western civilisation with his own spiritual unrest. Dostoevsky's power over the mind of his reader is emphasised by Carr in a reference to *The Brothers Karamazov*. The ordeal and trial of Dimitri in that work are a dominant theme and Dimitri becomes for the reader 'not merely the one figure in the novel', but the one being in the world; and we can look at the world through no other eyes but his. We attain, as we attained in *The Idiot*, to a 'spiritual sense of transmuted values'.[1]

The reader rarely surrenders so completely, for he cannot obliterate entirely memories of his own emotional experiences as well as reflections upon what he considers would have been himself, if he were placed in like circumstances to those described or suggested by the novelist. There is abundance of evidence to support this theory in the correspondence of Samuel Richardson and his circle, most of which forms a valuable commentary upon his novels. Richardson had produced an entirely new kind of novel of 'the affections', the phrase then used for what is now summed up in the less equivocal word 'sex'. And by relieving sex in fiction from the burden of being merely amusing or romantically 'moving', this London printer became the pioneer of the modern novel. He added dissection of the emotions to description of emotional behaviour, and if it had been possible for a novelist in the eighteenth century to be as frankly subjective, he might have anticipated his modern English namesake, Dorothy Richardson, or her French counterpart, Marcel Proust. The correspondence includes a large number of letters from his readers, both men and women, as well as his replies, and amid much gush and persiflage, it becomes clear that the popularity of the novels was the result of a psychological awakening. Men and women looked at Richardson's characters, and saw themselves. As one of them put it: 'Every man ... makes his own

[1] E. H. Carr, *Dostoevsky* (1931), 297.

character with Sir Charles Grandison, and is always believed good, till found otherwise.'[1]

The reading of fiction varies only superficially from time to time. Consciously or unconsciously, and perhaps oftener unconsciously, identification is the most prevalent demand. Sir Hugh Walpole, writing of the conditions of reading in the first half of last century, said 'The novel was then a newer art and the Reader was more credible of it, he also knew very clearly what he wanted.' This acted favourably upon the novelists, for 'what a novel reader wanted was to spend his time in the company of persons who, by their multiplied energies and activities, created a little world of their own. He definitely cheated himself into believing in them because of the fun he knew he was going to have'. Encouraged by this confiding attitude the novelists 'were able to persuade themselves of the reality of their little worlds'.[2]

xvii

But even novels of the ready-to-wear variety which are made for standard sizes of mind cannot always be guaranteed to fit. The confidence established between writer and reader may be upset by the vagaries of fashion or other involuntary change in condition of the reader, who, in the last resort, is arbiter. The appreciation of fiction, whether critical or uncritical, depends upon the equipment of the reader, and equipment is composed of knowledge and experience of life and art. Miss Rose Macaulay has pointed out that one of the problems of the novelist is this 'incalculable factor' of transmission, and she has penetrated a little further than most other professional commentators. Everything depends on how much the reader knows. 'For one reader, not all the novelist's skill and imaginative creation will avail to push a particular character into his realisation; for the rest it is done with a casual touch and no skill required. This is apparent whenever novels and people in them are discussed among a group of intelligent readers.'[3]

The full appreciation of fiction, as of poetry, history or drama, depends upon a skilled technique which in turn can only be obtained by constant watchfulness. The aim is the development of a ripe sensibility, capable of sensing the meaning within the meaning of

[1] Benjamin Kennicott, 9th May, 1754, *Correspondence of Samuel Richardson*. Ed. Anna Laetitia Barbauld (1804), ii, 184.   [2] Reading (1926), 89.   [3] Rose Macaulay, *The Writings of E. M. Forster* (1938), 236.

words and sentences. The skilled reader is not dependent on the adventitious aids of easiness or brightness; he is no longer, for instance, dependent upon plot for his enjoyment of fiction, or upon what is called 'actuality' or 'incident', or mere verisimilitude of description. Such things are elementary and they evoke but superficial feelings. They are for the callow reader, or for those moments when an easy escape from trial or tension is necessary. Imaginative experience should induce a sensitiveness towards inner meaning, towards understanding the subtlety and tenderness which an author experiences when he puts himself into plot or character or incident.

CHAPTER XII

BOOKS AS INTOXICANTS

'A true Reader, that is, one to whom books are like bottles of whiskey to
the inebriate, to whom anything that is between covers has a sort of
intoxicating savour . . .'—HUGH WALPOLE, *Reading* (1926), 43.

> 'Books—to intoxicate, to storm, to press
> The soul insatiate to unearthliness.'
>
> WALTER DE LA MARE, *Pleasures
> and Speculations* (1940), xv.

---

i

Nothing in familiar letters is so common as the desire to
explain anything between ordinary satisfaction and ecstasy
in terms of intoxication. It is a method of expression
acceptable to writers as well as to readers, neither of whom object to
the association of exaltation with less admirable forms of excitement.
Common acceptance of this apparent anomaly implies recognition
of a relationship between various states of intoxication, one of them
escaping the disadvantages of another. In the more reputable class
everything, it would seem, can be intoxicating according to mood
and circumstances; and this condition is accepted without challenge
as a legitimate means of approach to an infinitude beyond interference from the reasoning faculties or self-consciousness which
restricts the intuitive faculties and limits the opportunities of
inspiration.

Intoxication is a word with a variety of meanings, but the majority of the references to the use of the word given in this chapter are far removed from those forms of drunkenness which act as narcotics or otherwise limit consciousness. The spirit of Dionysos rather than that of Silenus is indicated. The word is associated in the minds of those who use it with enthusiasm, excitement, exaltation, with, in short, an acceleration of the feeling of wellbeing. Meredith called it a 'strengthening intoxication' whose secret is known to those who 'court the clouds of the South West with a lover's blood'.[1] The condition thus esteemed is physical as well as emotional. Intoxication, in the applications of the word I have cited, presumes a sensitised response to experience, a sense of power and a power of sense: the desire to receive and develop impressions, to produce that state of mind which encourages perception to express itself in immediate and gratifying sensation, and, where the ability to do so exists, in forms of art: images, patterns, pictures, which in turn are links in the processes of the whole of life. The related condition is called inspiration.

ii

There is no golden rule for the attainment of these exalted states of consciousness; for that reason and because the supply of natural ecstasy is irregular and uncertain, even writers of genius have hoped to tune themselves up to creative rapture by a variety of methods, from inward pondering to outward abandonment. There would seem to be no absence of opportunity for such short cuts to ecstasy. Not only may all the stars and all the heavens be tasted in a crust of bread, but those who seek inspiration may find it everywhere, from where the morning stars sing together to where the meanest flower that blows gives thoughts that often lie too deep for tears, provided that the sensibilities can be tuned in at the right moment.

Byron found the key to this mystery in love and sorrow, Robert Burns, Charles Lamb, and Francis Thompson in alcohol,[2] Coleridge,

---

[1] *The Egoist.*   [2] Not only the more exalted forms of alcohol, for, as George Meredith reminded us, 'You may get as royally intoxicated on swipes as on choice wine' (The Amazing Marriage, 162), and A. E. Housman, although a connoisseur of wine, probably found Juvenal and Manilius shorter cuts to ecstasy than alcohol, but in some of his most famous lines he set beer above poetry:

Oh many a peer of England brews
Livelier liquor than the Muse,
And Malt does more than Milton can
To justify God's ways to man.

> *A Shropshire Lad.* lxii.

Thomas De Quincey and Dante Gabriel Rossetti in laudanum. Coleridge was capable of auto-intoxication in many circumstances and from a variety of causes, and the condition was not always, if ever, imaginary, or the word a synonym for enthusiasm. The receipt of a letter from Southey, announcing the death of a friend's little daughter, had upon Coleridge 'the precise effect of intoxication by an overdose of some narcotic drug—weeping, vomiting, wakefulness the whole night in a sort of stupid sensuality of Itching from my Head to my toes, all night'.[1] Wordsworth got drunk on the idea of immortality; and he was wrought up by the friendlier aspects of nature as others have been enchanted by the austerities of alp and ocean, or bemused by what is remote. It does not appear to matter whether the inspiring object is an atom or a planet. William Blake needed only a grain of sand for heaven and an hour of time for eternity, and Thoreau was comforted by the thought that our planet was in the Milky Way! Even earthbound realists find (and perhaps seek) ecstasy in their work. Flaubert, whose talent flourished only in a frenzy of concentration, told George Sand that 'to get drunk with ink was wiser than to get drunk with brandy'.[2]

iii

The media for obtaining contact with the subconscious life are as varied as the desire to do so is widespread. The method of release from intellectual and material preoccupations knows no exclusions. It does not seem to matter whether the desired effect is produced by contemplation of what is commonly accepted as exalted: nature or humanity, the universe or God, music,[3] a passionate experience, a work of art, or by such mundane pleasures as good company[4] or a change of air.

But this universal desire for ecstasy is not always creative or intended to be so.[5] It is often frankly nihilistic, the negation not the

[1] Letter to his wife, 12th August, 1803, *Unpublished Letters*. Ed. E. L. Griggs (1932), i, 276. [2] *The George Sand–Gustave Flaubert Letters*, 1st January, 1869. [3] 'Weber intoxicated an entire generation (that of Gautier, Berlioz, Baudelaire) much as Wagner intoxicated ours.' Charles Ricketts, 1919, *Self-Portrait of Charles Ricketts, R.A.* Ed. Sturge Moore and Cecil Lewis (1939), 320. See Notes. [4] 'I can become intoxicated on good company as on drink.' Oliver St. J. Gogarty, *As I was going down Sackville Street* (1937), 88. [5] See Notes.

intensification of sensation, and it is consciously or automatically sought to lower the tension of being when pain or pleasure becomes unbearable.[1] Or to put it another way, intoxication is often no more than running away from self in an attempt to balance consciousness against boredom or anxiety. It is not the only way, and it may not always be the moral way, but it is certainly the most universally provoked or stimulated, the most widely dispersed and the most widely admitted means of escape for all kinds of people in all sorts and conditions of human life, from the primitive to the state of utmost sophistication. The word or its synonyms are in common though not always exact use, and everyone who is not insensitive to good and bad, to beauty and ugliness, to tragedy and comedy, has his own favourite intoxicant whether spirituous or sensuous.

There can be few objects or experiences which have not at one time been praised or condemned for this quality. Some, such as the pageant of spring, or the dawn of love, affect all, but the instruments of intoxication vary with time, place and person. Recreations, sports, holidays, are perhaps natural intoxicants, like the return of health after illness.[2] More and more men and women in our mechanised age get drunk on speed. Eric Linklater refers in *Poet's Pub*, to the 'epileptic intoxication of dancing'. George Moore relates that when he and George Russell (A.E.) were on a walking tour in Ireland, he found the sunlight so intoxicating that it was with difficulty that he kept himself from calling to A.E. that he felt certain the gods would hear and answer their wishes.[3] Such experiences were enjoyed by Anatole France who has, among many, a description of that 'master of method', the Abbé Perruque, tucking up his cassock and joining in a game of football 'with the zest of a cloistered peasant, drunk with air and exercise'.[4]

Love, the most familiar and universal of all stimulants, needs no elaboration; and there is no difference in the terminology which is

[1] There are probably phases of intoxication before the unconscious stage is reached when the perceptions become more acute than at normal times. An early defender of James Joyce seems to hold this view. 'It is possibly necessary', he thinks, 'to "trance" oneself into a state of word intoxication, fitting-concept inebriation, to enjoy this work [*Finnegans Wake*] to the fullest.' Robert McAlmon, in *Exagmination . . . of a Work in Progress* (1929), 114. [2] When Coleridge first went to Keswick after an illness he wrote 'I am settled with the voluptuous and joy-trembling nerves of a convalescent'. *Unpublished Letters*. Ed. E. L. Griggs (1932), i, 149. [3] *Hail and Farewell: Salve* (1912), 40. [4] *The Elm-Tree on the Mall*, 16.

used for the expression of sacred and profane love, for, say, the ecstasy of St. Bernard or Shelley. It is summed-up by Paul Valéry as 'the intoxication of the heart' and it has always played a predominant part in aesthetic enterprises. Byron is not the only poet who, on his own admission, never wrote anything worth mentioning till he was in love.[1] And closely related to the erotic stimulus is the love of power, which, in the worship of success and prosperity, has taken the place of religious ecstasy during the financial era which is at present in the melting-pot. This form of intoxication is not generally admired and is often looked upon as the prelude to destruction and chaos.[2] Two poets as wide apart in aim and method as Aubrey de Vere and Rudyard Kipling are equally concerned at the excessive engagement of the nineteenth century with mechanical progress and power politics. The older poet feared for an era which was 'intoxicated with the conquests of physical science',[3] and Kipling made the Diamond Jubilee of Queen Victoria the excuse to warn the nation against 'being drunk with sight of power'.

The idea of progress has made whole generations of intelligent people, if not exactly 'blind drunk', at least ecstatically indifferent to consequences. It is one of the ironies of history that many of those who have listened with most sympathy have added more sadness to 'the still, sad music of humanity'. 'Those who, in the eighteenth century, were first to voice it', says André Gide, 'appear to have been so much intoxicated thereby that they drove it, too quickly and too simply, to extremities.'[4]

Emerson, who was something of a specialist in ecstasy, saw a widespread love of intoxication of 'some sort' among Americans but the causes were different. 'One is drunk with whiskey, and one with party, and one with music, and one with temper. Many of them fling themselves into the excitement of business until their heads whirl and they become insane!'[5] The puritan rather than the mystic was speaking, for although Emerson was well aware of the mystical value of ecstasy his New England upbringing would not allow him

---

[1] See Byron's *Conversations with Medwin* (1824). [2] 'England, after forty years of peace, and four of intoxicating prosperity, was moving slowly into the Crimean war.' Edward Hallett Carr, *Karl Marx* (1934), 123. [3] Qt. Wilfrid Ward, *Aubrey de Vere* (1904), 19. [4] Qt. Pierre-Quint *André Gide* (1935), 293. 'Rousseau's social indifference permitted him to proclaim the intoxicating but misleading gospel that all men are spiritually equal, and the social consequences of that doctrine have made his descendants outlaws.' J. Middleton Murry, *Discoveries* (1934), 139. [5] *Journals* (1914), v, 413.

to give unqualified approval even to discriminate intoxication. At the same time, he would have been the first to understand his friend Thoreau, when that most abstemious of philosophers longed to be 'drunk, drunk, drunk—dead drunk to this world . . . for ever',[1] for he knew, as we do, that Thoreau could and did get drunk as readily on water, fresh air, or the resinous fragrance of pine bark, as on a passage from *Plato* or the *Mahabharata*.

iv

Without conscious longing for intoxication, but obviously in need of it, Jane Welsh Carlyle is wrought up by a snowfall in London. She had been to a theatre, and unlike most adults and particularly women, she exults in the mask of snow upon the streets. She walks and slides through it, her bonnet hanging on her back, and, still unsatisfied, takes a handful and eats it. 'In fact,' she says, 'that almost forgotten, Scotch-looking snow had made me perfectly *drunk*, or I should hardly have "tempted Providence" in such a distracted manner.'[2] George Gissing experienced a similar excitement on his first visit to the Vatican. He walked through the galleries in a 'state of exaltation', waving his arms and 'shouting in a suppressed voice'.[3] The Goncourt brothers were 'absolutely intoxicated' by a visit to the house at Auteuil, 'which they afterwards bought.[4] Rose Macaulay gets drunk over the beauty of Polperro in Cornwall. It has 'the eerie beauty of a dream or of a little foreign port', and 'such beauty, such charm, is on the edge of pain; you cannot disentangle them. They intoxicate, and pierce to tears'.[5]

The condition of a Gladstone overcome with the exuberance of his own verbosity,[6] is doubtless as authentic as the inebriation of a Mazzini over the idea of human progress; a James Russell Lowell falling for the temptations of the 'heavenly climate' of Naples, or a Coventry Patmore with his brain in 'a state of pleasant intoxication' over the 'pure and thin' air of Sussex;[7] a Charles Ricketts looking

---

[1] Qt. Channing, *Thoreau*, 15.   [2] *Letters and Memorials* (1883), iii, 38.
[3] *Letters* (1926), 261.   [4] 4th July, 1868, *Journals*.   [5] *Dangerous Ages* (1921).   [6] 'I remember being intoxicated with my own conversation and the manner in which I succeeded in making Arthur Balfour and George Pembroke, 13th Earl of Pembroke, join in.' Lady Oxford, *Autobiography of Margot Asquith* (Penguin Ed.), i, 157.   [7] Qt. Derek Patmore, *Portrait of My Family* (1935), 144.

forward to 'getting drunk on sound—as a sailor gets drunk on beer',[1] or a Keats longing for

> ... *a draught of vintage! that hath been*
> *Cool'd a long age in the deep-delvéd earth,*
>   *Tasting of Flora and the country green,*
>   *Dance, and Provençal song, and sunburnt mirth!*

> ... *a beaker full of the warm South!*
> *Full of the true, the blushful Hippocrene,*
>   *With beaded bubbles winking at the brim,*
>   *And purple-stainéd mouth;*

that he might 'drink and leave the world unseen', and 'fade away' with his nightingale 'into the forest dim'.

v

Writers of a sedentary habit seek inspiration in their inward lives, with the minimum of external aid. 'The world of imagination is shown us in Yeats's early poetry, as something infinitely delightful, infinitely seductive, as something to which one becomes addicted, with which one becomes delirious and drunken ...'[2] Contemplation of the abstract ideas of truth and beauty and good and evil has the inebriating effect of religious meditation, to which it is allied. The Puritans got as drunk on the thought of goodness as the Marquis de Sade and the Diabolonian poets of the Romantic Revival on the idea of evil.[3] Emerson noted that Bronson Allcott was 'intoxicated by pure beauty',[4] and the same could be said of Keats with his worship of 'the mighty abstract idea of beauty in all things', and indeed of all devotees of this faith, from Plato and Plotinus to Pater and Santayana. All kinds of excess, repressive as well as expressive, may contribute to this state, even impotence is said to promote its own sort of intoxication,[5] in much the same way as voluntary repression and inhibition of desires produces religious exaltation.

[1] Letter to Gordon Bottomley, 2nd October, 1916, *Self-Portrait of Charles Ricketts, R.A.* Ed., Sturge Moore and Cecil Lewis (1939), 59. [2] Edmund Wilson, *Axel's Castle* (1932), 30. [3] 'The intoxication of evil is certainly pathological.' Otto Flake, *Marquis de Sade* (1931), 159. Antony, in Conrad's *Chance* (p. 331), is intoxicated with 'generosity and pity'. [4] *Journals* (1914), viii, 519. [5] 'The excess of his own impotence acted like a sort of intoxication.' *Salavin*, Georges Duhamel, trans. Billings (1936), 283.

Writers are naturally intoxicated by their work. William Blake reeled intoxicated 'among the naked truths' that surrounded him.[1] Henry James found exaltation in the intensive study of manners and the passionate experience of hair-splitting in the process of transfusing what he had observed into words and sentences. His method was not unlike that of the doctrine-drunken schoolmen of the Middle Ages. He himself was conscious of this passion, for in *The Middle Years* he refers to an 'intoxicated vision of choice and range' in London society. George Moore brooded himself into feeling 'a little intoxicated by the ideas that were mounting' to his head,[2] and when Arnold Bennett was at his desk it seemed 'that he was almost drunk with work'.[3]

vi

The connection between ecstasy and religion is well known. All genuine religious experience has a common basis. John Bunyan's exaltation, which produced *Pilgrim's Progress* and *Grace Abounding*, is akin to the illumination of Swedenborg or William Blake, or 'God-intoxicated' Spinoza. The phenomenon of 'grace' is closely related to ecstasy and can be inspired by a similar variety of circumstances, yet: 'Through all the different forms of communion, and all the diversity of the means which help to produce this state, whether it be reached by a jubilee, by a general confession, by a solitary prayer and effusion, whatever in short be the place and the occasion, it is easy to recognise that it is fundamentally one state in spirit and in fruits.'[4] Ecstasy is essentially religious, and it would not be difficult to show how every form it has taken has been a means towards mystical or moral enchantment. And although the methods adopted within each theological system may be in greater or lesser degree political, or even scientific, every theology itself approximates to a work of art which, beginning as the intuitive expression of one person, is gradually developed by the creative projections and adjustments of its more powerful units, and the give and take of communal experience. If the arts are largely, perhaps entirely, the expression of individual subconsciousness, religion is the expression of what Jung called the 'collective unconscious'. The significance of a religion in this context is not what it

[1] Edward Dowden, *Fragments from Old Letters* (1914), 19.　[2] *Hail and Farewell: Vale* (1914), 233.　[3] Dorothy Cheston Bennett, *Arnold Bennett* (1935), 94.　[4] Sainte-Beuve, *Port Royal* (1867–70), i, 95 and 106. Abridged by William James, *The Varieties of Religious Experience* (1922), 260.

may be, as in the case of the Christian Church in the Middle Ages, a patron or dictator of the arts, so much as an art in itself, applied to the mastercraft of all arts: the art of living.

vii

Books have long been recognised as means towards the 'sort of intoxication' I am trying to define by a diversity of readers both ancient and modern, for if a writer may become intoxicated during the act of creation, so also may a reader become intoxicated by what has been created. And further, if, as Emerson believed, 'all the authors are enchanted men; intoxicated, plainly, with that stray drop of nectar or idealism they have imbibed,'[1] it is not surprising that their experiences are conveyed to others. This, indeed, is the only point of almost complete agreement between the old and new schools of literary appreciation. Here also, philistine and intellectual salute and fraternise. Men of learning meet across time and space in recognition of the pervading need. In America, nearly a hundred years ago, Emerson again was recording the intoxicating propensities of *Plotinus* and *Swedenborg*,[2] as Louis Untermeyer is recording to-day the intoxication to be enjoyed from reading *Whitman* and *Swinburne*.[3]

The moderns are perhaps more conscious of the intoxicating power of books than the writers of other times, or perhaps they are only more communicative—or romantic. Instances are embarrassing in both quality and variety. They range from Paul Verlaine, 'filled with ecstasy' by *Calderon*,[4] to Lowes Dickinson, 'sitting down with a sort of intoxication' to the *Aesthetics* of Hegel.[5] Nor is there any need for fastidious choice. Most of those readers who have recorded their experiences would seem to be addicted to vintage authors, and even then, to the more obviously intoxicating among them. André Gide thus came under the spell of Victor Hugo, Baudelaire, Sully Prudhomme and Heine,[6] and it is said that young men in Paris used to get 'intoxicated by the caressing eloquence of Daudet'.[7]

[1] *Journals* (1914), viii, 408. [2] *Ib.* vi, 496. Emerson was characteristically inconsistent in his faith in the efficacy of book-intoxication, and noted that people at one time (1850) were 'drugged with books for want of wisdom'. *Ib.* ix, 250. [3] American Poetry (1932), 596. [4] Havelock Ellis, *From Rousseau to Proust* (1936), 86. [5] Qt. E. M. Forster, *G. Lowes Dickinson* (1934), 86. [6] Pierre-Quint, *Op. Cit.* 17. [7] *Maupassant*, Ernest Boyd, (1926), 144.

Oliver Wendell Holmes told James Russell Lowell that the first reading of *The Ancient Mariner* produced a strange kind of intoxication';[1] Frederick Myers got drunk on Sappho;[2] Meredith's 'Love in the Valley' made Robert Louis Stevenson 'drunk like wine';[3] Frederick York Powell was intoxicated by Bunyan's prose,[4] Somerset Maugham by 'the colour and rareness of the fantastic words that thickly stud the pages of Wilde's *Salomé*,'[5] and the 'impassioned rhetoric' of Henry George's *Progress and Poverty* affected Bernard Shaw like 'strong drink', and incidentally converted him to socialism.[6]

It is not only politicians and high-powered salesmen who become inebriated with the exuberance of their own verbosity, for it is well known that the sound and beauty of words have an intoxicating effect upon both writers and readers. We have it on the authority of the present holder of the Chair of Poetry at Oxford that 'Every poet takes the intoxication of his own words',[7] and Logan Pearsall Smith refers to 'word-intoxicated' readers of Shakespeare who seem to behave as if Shakespeare 'sometimes used his plays merely for the opportunities they gave him of his lyric utterance'.[8] C. E. Montague was affected by 'special sequences of quite common words'; they 'can take hold of you with a high hand', he declared, 'thrilling your mind with a poignant ecstasy, a delicious disquiet, akin to the restlessness and the raptures of lovers.' When he was a boy at school he discovered these lines out of Scott,

> *Yet the lark's shrill fife may come*
> *At day-break from the fallow,*
> *And the bittern sound his drum,*
> *Booming from the sedgy mallow,*

and they made him so 'drunk with delight' that when on a railway journey he had 'to walk up and down empty compartments of trains, saying them over and over again, as incapable as a bluebottle either of sitting quiet or ceasing to hum'.[9]

[1] *Life and Letters of Oliver Wendell Holmes* (1896), ii, 133. [2] *Fragments of Prose and Poetry* (1904), 18. [3] *Letters* (1901), ii, 324. [4] Qt. Oliver Elton, *Frederick York Powell* (1906), i, 272. [5] W. Somerset Maugham, *The Summing-Up* (1938). [6] Frank Harris, *Bernard Shaw* (1931), 140. For further examples see 'Bibliobibacity with a Digression of Ecstasy', *The Anatomy of Bibliomania*. Holbrook Jackson (1931), Pt. x, Ch. 3, i, 218–226. [7] H. W. Garrod, *Keats* (1939), 106. [8] *On Reading Shakespeare* (1938), 75. [9] *A Writer's Notes on his Trade* (1930), 243–4.

viii

Poetry is commonly accepted as the product of a 'fine frenzy', and the poet is believed to be at his best when he is a master of ecstasy and capable of conveying that condition to his readers. Carlyle said we are all poets when we read poetry with understanding, but with many serious-minded people he confused understanding with ecstasy. The act of awakening or of illuminating consciousness which books are able to promote in certain circumstances, is, indeed, a form of ecstasy, like the rapture of adolescence or the renewal of life during convalescence. All renewals and revivals are reversions to the 'roses and raptures' of youth, to that 'continual intoxication' which was Rochefoucauld's conception of youth itself, to that intense feeling for life in which he saw the 'fever of reason'. Ecstasy is acute consciousness, and the condition is often achieved by a return to the more primitive sources of passionate energy. If therefore ecstasy can open the gates of the Kingdom of Heaven, the injunction that you cannot enter without becoming as a little child has a new meaning, for to see and to feel with few encumbrances, to look freshly upon life, to be widely and deeply interested, to see nothing common, never to be bored, is as near Heaven as mortals may hope to get, and it is under such conditions that poetry thrives.

ix

Coleridge who, like De Quincey, originally took opium to relieve pain,[1] associated the idea of literary intoxication with pleasure. He became intoxicated during the first reading of Gray's *Bard*, and later when that early rapture had worked itself out, he read the poem without pleasure and came even to consider it 'frigid and artificial'.[2] The attitude gives us a clue to the taste for literary stimulants. In his youth Coleridge still drew sustenance from classical as distinct from romantic poetry, and throughout his life his genius was the battleground of the antipathies of intellect and imagination. It was natural that he should be moved by Gray's poetry in which there

---

[1] 'Never was I led to this wicked direful practice of taking Opium or Laudanum by any desire or expectation of exciting *pleasurable* sensations; but purely by *terror*, by cowardice of pain, first of mental pain, and afterwards as my System became weakened, even of bodily Pain.' S. T. Coleridge to John H. Morgan, 15th May, 1814. *Unpublished Letters*. Ed. E. L. Griggs (1932), ii, 112. [2] See *Anima Poetae* (1895), 5, *Table Talk* (1874), 296.

are what appear to be glimmerings of the romantic revival, but it was to be supposed that the deepening romanticism of his own genius could not for long find exhilaration in that direction. The turbulence which was at work within him and which produced on the one hand the *Ancient Mariner* and *Kubla Khan* and on the other the *Biographia Literaria* and the *Confessions of an Enquiring Spirit* could not be expected to flourish on the 'sweet reasonableness' of even a para-romantic like Gray. The intellectual truce of the eighteenth century ended with Coleridge.

Nowhere in the whole range of English literature, and it is, perhaps, the outstanding characteristic of our poetry and prose, will you find that sense of ecstasy so pure and passionate as when it is associated with nature. Its highest expression is in Wordsworth:

> *For I have learned*
> *To look on nature, not as in the hour*
> *Of thoughtless youth; but hearing oftentimes*
> *The still, sad music of humanity,*
> *Nor harsh nor grating, though of ample power*
> *To chasten and subdue. And I have felt*
> *A presence that disturbs me with the joy*
> *Of elevated thoughts; a sense sublime*
> *Of something far more deeply interfused,*
> *Whose dwelling is the light of setting suns,*
> *And the round ocean and the living air,*
> *And the blue sky, and in the mind of man:*
> *A motion and a spirit, that impels*
> *All thinking things, all objects of all thought,*
> *And rolls through all things.*[1]

In this passage and in many less familiar Wordsworth has distilled emotion into a spiritual essence which is capable of handing on his ecstasy through all the generations of man.

x

Inspiration, or intuition, is invariably looked upon as the opposite of intellect, and even as the neuropathic opposite because it is allied with frenzy, delirium and other manic states. This deduction though supported by tradition is probably wrong. Yet, in the Middle

[1] 'Lines composed a few miles above Tintern Abbey.'

Ages, and even later, lunatics were believed to be inspired.[1] Shakespeare must have had that tradition in mind when he put into the same category poets, lovers and madmen.[2] Poets are borderline cases even in the popular mind, and their classification with lovers and lunatics has been accepted with general if amused approval. Scientific opinion[3] has gone further by pushing to its logical conclusion the ancient surmise that

> *Great wits are sure to madness near allied,*
> *And thin partitions do their bounds divide.*[4]

I am not here concerned with how near to madness genius is allied and only draw attention to an age-long contention because of its implied challenge to the popular approval of intellectual as distinct from intuitive processes. The challenge would be supported by many students of literature; but though genius is often neurotic few would go all the way with Nisbet, Lombroso and their followers, such as Max Nordau, who sometimes seem more intent upon establishing a theory than revealing a truth.

[1] 'We have had a poor unhappy girl in this village who drowned herself about a fortnight ago, that pretended to prophesy of earthquakes in England before a twelvemonth is at an end—one in London, one at Portsmouth, and one at Cowes. She was certainly a lunatic, poor soul; but yet many of her own rank here believe her a saint, and of course, have faith in her sayings.' Margaret Collier to Samuel Richardson, 31st December, 1755, *Correspondence*. Barbauld (1804), ii, 91. [2] The character of Hamlet shows that Shakespeare was keenly aware of the contest between the mental and intuitive processes: and it must not be forgotten that he endowed his fools with wisdom. [3] See *The Man of Genius*, Cesare Lombroso (1891); *The Insanity of Genius*, J. F. Nisbet (1891); *Degeneration*, Max Nordau (1895); *The Man of Genius*, Hermann Turck (1896). [4] Dryden (after Seneca), *Absalom and Achitophel* (1682), 163–4.

CHAPTER XIII

THE INTELLECTUAL COMEDY

'I saw in him [Leonardo da Vinci] the leading character in that Intellectual Comedy which, so far, has not found its poet, and which, to my mind, would be so much more precious a thing than the *Comédie Humaine* or even the *Divina Commedia*.'—PAUL VALÉRY, *Introduction to the Method of Leonardo da Vinci*. Trans. THOS. MCGREEVY (1929), 2.

> 'Our meddling intellect
> Mis-shapes the beauteous forms of things.'
> WILLIAM WORDSWORTH,
> 'The Tables Turned.'

'All *our* Thoughts are in the language of the old Logicians *inadequate*: i.e. no *thought*, which I have, of any *thing* comprises the whole of that Thing. I have a distinct Thought of a Rose Tree; but what countless properties and goings-on on that plant are there, not included in my thought of it?'—S. T. COLERIDGE, 13, x, 1806, *Unpublished Letters*. Ed. E. L. GRIGGS (1932), i, 354.

---

i

When Joseph Conrad said that 'our feelings have nothing to do with what we are pleased to imagine our wisdom', he showed that he was aware of the Intellectual Comedy and doubtless more disturbed than amused by it. He continually returns to the theme, as if he were trying to persuade himself that, in his own words, 'the best kind of knowledge' was 'most akin to revelation'. Often he found himself at war with his own unconscious elements which, fortunately for his art, he resisted unsuccessfully. This is borne out by an incident in connection with the publication of *The Secret Agent*. Edward Garnett drew his attention to an ambiguity which Conrad was already aware of but could not explain. He put it down to a 'defect of temperament'. At the time of writing he knew something had gone wrong, and it was 'a horrible grind', he said, 'to keep going with this suspicion at the back of the head'.[1] His novels often reflect some disturbance of the inner environment. They seem to dramatise, indirectly, the struggle between the intellect and all those non-intellectual forces and deposits which we call variously intuition and inspiration, instinctive and subconscious. He recognised the necessity of thinking vividly and correctly, but not as an end in itself. If we start from 'intelligible premises', he said, it must be with the object of arriving at 'an unsophisticated conclusion'. He remarks this characteristic in Guy de Maupassant with approval and his own novels represent, among other things, the half-conscious struggle of instinct with sophistication of which his own unrest was a focusing point. Conrad's attitude may be the symptom of a resistance of ancient descent: a long-standing effort to transcend the dictatorship of the intellect.

ii

Much has been written about the old feud between the mind and the soul of man, and although there is no general agreement upon the characteristics of the combatants, and although there are some who still refuse to differentiate them, it is commonly believed that not only is there a difference, but that the two states of consciousness are fundamentally as well as functionally opposed. This belief is implicit in much speculative philosophy and in most poetry, and although psychologists have introduced some new points of view and several new concepts and definitions, they have succeeded, so far, in doing little more than extend the area of dispute. Apart from the introduction of new methods in the diagnosis and treatment of disease, the contribution of psychology to modern thought is an attitude or method of approach. There is nothing new, for instance, in the recognition of a subconscious realm of unemployed desires which may flare up at any moment with surprising results. What is new is the designed extension of consciousness into that realm.

---

[1] *Letters from Conrad*, Ed. Garnett (1928), 211.

One of the novelties of speculative science is the recognition of an age-long but hitherto only timidly admitted desire of intelligent people to penetrate into the hinterland of mental processes, not so much to abandon as to get beyond thought. The reasoning processes have lost some of their supremacy, as we incline to believe with William James that 'Knowledge about life is one thing; effective occupation of a place in life, with its dynamic currents passing through your being, is another'.[1] The intellect is thus a suspected if not yet an out-moded instrument, and an increasing number of observant people agree with H. G. Wells that 'the forceps of our minds are clumsy forceps, and crush the truth a little in taking hold of it'.[2]

iii

Many attempts have been made to explain the relationship between intellect and inspiration, but I know of only two writers who have succeeded in giving anything like a convincing account of the process of aesthetic creation on the evidence of their own experience. They are as wide apart as Wordsworth and Proust. Both approached the art of writing as a means of self-realisation based upon memory working intuitively upon past experiences. 'All good poetry is the spontaneous overflow of powerful feelings,' but 'Poems to which any value can be attached were never produced on any variety of subjects but by a man who, being possessed of more than usual organic sensibility, had also thought long and deeply. For our continued influxes of feelings are modified and directed by our thoughts, which are indeed the representatives of all our past feelings; and, as by contemplating the relation of these general representatives to each other, we discover what is really important to men, so, by the repetition and continuance of this act, our feelings will be connected with important subjects, till at length, if we be originally possessed of much sensibility, such habits of mind will be produced, that, by obeying blindly and mechanically the impulses of those habits, we shall describe objects, and utter sentiments, of such a nature, and in such connection with each other, that the understanding of the reader must necessarily be in some degree enlightened, and his affections strengthened and purified'.[3]

[1] *Varieties of Religious Experience* (1922), 489. [2] 'Scepticism of the Instrument,' *A Modern Utopia* (1905), Appendix 382. [3] Wordsworth, Preface, *Lyrical Ballads* (1798–1802), *Prose Works* (1876), ii, 82.

Proust is more practical. He gets down to the actual process of recovery from the unconscious reserves of memories which are stored 'like albumen in the ovule of a plant'. It is upon this reserve that a writer draws for the sustenance of his art, much as 'a plant draws its nourishment in order to transform itself into seed'. What amounts to 'chemical phenomena' is going on in secret and embryonic seeds or sentences are being prepared for release by a process of germination.[1] In the art of writing release comes about by consciousness of the implications in time of memories which have been germinating in most instances since the impressionable days of childhood. The twelve volumes of Proust's *Remembrance of Things Past* are built up on half a dozen such memories which are constantly being recalled as starting points for the recovery of the main incidents and experiences of his life, and unless this process is realised clearly the novel cannot be understood. The points of memory, sprung by some recent impression, are in themselves slight, even commonplace, but they increase in importance as the genius of the writer fits them into the jigsaw portrait of his introspective hero, who is a fictional symbol of himself.

On one occasion towards the end of his life Proust arrives late at a musical recital given by the Princesse de Guermantes at her Paris mansion, and he is shown into 'a small boudoir-library adjoining the buffet until the piece then being played had come to an end, the Princesse having given orders that the door should not be opened during the performance'. On his way to the recital various memories had been recalled, particularly the sensation he once felt in St. Mark's when he stumbled slightly over an uneven slab of pavement. This incident brings up pictures of Venice which he had hitherto failed to get into words, a circumstance which had caused him to doubt his literary ability. The working of this sensitive process is revealed in what passes through his mind whilst waiting in the ante-room for the doors to open. 'The servant in his ineffectual efforts not to make a noise had knocked a spoon against a plate. The same sort of felicity which the uneven paving stones had given me invaded my being; this time my sensation was quite different, being that of great heat accompanied by the smell of smoke tempered by the fresh air of a surrounding forest and I realised that what appeared so pleasant was the identical group of trees I had found so tiresome to observe and describe when I was uncorking a bottle of beer in the

---

[1] *Time Regained*. Trans. Stephen Hudson (1931), 251.

railway carriage and, in a sort of bewilderment, I believed for the moment, until I had collected myself, so similar was the sound of the spoon against the plate to that of the hammer of the railway employee who was doing something to the wheel of the carriage while the train was at a standstill facing the group of trees, that I was not actually there. One might have said that the portents of the day were to rescue me from my discouragement and give me back faith in literature.' While thus ruminating he is recognised by a servant who brings him some cakes and orangeade, and the stiffness of the napkin with which he wipes his mouth recalls a table in an hotel during a holiday years ago at the seaside, a memory which, at its inception not particularly happy, has been mellowed by time. He felt that he could walk out on to the sea-wall because 'the napkin upon which I was wiping my mouth had exactly the same kind of starchiness as that with which I had attempted with so much difficulty to dry myself before the window the first day of my arrival at Balbec and within the folds of which, now, in that library of the Guermantes mansion, a green-blue ocean spread its plumage like the tail of a peacock. And I did not merely rejoice in those colours, but in that whole instant which produced them, an instant towards which my whole life had doubtless aspired, which a feeling of fatigue or sadness had prevented my ever experiencing at Balbec, but which now, pure, dis-incarnated and freed from the imperfections of exterior perceptions, filled me with joy.'[1]

These recoveries of past time are made intuitively; the unconscious reserve of memory is explored by a process of experimentation: 'intuition for the writer' being 'what experiment is for the learned'. Proust compares the hidden resources of the self to a book of unknown signs which cannot be read by any rule: 'its reading consists in an act of creation in which no one can take our place and in which no one can collaborate'. As with Wordsworth the method is that of emotion remembered, but not always in tranquillity— Proust is not philosopher enough for that—but remembered or crystallised, after a period of germination, by the irresistible force of instinct. 'The artist must at all times follow his instincts, which makes art the most real thing, the most austere thing in life and the true last judgment. The book, which is the most arduous of all to decipher, is the only one which reality has dictated, the only one printed within us by reality itself. The ideas formulated by the

[1] *Ib.* 212–3.

intellect have only a logical truth, a possible truth, their selection is arbitrary. Our only book is that one not made by ourselves whose characters are already imaged. Intuition alone, however tenuous its consistency, however improbable its shape, is a criterion of truth and, for that reason, deserves to be accepted by the mind because it alone is capable, if the mind can extract that truth, of bringing it to greater perfection and of giving it pleasure without alloy.'[1] The conclusion is that it is the business of the writer not to invent but to interpret that which is already within him.[2]

The subconscious element operates in all these creative acts as a reserve and intuitively as a release or recovery, but before that the impressions to be taken for future use if required or recalled are not always the result of deliberate acts of observation or particularly deep impressions. A writer may at times give the impression of absent-mindedness when he is only ignoring the obvious and absorbing what is significant. When the time comes for recovery 'He recalls only what is general. Through certain ways of speaking, through a certain play of the features and through certain movements of the shoulders even though they had been seen when he was a child, the life of others remains within himself and when later on he begins writing, that life will help to recreate reality, possibly by that movement of the shoulders common to many people. This movement is as true to life as though it had been noted by an anatomist, but the writer expresses thereby a psychological verity by grafting on to the shoulders of one individual the neck of another, both of whom had only posed to him for a moment'.[3]

iv

It is not my business, even were it within my capacity, to travel far into the realms of psychology, but it is necessary to state my own understanding of the aesthetic process in order to make clear some of the theories expounded in this and relative chapters. In my understanding of the processes inspiration and intellect, though functionally distinct, are complementary when suitably balanced and exercised. Inspiration draws upon the interior environment, which is the subconscious storehouse of memories, undivulged desires, and the resentments engendered by disappointments and unsatisfactory experiences. Intellect is concerned with what is learnt or observed.

[1] *Ib.* 226-7. [2] *Ib.* 240. [3] *Ib.* 252-3.

Inspiration's allies are instinct, feeling and passion; intellect's, reason and observation. It is, in short, the job of intellect to test, use, and, when necessary, curb the impetuosities of inspiration, but not to supplant them. Art is inspiration formalised: science is intellect methodised.[1]

From this brief attempt at differentiation, it will be seen how the eternal clash between the two comes about, particularly in the arts. The intuitions or inspirations of the artist are subject not only to the tests of criticism however imposed, they first and always must risk something of their independence to the circumstances and conditions of established technique and convention. Whether we like it or not, all literature is thus tempered: even the wildest attempts to conquer sophistication cannot do without recognisable, or ultimately recognisable forms. Poetry is generally supposed to be wholly inspired, but poets have shackled themselves with formal methods of expression which might have been resented if imposed upon them by critics or academies, yet not only are traditional forms in prosody accepted by the majority of poets and their readers, but revolutionary attempts to abolish them are fiercely opposed or resentfully ignored, and when an old form is broken or discarded a new one takes its place. At the same time the war between intellect and instinct is not solely external. War is a constant condition inwardly and outwardly. The artist is both Dionysos and Apollo. His Dionysian daemon is always subject to the correction of his Apollonian intelligence. A masterpiece is a truce not a victory, its acceptance as a classic, as I show elsewhere in this book, being challenged at all stages of its history.

v

Inspiration and reasoning are different and may also be divergent processes. If it is possible for one to help the other, it is certain that one can hinder the other. You can reason about a poem but you cannot reason a poem into existence. It is a mistake, however, to assume that the two processes are fundamentally opposed. They move along parallel lines, and are only opposed if attempts are made to substitute one for the other. The best literature is the result of inspired observation of external and internal phenomena combined with appropriate technique. The intellect can do no more for a work

[1] 'Art is always instinctive.' John Ruskin, Pref. *St. Mark's Rest* (1879).

of art than give it finish. Even ideas are born, not made,[1] and men of action no less than men-of-letters work all the better if their intuitions as well as their intellects are intact and on friendly terms. But there is a tide in the affairs of art when the partnership is temporarily suspended. It is the moment when the intuition tells the artist that he can add no more to his poem, or his picture, or his sonata. If he is wise, that is, if he is an artist, he will obey. The time to conclude a work of art is a matter of taste about which you can argue interminably without arguing it away. Intuition decides taste, but exposition of taste is the business of the intellect, for although, as Bergson pointed out, 'the intellect is characterised by a natural inability to comprehend life,'[2] it may help us to comprehend art.

Writers are aware of the recalcitrances of an art which will not readily permit them to have all their own way, and they are forced to recognise that much of their work springs accidentally or automatically from unconscious sources: the product of circumstances or mood rather than deliberation.[3] Indeed, all literature, whether inspired or not, is subject to invasions from the subconscious. 'When the mood leaves me', said Charlotte Brontë, 'I put back my MS. and wait till it comes back again.'[4] We are no more surprised at such a confession from the author of *Jane Eyre* than we are when the author of *The Great God Pan* declares that a writer 'is unconscious while he is writing'.[5] It is unexpected, however, to find Anthony Trollope in the same boat. In one of the franknesses which for so many years undermined the faith of those who should have been enjoying the fruits of his genius, he confessed that he never found himself thinking about his work until he was doing it, and that he had 'almost abandoned the effort to think', trusting himself 'with the narrowest thread of a plot, to work the matter out when the pen was in his hand'. But, he added, with an intuitive grasp of

---

[1] 'The most valuable thoughts which I entertain are anything but what I thought. Nature abhors a vacuum, and if I can only work with sufficient carelessness, I am sure to be filled.' H. D. Thoreau, *Journal: Spring* (1883), 35. [2] *Creative Evolution*. Trans. Mitchell (1911), 174. [3] 'When I come to write poetry I seem—I suppose it is all instinct with me—completely ignorant. I wrote once "I would be ignorant as the dawn" but now I want to explain and cannot.' W. B. Yeats to Dorothy Wellesley, 14th June, 1935, *Letters on Poetry* (1940), 5. [4] *Life*, Gaskell (1857), ii, 237. [5] Arthur Machen, *Hieroglyphics* (1902), 138. This essay argues that ecstasy and not reason or artifice determines the character of what he calls 'fine literature'.

the function of the intellect, 'my mind is constantly employing itself on the work I have done.'[1]

vi

Contemporary writers have been peculiarly aware of the phenomenon of being possessed by this mysterious creative force. Joseph Conrad was so dependent upon these indwelling energies that he found great difficulty in correcting what had been written under their spell: 'All my work is produced unconsciously (so to speak) and I cannot meddle to any purpose with what is within myself. . . . It isn't in me to improve what has got itself written.'[2] George Russell (A.E.), as might have been expected, attributed his poems to 'an internal creator' who floods the 'superficial consciousness' with a light from within with results often surprising to the author. 'The words', he says, 'often would rush swiftly from hidden depths of consciousness and be fashioned by an art with which the working brain had but little to do.'[3] George Moore records a similar experience, when, in his last work, *A Communication to my Friends* (1933), he said 'all that goes down on the canvas and the paper comes from within, unconsciously.'[4] D. H. Lawrence took advantage of the automatic element in authorship by making it a part of his technique. It had its difficulties, for sometimes he feels as though he were writing in an inadequately known foreign language, so that he 'can only just make out what it is "about".' Aldous Huxley, who had many opportunities of observing him at close range, says Lawrence was 'determined that all he produced should spring direct from the mysterious, irrational source of power within him', and not to allow 'the conscious intellect . . . to come and impose, after the event, its abstract pattern of perfection.'[5]

vii

In ancient times these subconscious forces were attributed to a Daemonic force, an idea which was introduced to modern thought

[1] *Autobiography*. Ed. Sadleir (1923), 142. [2] *Letters from Conrad*. Ed. Garnett (1928), 15. [3] *Song and its Fountains* by A.E. (1932), 62, 24.
[4] 'Shelley did well to speak of the unpremeditated song of the lark—his own song was unpremeditated; he could hardly have been aware of his poetry while it was being written, and afterwards, when he studied it, he must have wondered how it had come to be thére.' George Moore, *Op. cit.* 85. [5] Preface, *Letters of D. H. Lawrence* (1932).

by Goethe. The idea is still current, and quite recently Rùdyard Kipling attributed much of his best work to his Daemon. 'When your Daemon is in charge', he said, 'do not try to think consciously. Drift, wait, obey.'[1] Sometimes he substituted 'pen' for 'Daemon'; when, for instance, he was·writing the *Jungle Books*, 'the pen took charge and I wanted to begin to write stories about Mowgli and animals . . .'[2] Kipling seemed to think that his Daemon could do no wrong, but Goethe's faith was not so complete. He believed that although a Daemon may be a powerful and indispensable accession to genius, its judgment was by no means infallible or always acceptable. 'The higher a man is,' he told Eckermann, 'the worse he is under the nightmare of Daemons, and he must take heed lest his guiding will counsel him to a wrong path.'[3] In Goethe's conception there is something Puck-like and impish in this unseen force which delights in misleading its victims until in the end they destroy themselves. 'Thus it was with Napoleon and many others. Mozart died in his six-and-thirtieth year. Raphael at the same age. Byron only a little older.' But this high-handed procedure is not wholly bad, for these Daemonic geniuses 'had perfectly fulfilled their missions; and it was time for them to depart, that other people might still have something to do in a world made to last a long while'.[4] At other times they delight in setting up unattainable ideals 'to tease and make sport of men'.

But in spite of disadvantages Goethe concludes that a Daemon is an indispensable part of the equipment of genius, including his own. 'In poetry, especially in what is unconscious, before which reason and understanding fall short and which therefore produces effects far surpassing all conception, there is always something Daemonic.'[5] Yet this Daemonic 'something' which can inspire and guide equally a Napoleon or a Paganini, a Shakespeare or a Mozart, 'is that which cannot be explained by Reason or Understanding; it lies in my nature,' he says, 'but I am subject to it.'[6] We may 'adore' without being able to explain, and use without being able fully to control.[7] At the same time Goethe was not always inclined to give way to his

---

[1] *Something of Myself* (1936), Albatross Ed. 107.   [2] *Ib.* 193. George Russell (A.E.) held a similar idea but believed that it took the form of 'a being of pre-natal wisdom' which 'exists in all of us trying to become self-conscious in the body'. *Song and its Fountains,* by A.E. (1932), 52.   [3] 24th March, 1829, *Conversations of Goethe with Eckermann.* Trans. John Oxenford.   [4] *Ib.* 11th March, 1828.   [5] *Ib.* 8th March, 1831.   [6] *Ib.* 2nd March, 1831.   [7] *Ib.* 18th February, 1831

Daemon. He was far too imperious for that, but he knew that in a direct attack he would be defeated, so got his own way as he imagined by an outflanking movement. 'I sought to escape from this terrible principle', he records in his autobiography, 'by taking refuge, according to my wont, in a creation of the imagination.'[1] It is probable that Goethe was deceiving himself for he had no unquestioning faith even in an imaginative faculty which in his opinion needed the control of art. 'Nothing', he said, 'is more frightful than imagination without taste,'[2] that is, without correction of the intellect.

Edward Dowden was the first English critic to point out that Goethe's work was handicapped by undue emphasis on the mental rather than the intuitive faculties. 'His intellect and deliberate self-consciousness', Dowden says, 'took up his instincts and spontaneous movements of imagination, and in the end overpowered them.' The case of Goethe was further complicated because he applied that principle to his life: 'His intellect and dominant will controlled his impulses, in a certain cruel way at times, so that these impulses fled from his life into his art, where they were again pursued by his self-consciousness. Meanwhile his life lost something ... He had a dominant intellect, and he subdued every feeling which would fatally interfere with his true tendency.' It is interesting and significant to note that Goethe 'did not admire his intellect from a distance, but actively served it as a servant serves a master'.[3]

viii

What I have said in this chapter is to define not to disparage intellect or to give intuition a higher value than it already possesses. Both have their functions and their methods of expression, and neither is immune from error. It is too readily assumed that inspiration is always right and intellect ultimately wrong, whereas either is capable in its own way of distorting as well as sublimating the records of the senses. The terms have become confused through lack of exact definition. It might be possible to use the words 'art' and 'craft' to distinguish the two methods of expression, remembering always the possibility of incursions of craft into art and art into craft. Differences between the two are relative. At a point, not always

---

[1] *Poetry and Truth from My Own Life.* Trans. Oxenford and Morrison, revised by Minna Steele Smith (Bohn Ed. 1908), ii, 301. [2] *Maxims and Reflections.* Trans. Bailey Saunders (1893), 173. [3] *Fragments from Old Letters* (1914), 17th December, 1872.

easy to define and not immediately evident even to the expert observer, craft and art are appropriately united, and perhaps, as I have hinted, at no time is the line of demarcation complete. A genuine difference occurs only on the decontrol of the intellectual processes and their replacement by intuition. I am here using the word 'craft' in its widest application so that it shall include all forms of technical and 'professional' activity, workmanship, sport and even administration. I believe that an unconscious element enters more widely into our actions, at their best, than is generally supposed;[1] the difference between the inspiration which goes to the making of any useful piece of goods, provided that there is inspiration, and that which goes to the making of a poem, is one of degree rather than of kind.

The paradox of art and craft is often elucidated in the common remark that one who is doing a job of work well is an artist. The precise working of this influence—'the influence' in the words of Siegfried Sassoon, 'of that unchartable element the subconscious mind which . . . knows a lot more than the conscious one'—is not known; but we are familiar with its activities. A certain automatism in connection with technique is a condition of all expressions of the subconscious. Siegfried Sassoon states the case clearly for the poet. He says: 'The poets themselves admit that in their best lines they discover meanings and metaphors of which they knew nothing while composing them. There was more in it than they knew at the time. Technique had been instinctive; *thought* had been somehow uncensored. The brain-work was there, but it had been fundamentally mysterious!'[2]

Stephen Reynolds has an illuminating passage on this kind of interpretation in *A Poor Man's House*. He is describing the skill of the fishermen among whom he lived and he points out that although they may be deficient in theory compared with him, they hook fish whilst he, the theorist, is thinking about it. 'The fisherman', he says, 'is an artist none the less because his skill is partly inborn; because he sails his boat airily and carelessly, yet grimly—for life and the bread and cheese of it.'[3] The reason for that efficiency is not, however, that the skill is 'partly inborn' but that the fisherman through experience, tradition and inheritance, is adept enough to be able to abandon self-consciousness and by so doing to allow his instinct for the right things to have free play.

[1] See Notes. [2] *On Poetry* (1959), 7. [3] *A Poor Man's House* (1908), 48–9.

The process applies equally to any activity requiring skill,[1] and since all art is dependent upon auto-intoxication during which technique becomes automatic, the cricketer and the cabinet-maker, the poet and the pianist, the surgeon and the mathematician, the mason and the lumberjack, become artists when their technical skill is so perfect that they can afford to forget it. Maurice Hewlett found this principle effective both as a novelist and a barrister. He put no 'conscious or deliberate brainwork' into his books, and when earlier in life he practised at the Bar he prepared cases in 'exactly the same way—all the close searching and arrangement of evidence' being 'the result of inspiration and brainwork done unconsciously'[2]. Paderewski, master of a far different art, used to say that unless he practised for many hours a day his recitals suffered. The drudgery kept his technique in such perfect condition that he was able to forget it on the platform and so give his genius its head when he appeared before the public. Art is thus inspiration plus technique but minus the consciousness of technique. An artist should be as unaware of his aesthetic processes as we are unconscious of our bodily processes when we achieve that well-balanced condition which we call 'good health'. If a craftsman allows his technique to get in the way of his inspiration he is a technician not an artist.

And what is true of art and craft is true also of reading. If the reader is to become an artist he also must be capable of forgetting his technique, indeed, in the last resort, of forgetting his book! Coleridge, who read as greatly as he wrote, crystallised this conception of the art of reading, when in one of his lectures on Shakespeare he said that 'imagination acts by so carrying on the eye of the reader as to make him almost lose the consciousness of words'.

ix

The means of expressing or interpreting the inner world, which is the special province of the intuition, is by art. The intellect concerns itself with the external world. It observes and organises: builds where intuition creates. But intellect also disorganises and deduces without special regard for what has been observed, and it is here, in the exercising of the reasoning faculty, either in the form of analysis or criticism or classification, that the intellect becomes most pure and most passionate and furthest removed from the intuition.

[1] See Notes [2] *Letters of Maurice Hewlett* Ed. Laurence Binyon (1926), 85.

It is here that art and craft part or fight. The writer must de-intellectualise himself if he would be an artist. During the practice of his art, at least, he must not yield to the temptations of the intellect. 'They and they only can acquire the philosophic imagination, the sacred power of self-intuition, who within themselves can interpret and understand the symbol, that the wings of the air-sylph are forming within the skin of the caterpillar; those only, who feel in their own spirits the same instinct, which impels the chrysalis of the horned fly to leave room in its involucrum for antennae yet to come. They know and feel, that the *potential* works *in* them, even as the *actual* works on them.'[1] After he has yielded to the sacred power of inspiration, he may take up his intellect again and use it as a tool to criticise what he has created, to give it a final polish before sending it out into the world, for one of the most useful services of the intellect is to be the finishing school of inspiration. The intellectual comedy is the human comedy. It begins when the finishing school is exalted to the status of a cathedral.

[1] S. T. Coleridge, *Coleridge and S.T.C.* Stephen Potter (1935), 80–1.

CONCLUSION

i

I have been tempted in conclusion to offer a little pocket-wisdom, a few portable rules for readers about to become fit, but I have resisted because of a feeling that those who have accompanied me so far are already fit enough to formulate their own rules. They, I think, will be the first to release me from any further complicity in their bookish enterprises. It may, however, be asked to what end is all this fitness, this reading between the lines and behind the words, this tracking down of a writer to the innermost meaning of his words, phrases, poems, narratives and dissertations? There are many answers, and several of them are given or hinted at in the body of the book. These may be summed up, briefly, in the phrase—for the reader's greater content. The justification of the fit reader in accordance with what I have already said is the capacity to endow himself with a refined and enriched sensitiveness, so that living may be deeper and fuller than it might otherwise have been, the art of reading, as I understand it, and as I have tried to expound it, being a method of further implementing the art of living, by enriching the mind, sharpening the wits, and refining the senses.

These faculties are important at all times but doubly important at a time when the right to read what one likes in one's own way has been challenged once again and on a scale which makes the intellectual tyrannies of the past look insignificant. I believe the fate of civilisation as we understand it is bound up with the fate of books, and I believe further that the fate of books depends upon the existence of a permanent nucleus of fit readers, that is to say, of readers who are artists in their approach to books and determined to remain so whatever restrictions are attempted or imposed. These will be the guardians of human consciousness, trustees of the arts of living, to whom writers who are artists will appeal and be responsible.

CONCLUSION

Readers have rights as well as whims and prejudices, although it may be difficult to separate one from the other. That, however, is not the main difficulty; the main difficulty is that fit readers are often diffident and reclusive and not inclined to assert their rights even when they have come to the point of recognising that there are such things as rights. There are readers who rise above the common average but not enough of them in an acquisitive society to prevent serious lapses from literary grace. The average reader seems to be content to have his tastes and opinions formed for him by the popular press, which is natural and on the whole beneficial, but that is no reason why all readers should be reduced to the same condition.

The reading which I have expounded in this book may not appear to be in any real danger. But we must not allow ourselves to be misled by appearances. It is too readily assumed that reading is immune from outside interference, because it keeps itself to itself. At the present time a new battle of the books is in progress and this time it is no mere skirmish between critics and scholars. It is an integral part of the world revolution which began in 1914. What people think is as important as what they do. Thought mobilised by propaganda is an inevitable instrument of war, and in war it is tolerable because of the assumption that sacrifices made for victory will be made good when peace comes. That is the intention, but there is always a hang-over after an orgy, and since it is easier to lose a freedom than to gain one the guardians of books should be alert, however much they may be inclined to yield in a national emergency.

The world is in a ferment of New Deals and New Orders and their promoters have a common faith in the necessity of controlling private as well as public affairs. The individual under these ideologies and interests no longer belongs to himself, he belongs to the state or to big business, and once the right to say what you like has gone, it will not be long before the right to read what you like follows. The danger is all the greater because, as I have said, there are groups of writers who advocate writing (and therefore reading) within the limits of a definite doctrine. The idea is not new. It has always existed under authoritarian rule, whether aristocratic or theocratic, but it has never before been applied to a modern political state—and with the apparent permission of the people, aided and abetted by their writers. In the past there have been suppressions and censorships, but generally these have been opportunist and temporary. Never before has there been a theory of limitation openly formulated by writers and accepted with apparent enthusiasm by those who must ultimately be its victims.

iii

In addition to suffering from political and economic restrictions, reading is in danger from the pressure of material possession and mechanical prepossession. The desire to accumulate property and the anxieties of protecting such accumulations, together with the widespread mechanisation of human operations, are said to be limiting the desire for books, but that perhaps is not so evident or so serious as it might seem to be at first glance. Books were never more accessible or in greater demand and anyone who has the inclination can find time to read and places to read in. The main dangers to reading in the immediate future must be looked for elsewhere and are not difficult to find.

The future of books is menaced mainly by conditions which have their origin in the political, commercial, mechanistic and educational customs and peculiarities of our time. These four categories are named for the sake of convenience, they are not to be looked upon as the sole influences, still less as separate entities each with its own power of independent action. They arise out of each other and contrive to overlap and influence one another. For instance, in a commercial state which makes buying and selling for profit the qualification for social survival, it is obvious that both politics and education will be given a commercial bias and that the scientists who invent mechanical means of communication and entertainment may be exploited for profit rather than used for developing the potential excellences of human beings. At the same time each has still its own technique and contributes its own quota of energy to the undermining of the free and intelligent pursuit of reading.

iv

Apart, however, from the changes and difficulties brought about by controls and censorships, changes in habits and conditions of living will inevitably be reflected in reading. If, for instance, the cinema destroys the theatre, it is probable that drama will be read rather than heard and seen. Reading aloud to satisfy the desire for dramatisation may develop. It is not likely that fiction would in such circumstances take the place of drama. If that had been possible it would have happened long ago as books are always more accessible than theatres. It is also possible that even fiction, the oldest of our substitutes for living, may lose caste with any development of a more organic life in which living as we understand it is more intimately related with being in the universal sense. If social life is full and satisfying substitutes for living will no longer be necessary.

Mr. Wells has already foreseen some such variation. He thinks that as mankind settles down into the security of a world-state and 'as men's minds escape more and more from the harsh urgencies and feelings of a primary struggle, as the conception of the modern world-state becomes the common basis of their education and the frame of their conduct, the discussion of primary issues will abate and the analysis of individual difference again become a dominating interest . . .' then people 'will be less round-about in their approach to expression and the subterfuge of fiction will not be so imperative as it is today'. He has no very great opinion of the power of the novel or the drama to affect the moral and social preconceptions of the public. 'Stupid people', he says, 'will never read anything with which they do not agree, so what is the good of trying to write down to them? And even quite intelligent people will read and consider an account of strange defiant behaviour only if it is neither glorified nor extenuated, but put before them simply as a vitalised statement.'[1] All a novelist or playwright can do apparently is to arrest attention in the hope of arousing interest, and if that is achieved so as to induce free judgment without resentment, no more can be expected.

v

It is doubtful whether a writer can give anything to a reader that is not already there in some measure. All he can do is to make him conscious or more deeply conscious of what he already possesses by stimulating apprehension, by smoothing or ruffling the surface of consciousness, and, in rare instances, by striking below the surface and opening the way to vision or revelation. Books at their best and in their most favourable moments of reception revitalise. The end of reading is not more books but more life. Reading in the last resort should not be only literary, any more than art should be merely

---

[1] *Experiment in Autobiography* (1934), ii, 548–9.

artistic: reading should tend towards vitality rather than bookishness. The pleasure of bookish associations are not, however, to be denied. Such associations with what wise men or artists have said or sung are among the rewards of reading, but not solely for what they prove or teach. They are interesting for what they are and our appreciation of their quality is an experience not to be despised; although an experience of the kind is not easy to define. You know it when you feel it, and most readers and writers are content to leave it at that. Allusions to the rewards of reading in memoirs or essays are apt to abstract themselves into vague references to illumination, revelation, uplifting and other indications of emotional or imaginative disturbance.

There are critics and readers who would insulate literature from common experience, advocates of 'art for art's sake', 'pure poetry', and the 'Ivory Tower'. They dwell upon style and are connoisseurs of all those qualities which are remote from contemporary problems and disturbances. Such experiences as they indulge are self-contained and removed as far as possible from the common life. This attitude is not new; every period has its examples, but it has not been seriously opposed until our own time when it has had to combat a widespread objection to escapist literature. Readers of this class may refer to their reading as experiences, but they are experiences which have become things in themselves—experiences for experience's sake, not experiences for life's sake. They are abstracted from life and the word 'experience' thus used represents an idea rather than an event.

Insulated art is decadent when it attempts to remove consciousness from the common stream of life which is as necessary to us as the blood stream to the body. Life is communalised experience and any attempt to side-track that experience to your own whim for seclusion, though bound in the end to fail, is theft or sabotage or both. There are limits. The Ivory Tower is permissible as an occasional retreat but not as a permanent abode. Art for art's sake should not be a substitute for art for life's sake. It is better to live in a beautiful city without an art gallery than in a noisome factory town with an art gallery of distinction.

In recent years there has grown up a considerable dissent from insulated and escapist art and letters, which are supposed with some justice to represent a bourgeois attitude. If art is to be divorced from life and action in ideas and affairs, few experiences are left, it is contended, but those concerned with the personal sensations, emotions, and conduct of 'the parasitic class'. 'Such art is produced today by bourgeois writers' who are 'class-conditioned' and 'pretend that their values are the values of humanity'.[1] To say, however, that these writers 'pretend' to universality is to dodge the issue. It is far more likely that they believe what they assume.

vi

Finally, I hope I have not made the art of reading appear to be more troublesome or less pleasant than I have found it, for that was not my intention. Reading is no more troublesome and no less enjoyable than any other art once you have mastered and become unconscious of your technique. But, on the other hand, if the technique of reading which pleases me only vexes you then there is nothing left but for us to part. I have not (or hope I have not) played the part of advocate. Proselytising is not my aim, nor is it necessary, for the convertible are already converted. Nor, believing as I do that there are several other methods of reading beyond my experience or outside of my interests, probably as good as mine and possibly better, I have no reason for being dogmatic. All I have tried to do is to present a point of view—my own. I have done no more, perhaps, than explain—in part, for much more could have been said—what kind of reader I am, hoping that what I have said about books, their makers, and their readers, may interest like-minded bookmen, and possibly help to awaken in others a desire to develop a hidden capacity towards sound (or at least individual) bookmanship, for that in the long run will save his and the common Right to Read.

[1] Joseph Freeman, *Proletarian Literature in the United States*. Intro., 12.

NOTES

Page 16. *Taste is perception, assimilation and understanding.*

Coleridge divides readers into four classes:

'1. Sponges, who absorb all they read, and return it nearly in the same state, only a little dirtied.

2. Sand-glasses, who retain nothing, and are content to get through a book for the sake of getting through the time.

3. Strain-bags, who retain merely the dregs of what they read.

4. Mogul diamonds, equally rare and valuable, who profit by what they read, and enable others to profit by it also'. *Lectures on Shakespeare and Milton.* (1811–12). Lecture ii.

Page 17. . . . *the desire to escape from the fever and fret of life has been the most dominant of all literary stimuli* . . .

'The desire to decorate existence in some way or other with more or less care is nearly universal. The most sensual and the meanest almost always manifest an indisposition to be content with mere material satisfaction. I have known selfish, gluttonous, drunken men spend their leisure moments in trimming a bed of scarlet geraniums, and the vulgarest and most commonplace of mortals considers it a necessity to put a picture in the room or an ornament on the mantelpiece. The instinct, even in its lowest forms, is divine. It is the commentary on the text that man shall not live by bread alone. It is evidence of an acknowledged compulsion—of which art is the highest manifestation—to *escape*'. Mark Rutherford, *The Deliverance* (1885), 33.

Page 20. *Even books which are technically bad* . . .

The influence of aesthetically bad books is worth investigating and Sir Osbert Sitwell has made a start in an essay reprinted in *Sing High! Sing Low!* (1944) on the evil effects of Henri Murger's *La Vie de Bohême* on the destiny of the country once called Bohemia and now known as Czecho-Slovakia. 'Perhaps', he says, 'a worthless book . . . can achieve more ill than a good book can ever achieve good,' and upon 'this seeming paradox', he goes on to demonstrate 'beyond the power of any scepticism to disprove, how a bad writer, by means of his bad writing, can influence the fate of a whole country, and how, by advocating false ideals through the medium of cheapened words, and thereby still further debasing the verbal currency—, the author of a fifth-rate romance can, ninety years after he has written it and eighty'years after his own death, become responsible for the destruction of a flourishing and famous land.' 'A Rose by any other Name,' *Sing High! Sing Low!* (1944) 94. The land is, or was, Bohemia, and its character and status have, according to Sir Osbert, been sadly shaken, if not destroyed, because, owing to Murger's debasing of the currency of the word *Bohemian*, it had to abandon its historic name and with it its vital links with an honourable and distinctive past. The argument is suggestive if somewhat whimsical, but it contains a half-truth which should be a warning to those who are indifferent to verbal lapses from usage and tradition. To realise the value of such an essay it is only necessary to imagine what we should say if some novelist made British a synonym for 'moral obliquity and lack of manners' for anyone who 'never paid a debt, or who lounged about the world, never doing anything and getting in the way of those who did.' The remedy he suggests for the word discussed is never to use *Bohemian* 'except for an inhabitant of the country Bohemia, and by calling "a waster" and a drunkard, "a drunkard"—or, if you like "a drunk".' *Ib.* 97.

Page 31. . . . *a manifesto . . . exhorting the Venetians to destroy their festering antiquities . . .*

An English translation of the document was circulated in which it was announced that certain futurist painters 'having gone to Venice, climbed the clock tower from the top of which they threw down on the howling agitation of the enormous crowd filling St. Mark Place, 200,000 multi-coloured manifests'. The following is the official translation: 'We repudiate the ancient Venice extenuated by morbid secular voluptuousness, though we have loved it long and possessed it in the anguish of a great delightful dream.

We repudiate the ancient Venice of strangers, market to fraudulent antiquaries, magnetical pole for all the snobs and imbeciles of the world, the sunk in bed of innumerable caravans of lovers, precious gemmed tub of cosmopolitan adventuresses.

We want to cure and cicatrize this rotting town, magnificent wound of the past. We want to enliven and ennoble the Venetian people declined from its former grandeur, morphinised by a disgusting cowardice and abased by small dishonest traffic. We want to prepare the birth of a commercial and military Venice, able to brave and affront on the Adriatic Sea our eternal enemy: Austria.

Hasten to fill its small fetid canals with the ruins of its tumbling and leprous palaces.

Burn the gondolas, those swings for fools and erect up to the sky the rigid geometry of large metallic bridges and manufactories with waving hair of smoke, abolish everywhere the languishing curves of the old architectures!

May the dazzling reign of divine Electrical Light at last free Venice from her venal furnished room's moonshine.'

Page 56. *Even the most original of writers is largely conditioned by the characteristics of his own age. . . . Every reader is both debtor and creditor to his period.*

'At the moment when the creative writer sits at his desk and composes his verses or his novel or his play, he may have the illusion that he is writing his work for its own sake. But without his past life, without his class education, prejudices, and experiences, that particular book would be impossible. Memory, the Greeks said, is the mother of the muses; and memory feeds not on the general abstract idea of absolute disembodied experience, but on our action, education, and knowledge in our specific social milieu. As the poet's experience changes, his poetry changes. The revolutionary Wordsworth, Coleridge, and Southey become reactionary with age and advancement by the ruling powers; the Goethe of Goetz becomes the Goethe of Weimar; the T. S. Eliot of *The Hippopotamus* becomes the T. S. Eliot of *Ash Wednesday*; the Lewis of *Babbitt* becomes the Lewis of *Work of Art*; the O'Neill of *The Hairy Ape* becomes the O'Neill of *Days Without End*.' Joseph Freeman, *Proletarian Literature in the United States*. Introduction, 15, 16.

Page 69. *William Michael Rossetti has shown that the 'Ode to a Nightingale' is a tangle of inaccuracies—yet it remains a noble poem.*

'Unless perhaps in "La Belle Dame sans Merci", Keats has not, I think, come nearer to perfection than in the "Ode to a Nightingale". It is with some trepidation that I recur to this Ode, for the

invidious purpose of testing its claim to be adjudged "faultless",
for in so doing I shall certainly lose the sympathy of some readers,
and strain the patience of many. The question, however, seems to be
a very fair one to raise, and the specimen a strong one to try it by,
and so I persevere. The first point of weakness—excess which becomes weak in result—is a surfeit of mythological allusions: Lethe,
Dryad (the nightingale is turned into a "light-winged Dryad of the
trees"—which is as much as to say, a light-winged *Oak*-nymph of
the *trees*), Flora, Hippocrene, Bacchus, the Queen-moon (the
Queen-moon appears at first sight to be the classical Phoebe, who is
here "clustered around by all her starry Fays", spirits proper to a
Northern mythology; but possibly Keats thought more of a Faery-
queen than of Phoebe). Then comes the passage (already cited in
these pages) about the poet's wish for a draught of wine, to help him
towards spiritual commune with the nightingale. Some exquisite
phrases in this passage have endeared it to all readers of Keats; yet I
cannot but regard it as very foreign to the main subject-matter.
Surely nobody wants wine as a preparation for enjoying a nightingale's music, whether in a literal or in a fanciful relation. Taken
in detail, to call wine "the true, the blushful Hippocrene"—the
veritable fount of poetic inspiration—seems both stilted and re-
pulsive, and the phrase "with beaded bubbles winking at the brim"
is (though picturesque) trivial, in the same way as much of Keats's
earlier work. Far worse is the succeeding image, "Not charioted by
Bacchus and his pards"—*i.e.*, not under the inspiration of wine: the
poet will fly to the nightingale, but not in a leopard-drawn chariot.
Further on, as if we had not already had enough of wine and its
associations, the coming musk-rose is described as "full of dewy
wine"—an expression of very dubious appositeness: and the like
may be said of "become a sod", in the sense of "become a corpse—
earth to earth". The renowned address—

> *Thou wast not born for death, immortal bird!*
> *No hungry generations tread thee down,*

seems almost outside the region of criticism. Still, it is a palpable fact
that this address, according to its place in the context, is a logical
solecism. While "youth grows pale and spectre-thin and dies",
while the poet would "become a sod" to the requiem sung by the
nightingale, the nightingale itself is pronounced immortal. But this
antithesis cannot stand the test of a moment's reflection. Man, as a
race, is as deathless, as superior to the tramp of hungry generations,

as is the nightingale as a race: while the nightingale as an individual bird has a life not less fleeting, still more fleeting, than a man as an individual. We have now arrived at the last stanza of the ode. Here the term "deceiving elf", applied to "the fancy", sounds rather petty, and in the nature of a make-rhyme: but this may possibly be a prejudice.' William Michael Rossetti, *Life of John Keats* (1887), 200-2.

Page 73. *The writer expresses himself in a book, the reader through a book.*

An interesting reflection upon the interaction of author and reader occurs in John Galsworthy's novel *Flowering Wilderness* (1932, Globe Ed., 261-2). Michael Mont has been wondering at the success of his friend Wilfrid Dersert's book of poems. It has become a 'best seller' without having any of the ingredients of popularity, but one poem 'The Leopard' contains the author's confession that on a journey in Arabia he renounced Christianity in favour of Mohammedanism under threat of death. Michael 'fell to considering what was really making the public buy a book not concerned with sex, memoirs, or murders. The Empire! The prestige of the English! He did not believe it. No! What was making them buy it was that fundamental interest which attached to the question how far a person might go to save his life without losing what was called his soul. In other words, the book was being sold by that little thing —believed in some quarters to be dead—called Conscience. A problem posed to each reader's conscience, that he could not answer easily; and the fact that it had actually happened to the author brought it home to the reader that some awful alternative might at any moment be presented to himself. And what would he do then, poor thing?'

Page 78. . . . *tales about crooks.*

'An interest in crime literature is intellectually flattering to the reader. It is his own intellectual superiority to himself. His social happiness is based on an exchange of compliments with other members of the society. As a member of that society it is his duty to it and to himself to be shocked at the commission of a crime. As a reader of crime literature he enjoys the crime as a joke against himself, an insult to himself. The insult does not affect his social self-esteem, the joke does not affect his social solemnity. Death itself is the joke, the joke against himself that he can make in private comfort because he is alive. Death is not officially acknowledged in his society; the social mind is interested only in life. Thus, the pleasure in crime literature is more absolute where the crime involves death.' Laura Riding, *Epilogue*. Ed. Laura Riding and Robert Graves. (1936). ii, 11.

Page 81. . . . *cause and effect* . . . *are reciprocal only when writer and reader happen to be going the same way.*

'We remember many of Bunyan's scenes because he tells us so little about them. Of the Hill of Difficulty he tells us nothing but that it was a hill and steep; of the footpath across the Giant's Despair demesne he tells us little but that it ran hard by a hedge; and we remember these things because we have all seen steep hills and hedgerow paths, and because we at once adopt a hill or a path from the pictures in our memories. It is small wonder, then, that these pictures are real to us. They *are* places we know, but they are *our* places, not Bunyan's, and real as they are to me, and real as they are to others, they are not the same to any two of us. Macaulay's Valley of Humiliation, Doubting Castle, and Hell Gate are not mine and yours. Each of us paints his own picture, puts it into Bunyan's frame, and cries "wonderful".' Robert Blatchford, *My Favourite Books* (1900), 213–4.

'The poet describes a flower differently from a botanist, a war differently from a general. Ernest Hemingway's description of the retreat from Caporetto is different from the Italian general staff's; Tretiakov's stories of China are not the same as the resolution on that country by a Comintern plenum. The poet deals with experience rather than theory or action. But the social class to which the poet is attached conditions the nature and flavour of his experience. A Chinese poet of the proletariat of necessity conveys to us experiences different from those of a poet attached to Chiang Kai Shek or a bourgeois poet who thinks he is above the battle. Moreover, in an era of bitter class war such as ours, party programs, collective actions, class purposes, when they are enacted in life, themselves become experiences—experiences so great, so far-reaching, so all-inclusive that, *as experiences*, they transcend flirtations and autumn winds and stars and nightingales and getting drunk in Paris cafés.' Joseph Freeman, *Proletarian Literature in the United States*, Introduction, 11–12.

NOTES

Page 89. *All that has happened is that it has been thrown into relief.*

This is shown by our willingness to see with the eyes of a dominant painter, or a new mechanical process. We speak of the Rossetti woman or the Gibson girl, and believe that the artists named have created those types of women when the types already existed, but were unnoticed until the observation of the artists indicated them.

Mechanical processes of visual reproduction have the same effect, and because of their widespread use they alter our way of looking at things on a universal scale. The film producer exhibits a Greta Garbo or a Clark Gable and these types appear immediately in all the cities of the world. A similar effect, on a much smaller scale, was produced by the invention of photography. The camera changed the technique of observation. Jacques-Emile Blanche told Charles Ricketts that it was difficult for us 'to vision things broadly, however much we may try to do so, owing to the alteration of the modern eyesight brought about by photography. We are all influenced by it and dislike its dread effects.' *Self-Portrait of Charles Ricketts, R.A.* Ed. T. Sturge Moore and Cecil Lewis (1939), 98. The same could be said of other methods of pictorial reproduction. Chromo-lithography probably inspired the cruder colour-schemes of the mid-Victorian period, and it is probable that the naturalistic detail of pre-Raphaelite pictures owes more to the invention of the Daguerreo-type than to the methods of Ford Madox Brown and Holman Hunt.

Page 98. *The greater the writer the greater the faculty of observation.*

'On *a priori* grounds it seems safe to say that Shakespeare's characters were the result of observation, for they possess that convincing quality of figures drawn from life. Most revealing to my mind is a remark of Falstaff's, who, after a subtle analysis of Shallow's character, goes on to say: "I will devise matter enough out of this Shallow to keep Prince Henry in continual laughter for the wearing out of six fashions." We cannot but feel that Shakespeare's disreputables, his bawds, and pimps, and boasters, his nincompoops and fools and dullards, his complacent old shallow-pates, were drawn from living models.' Logan Pearsall Smith, *On Reading Shakespeare* (1924), 118.

Page 106. . . . *the general background of culture and experience forces us to see things differently* . . .

Observation is not dependent upon perfect eyesight; on the contrary, being an act of the will it can conquer myopia by taking advantage of it. The accident of short sight by enforcing attention accentuates the impression of things seen. 'We often see children with imperfect eyes take more of an interest in visual things. They develop a keen faculty in this way. We see Gustav Freitag, a great poet who had poor, astigmatic eyes, accomplishing much. Poets and painters often have trouble with their eyes. But this in itself often creates greater interest. Freitag about himself: "Because my eyes were different from those of other people, it seems that I was compelled to use and train my fantasy. I do not know that this has helped me to be a greater writer, but in any case as a result of my eyesight it has come about that I can see better in fantasy than in reality."

If we examine the personalities of geniuses we shall often find poor eyes . . . . In the history of all ages even the gods have had some deficiency such as blindness in one or both eyes. The fact that there are geniuses who though nearly blind are yet able to understand better than others the differences in lines, shadows, and colours shows what can be done with afflicted children if their problems are properly understood.' Alfred Adler, *The Science of Life* (1930), 69–70.

Page 108. *Still fewer are capable of responding to any but the coarser smells . . .*

'As for smell, scent, perfume, fragrance, aroma—no perfect gentleman, of course, would acknowledge that he has inherited or been given a nose for any other purpose than the enjoyment of his Stilton or his pheasant or his tweeds; his claret and old brandy and perhaps his China tea. It is effeminate to rhapsodize on scents and odours. That being so, most of the poets, unhappily enough, who have written about flowers have proved to be gentlemen. Nevertheless, faint, sweet, fresh, sour, dry, hot, aromatic, liquid, composite are words that come trippingly enough to the tongue via that nose when, gentility either lacking or forgotten, one happens to be straying through even the smallest of gardens in the spring or summer. Indeed, in any season, hour or weather.

But the smell of many flowers and of most herbs is as exquisitely difficult of analysis as is that of the dust after rain, or of mown grass in a meadow. One must pause, heed and ponder—curiouser and curiouser: Old man or southern-wood, rue, "wine-sweet musk rose", rosemary, fennel, spiced gillyflower, balm, the little thyme, verbena, geranium, tansy, jasmine, camphor, menthol, wormwood, sage, mint and peppermint, hawthorn, lilac, chives, carrot, juniper, cowslip, spurge. Are these, as we read them in this haphazard list, only mere names of the irrecallable, or does the most nebulous ghost of their originals and their soft incense haunt the printed page?' *Pleasures and Speculations*, Walter de la Mare (1940), 228.

Page 108. . . . . *still fewer are sensitive to the subtleties of taste or touch*

'I prayed by the thyme, whose little flowers I touched with my hand; by the slender grass; by the crumble of dry chalky earth I took up and let fall through my fingers. Touching the crumble of earth, the blade of grass, the thyme flower, breasting the earth-encircling air, thinking of the seas and sky, holding out my hand for the sunbeams to touch it, prone on the sward in token of deep reverence, thus I prayed that I might touch to the unutterable existence infinitely higher than deity.' Richard Jefferies, *The Story of My Heart* (1883), 6.

Page 111. *The unheard melodies of the human voice evoke responses through the printed word.*

'If I were advising any youth of high aims, who might entertain the ambition of reviving the dead art of the English drama, or the dying art of the English novel, I should suggest to him . . . that he should study above all the speech-rhythms, the syntax, the hesitations, the tricks of phrase and verbal sing-song of the people with whom he talks; for this shimmering texture of speech, significant as it is both with the states of the soul and with the meanings and tensions and clashes of human beings in their relation with each other, is, for the writers of drama or fiction, the very stuff of life, the stuff out of which are woven plays like those of Shakespeare, novels like those of Jane Austen, Scott, and Dickens.' Logan Pearsall Smith, *On Reading Shakespeare* (1934), 135.

Page 130. *Although a vocabulary is common to all, each of us has one of his own which has been inherited from family or school, or acquired by contact with particular groups of associates in either office or workshop* . . .

All such vocabularies or 'languages' have a common origin in needs, often hidden, in individual unconsciousness—a subject with interesting possibilities for philosophical research—particularly in the fields of 'private' or 'little' languages. Edmund Wilson, in the following extract, is suggestive on the 'much vexed' phenomenon of the 'private' language which James Joyce dug out of his own unconscious for *Ulysses* and later, and more formidably, developed in *Finnegans Wake*:

'The best way to understand Joyce's method is to note what goes on in one's own mind when one is just dropping off to sleep. Images —or words, if one thinks in words like Joyce—which were already in the conscious mind will suddenly acquire an ominous significance which has nothing to do with their ordinary functions; some vivid incident which may have taken place just before one went to bed will begin to swell with a meaning, an emotion, which at first we do not recognise because it has come up from the submerged part of the mind and is attempting to pass itself off in the clothes of immediate experience—because it is dissociated from the situation out of which it originally arose . . . the images which our waking mind would keep distinct from one another incongruously mix in our sleep with an effect of perfect congruity. A single one of Joyce's sentences, therefore, will combine two or three different meanings— two or three different sets of symbols; a single word may combine two or three . . . but we are not, I take it, to suppose that Joyce's hero necessarily frames all these sentences to himself. Except when he dreams he is reading something or carrying on a conversation, the language is merely a literary equivalent for sleeping states not even articulate in fancy. Nor are we to assume that Joyce's sleeper is actually master of all the languages or understands all the allusions of which Joyce makes him avail himself in his dream. We are now at a level below particularised languages—we are in the region whence all languages arise and where the impulses to all acts have their origin.' *Axel's Castle*, Edmund Wilson (1932), 228–9.

It must be a dull family which has not indulged in the impulsion towards expression, however elementary, in a 'little' language. Everyone knows of Jonathan Swift's whimsies in his epistolary *Journal to Stella*, but this form of word-play has fewer records in the annals of literature than it deserves, so I make no excuse for giving particulars of the 'little' language of the Baring-Ponsonby family recorded in Sir Edward Marsh's autobiography, *A Number of People* (1939). He believes it was started by Maurice Baring's mother and her sister, Lady Ponsonby, when they were little girls and continues down to today. 'In the course of two generations', he says, 'it had developed a vocabulary of surprising range and subtlety, putting everyday things in a new light, conveying in nutshells complex situations and states of feeling, cutting at the roots of circumlocution.' The words are derived from incidents associated with the two families and from the names of friends. Although the words often possess a subtlety of expression, they are sometimes merely playful substitutes for words in ordinary use. One of the best examples of the first group is *pointful* as the opposite of *pointless*. This word is used, Sir Edward reminds us, by Desmond MacCarthy in his critical essays. Another useful word is *floater*, 'which means anything which gives rise to an awkwardness.' Among words derived from proper names may be mentioned, an *Edmund*, after Edmund Gosse: 'a display of undue touchiness'; and a *Hubert*, after Hubert Cornish, for dawdling.

Page 144. . . . *words as 'patterns' become more important than content and weariness.*

Among contemporary novelists Elizabeth Bowen takes a pleasure in putting new words through their paces and in teaching old words new tricks. But although verbal self-consciousness is obvious its expression is not allowed to get out of hand. Thus her experiments and adventures rarely result in conceits or preciosities. An analysis of her novel *Death of a Heart* (1938) shows her to be on easy terms with the vogue-word, without going too far: *phony, dim, distaste, amusing, goofy* and *pattern,* are examples, only the last being slightly overdone. But she does not depend upon fashion for her effects, unless novelty is fashionable. She is both diligent and enterprising in the pursuit of novel words and contexts, wielding the unique word with skill, and when that fails her she can invent her own words even more skilfully. Among unique words she has ladies' faces '*flowering* on fur collars'; a scene '*varnished* with spring light'; an alabaster pendant that 'poured *choked* orange light' on the head of one of her characters; a lady who slept *voraciously*; another who 'put on her hat with an *immune* little smile'; children who '*scuttled* about'; and a '*salty*' seaside sun.

Her invented and curiously used words are nearly always functional and associated with movement and sound such as, 'Doris . . . *nimbled* in with the tray'; Daphne's feet, in mules, '*clip-clopped* across the landing'; 'they all three *scrabbled* up a . . . shingly incline'; a lady in a library is observed '*dithering* around a table of new novels'; others '*doddered* off with their books'; and there are 'waxy *demi-monde* flowers'; wicker chairs that '*whicker*'; a church congregation that '*jumbled* happily out'; and a woman who looked 'after dark . . . like a governess gone to the bad, in a Woolworth tiara, *tarted* up all wrong'.

Page 153. *Moods and feelings, dreams and reveries, take charge of writers . . . and for the same reasons readers are equally bemused by the image of themselves which they see reflected in all kinds of books.*

'We set a value on things as they have cost us dear: the very limitation of our faculties or exclusiveness of our feelings compels us to concentrate all our enthusiasm on a favourite subject; and strange as it may sound, in order to inspire a perfect sympathy in others or to form a school, men must themselves be *egotists*! Milton has had fewer readers and admirers, but I expect more *bigoted* ones, than ever Shakespeare had: Sir Walter Scott has attracted more universal attention than any writer of our time, but you may speak against him with less danger of making personal enemies than if you attack Lord Byron. Even Wordsworth has half-a-dozen followers, who set him up above everybody else from a *common idiosyncrasy* of feeling and the singleness of the elements of which his excellence is composed. Before we can take an author entirely to our bosoms, he must be another self; and he cannot be this, if he is 'not one but all mankind's epitome'. It was this which gave such an effect to Rousseau's writings, that he stamped his own character and the image of his self-love on the public mind—*there* it is, and there it will remain in spite of everything. Had he possessed more comprehension of thought or feeling, it would only have diverted him from his object. But it was the excess of his egotism and his utter blindness to everything else, that found a corresponding sympathy in the conscious feelings of every human breast, and shattered to pieces the pride of rank and circumstance by the pride of internal worth or upstart pretension.' William Hazlitt, *Conversations of Northcote*, 1830. Gosse (1894), 186–7.

Page 225. *H. G. Wells's art is a projection of himself into novels, stories and sociological essays.*

'In a social order where all the good things go to those who constitutionally and necessarily, watch, grab and clutch all the time, the quality of my father, the rich humour and imagination of my brother Frank, were shoved out of play and wasted altogether. In a world of competitive acquisitiveness the natural lot of my sort of people is to be hustled out of existence by the smarties and pushers.

A very strong factor in my developing socialism is and always has been the more or less conscious impulses, an increasingly conscious impulse, to anticipate and disarm the smarty and the pusher and make the world safe for the responsive and candid mind and the authentic, artistic and creative worker. In the *Work, Wealth and Happiness of Mankind* I have written about 'Clever Alec'. He's 'rats' to me and at the smell of him I bristle. I set the highest value on people of my own temperament, which is I suppose, a natural and necessary thing to do, and I believe in the long run our sort will do better than their sort, as men do better than rats. We shall build and what we build will stand at last.' H. G. Wells, *Experiment in Biography* (1934), i, 196.

Page 231. *He merges himself into the experiences of the novelist . . .*

'Our friend Mrs. Harrison is a perfect example of this dramatisation business—and is quite capable of dramatising herself in two totally inconsistent directions at once, rather like the Victorian age. Any attitude that appeals to her sense of the picturesque she appropriates instantly, and, I really believe, with perfect sincerity. If she reads a 'piece in the paper' about the modern woman who finds spiritual satisfaction in a career, she *is* that woman; and her whole life has been ruined by having had to give up her job at the office. Capable, intelligent, a comradely woman, meeting male and female on a brisk, pleasant, man-to-man basis—there she is! If, on the other hand, she reads about the necessity of a 'complete physical life' for the development of personality, then she is the thwarted maternal woman, who would be all right if only she had a child. Or if she gets a mental picture of herself as a Great Courtesan (in capital letters), she is perfectly persuaded that her face only needed opportunity to burn the topless towers of Ilium. And so on. What she really is, if reality means anything, I do not know. But I can see now, what I didn't see before, that this power of dramatisation, coupled with a tremendous vitality and plenty of ill-regulated intelligence, has its fascination. If ever she found anyone to take one of her impersonations seriously, she would probably be able to live very brilliantly and successfully in that character for—well, not all her life, perhaps, but for long enough to make an impressive drama of it. Unfortunately, the excellent Harrison is not a good audience. He admires, but he won't clap, which must be very discouraging.' *The Documents in the Case*, Dorothy L. Sayers and Robert Eustace, 42.

Page 238. . . . music . . . .

Music intoxication is so well known as to need no more than a passing reference. The general attitude toward music recognises its power to overcome ordinary forms of consciousness, whether the desire is to arouse martial, religious, or aesthetic ecstasy. The methods of composers of marches, hymns, convivial songs or lullabies are conventional and ready for use as required. But apart from the functional inebriety of music, the musical pose implies a break with normal consciousness. It reveals itself in a form of facial expression peculiar to the appreciators of music and in a tendency to exaggerated applause. Two examples of unbridled applause are common objects, 'features' in fact, of the Promenade Concerts, and productions of the Savoy Operas. The applause at the conclusion of a Promenade Concert often lasts for half-an-hour and it is not unusual for six encores of a popular air to be demanded by an excited Gilbert and Sullivan audience. Nor are these manifestations peculiar to England. At the Max Reinhardt production of *The Mikado* in Berlin I heard 'Tit Willow' encored seven times.

Page 238. . . . *this universal desire for ecstasy is not always creative or intended to be so.*

Although some artists are supposed to work better under the influence of drink or drugs, few have adopted one or the other as regular implements of their craft. Neither Coleridge nor De Quincey used opium as a literary stimulant. The origin of the habit in each case was medicinal, and *Kubla Khan* and the dream-passages in *The Confessions of an English Opium Eater* were by-products. Both Coleridge and De Quincey deprecated the habit. Coleridge thought so little of the effects of imposed ecstasy that he once apologised for an opinion because it was expressed 'under the inebriation of self-conceit'. *Unpublished Letters of S. T. Coleridge.* Ed. L. E. Griggs (1932), ii, 335. On the other hand the majority of expressions I have quoted are enthusiastic comments upon a condition which apparently is so desirable as to need no apology.

'Alcohol leads, by an apparently inevitable process, to the exchange of confidences. Reserved people, unsophisticated people, get together in corners and bare their hearts to one another. In wine, the subconscious or the semi-conscious floats to the surface, and alcoholic tears oil the joints of self-revelation. The need to exteriorize oneself, as the French say, becomes an immediate necessity, and the deep-seated desire, the hidden complex, the secret sin are unveiled in the presence of the chosen confidant. Fortunately, the chosen confidant is himself too far gone to take notes. Indeed, he is hardly interested; he only listens out of politeness, awaiting his own turn to unbosom himself to his particular father-confessor. Among very sophisticated people this relief is difficult. They already know all there is to know about one another, since sexual aberrations are the main topic of their daily conversation. Each regards the other as a pathological case, already diagnosed and classified. Therefore such people—the artistic cosmopolitan coteries of Paris, for example—transfer their exhibitionism to another plane; the spiritual gives place to the physical, soul yields to body. In a word, they tend, when under the influence of drink, to undress themselves, a curious phenomenon which, at Pierre Fort's party, had already begun to happen.' *James Laver, Nymph Errant,* Evergreen Books (1941), 91.

Page 260. . . . *an unconscious element enters more widely into our actions, at their best, than is generally supposed.*

The following passage from the title-story of C. E. Montague's *Action* (1928) illustrates the idea from the point of view of a Harley Street specialist named Gollen who meets Christopher Bell under dramatic circumstances whilst climbing in the Alps. Bell in fear of paralysis decides to meet death in a last climb. He chooses an impossible setting for his adventure on a wall of ice with a perilous bulge near the top. Just as his strength is giving out he becomes aware of other alpinists above him on the ice face and obviously in trouble. It is Gollen and his wife—the woman had lost her foothold and was hanging by the rope held by her husband who was calling for help—rather hopelessly in the circumstances. Bell forgets his own peril and in an ecstasy of humane action he saves Gollen's wife and incidentally himself. During the effort the numbness which had made Bell fear paralysis disappears. Gollen asks him whether the numbness had cramped him that day; Bell admits it had gone at the moment of crisis in the climb. Gollen hints that this was due to going into action:

'I don't mean just doing things out of doors—pressing triggers or lassoing cows. I mean getting every Jack fibre there is in your nature alive and utterly turned on to something outside you—absorbed in it, lost in it—every bit of your consciousness taken up into some

ecstasy of endeavour that's passion and peace . . . . I guess the great
artists—all sorts of them—know how to bring the fit on, or it comes
when they're at the top of their form—they seem to get further and
further above themselves—hold the note out in a way that we can't
—bring every tissue they have in their being to bear on the effort to
get a wee touch to come right. Saints, too, I suppose—the pukka
ones . . . they have the knack too: they can get more alive; they've
found how to exist at a sort of top pressure. I fancy all of us get just
a glimpse of the thing now and then—of what living might be, you
know—at a great turn in a game, or when we're in love, or if some
beautiful thing in a book bowls us over. Only, we can't hold the
note, or we can't do it yet: the pitch is too high for our reach; so we
flop back into flatness. But we shall get there . . . what we've done
since we started as jelly-fish is to get more and more of ourselves into
action, and we shall go on until we are as much more in action—real
true action—than now, as we are now than when we were jelly-fish.
Why, in a few thousand years we may well be able to live half our
time as you lived to-day for ten minutes.'

Page 261. *The process applies to any activity requiring skill.* . . .

'Some weeks ago I went to a prize fight at the Albert Hall. How
refreshing to see the British public face to face with *an art* (an art,
mind you), and possibly genius that they *liked and understood*. There
was the same warm, tense, embracing silence, the same sudden
tremor and irrepressible ripple of appreciation, the same unchok-
able outburst of applause, face to face with a clever piece of foot-
work, an inspired punch, a subtle feint, a faultless piece of timing,
as you find in a French theatre when an actor of genius is speaking
Racine, or in a German concert hall, where a violinist in a quartet
is phrasing as if the composer were whispering in his ear. . . .'
Maurice Baring to Dame Ethel Smyth, 29th July, 1925. *Maurice,
Baring*. Ethel Smyth (1928), 322.

INDEX

Ade, George, 135
Adler, Alfred, 179, 275
A. E., See George Russell
Agate, James, 60, 165
Alcott, Bronson, 242
Aldington, Richard, 209
Amiel, Henri-Frédéric, 37
Andersen, Hans Christian, 159
Anderson, Sherwood, 87, 158
Andreyev, Leonid, 217
Angelo, Michael, 56
Apollinaire, Guillaume, 168
Ariosto, 18
Arnold, Matthew, 19, 63, 100, 155
Arnold, Sir Edwin, 63
Ashford, Daisy, 137
Asquith, Margot (Lady Oxford), 241
Auden, W. H., 62
Austen, Jane, 76–7, 136

Bach, J. S., 115
Bacon, Francis, 18, 82, 160, 167
Bailey, John, 200
Bakunin, Michael, 161
Balfour, A. J., 241
Balzac, Honoré, 74
Bamford, Francis, 136
Bancroft, Edward, 21
Barbauld, Letitia Anna, 181, 234, 248
Baring, Maurice, 81, 278, 284
Barnes, William, 50
Barrès, Maurice, 80
Baudelaire, Charles, 215, 244
Beardsley, Aubrey, 139, 141, 145
Beattie, James, 30
Beerbohm, Max, 137
Beethoven, 56
Belloc, Hilaire, 153, 167

Bennett, Arnold, 150, 243
Bennett, Dorothy Cheston, 150, 243
Benson, Archbishop, 21
Benson, Arthur Christopher, 21
Bergson, Henri, 256
Bernard, St., 171, 240
Besant, Sir Walter, 74
Bickley, Francis, 174
Billings, Gladys, 154
Binyon, Laurence, 261
Biran, Maine de, 160
Biryukov, Paul, 161, 206, 215–6
Blake, William, 105, 142, 147, 173, 199, 238, 243
Blackstone, Sir William, 14
Blanche, Jacques-Emile, 225, 275
Blatchford, Robert, 274
Borrow, George, 117, 133, 209
Bosanquet, Theodora, 176
Boswell, James, 132, 157, 181
Bottomley, Gordon, 242
Bourgeois, Maurice, 157
Bourzes, Father, 36
Bowen, Elizabeth, 279
Boyd, Ernest, 244
Bozman, E. F., 128, 208, 232
Bradlaugh, Charles, 173
Bradley, F. H., 122
Bradley, W. A., 124
Bradshaigh, Lady, 136
Bridges, Robert, 50, 85, 103, 117, 170–1, 185
Brontë, Charlotte, 217, 232, 256
Brooke, Rupert, 104, 138, 142
Brooks, Van Wyck, 21, 67, 158–9, 195
Brown, Ford Madox, 275
Brown, T. E., 166
Brown, W. Sorley, 194

285

INDEX

INDEX

The University of Illinois Press
is a founding member of the
Association of American University Presses.

University of Illinois Press
1325 South Oak Street
Champaign, IL 61820-6903
www.press.uillinois.edu